Why New Systems Fail
Theory and Practice Collide
By Phil Simon

About the Author

Phil Simon began independent software consulting in 2002 after six years of related corporate experience. He has cultivated over twenty clients from a wide variety of industries, including health care, manufacturing, retail, and the public sector.

Phil has worked with a wide variety of applications, both mainstream and homegrown. He has assisted organizations in all phases of system implementations, including vendor selection, project management, business needs analysis, gap analysis, system design, application training, system testing, interface and custom report development, and documentation.

He is a graduate of the School of Industrial and Labor Relations at Cornell University (MILR) and of Carnegie Mellon (B.S., Policy and Management). An avid—but poor—golfer and a respectable tennis player, Phil lives in Northern, NJ, USA.

Acknowledgments

I am grateful to Michael, Brian, Mike, and Thor for their years of sage advice and friendship. My primary editor and frequent tennis partner Steve did a fabulous job as did the rest of my editing staff: Heather, Mike, and Mary. Mark, John, and Bill provided great content for the book. Jordan, John, John, Mike, James, Geddy, Alex, and Neil have given me many years of creative inspiration through their music. My friend, fellow author, and annual basketball teammate Scott provided an abundance of advice and encouragement about writing. Maybe he'll let me shoot the ball a little more next time we play.

Special thanks go to my parents, Linda and Sandy, who provided me with emotional and financial support while I was trying to figure things out.

AuthorHouse™
1663 Liberty Drive, Suite 200
Bloomington, IN 47403
www.authorhouse.com
Phone: 1-800-839-8640

First published by AuthorHouse 02/02/2009

ISBN: 1-9781-4389-4424-1

Printed in the United States of America
Bloomington, Indiana

This book is printed on acid-free paper.

To err is human, but to really foul things up requires a computer.

-Farmers' Almanac, 1978

Table of Contents

List of Tables and Figures in Book

Trying is the first step to failure.

-Homer Simpson

CHAPTER 1: INTRODUCTION

With regard to new systems, Homer Simpson is usually right.

Specifically, over than three in five IT projects do not do what they were supposed to do for the expected costs and within the expected timeline.[1] More gloomy stats include the following:

- 49 percent suffer budget overruns.
- 47 percent result in higher than expected maintenance costs.
- 41 percent fail to deliver the expected business value and ROI.

Ouch. Or, as Homer says, "D'oh!"

The process of implementing systems can hardly be called a recent business development. If it were, then perhaps the failure rate would be understandable. It is not. Organizations have been using major enterprise systems for decades but, as a percentage, few have met their original goals and promise. Reflecting on more than a decade of implementing systems in many countries, industries, and organizations, I have come to one conclusion:

The statistics above are probably understated.

I have many reasons to question these numbers. For one, many executives do not want to admit that their pet projects ran over budget and/or missed deadlines. What's more, the simple time and money criteria mask less obvious system failures. The project that "makes its date and hits its numbers" may still not give the organization the expected bang for its buck. Many end-users fail to use the new system's enhanced functionality and revert to old habits. The average CIO probably does not have the following in mind prior to implementing a new system: spending an enormous amount of money essentially to replicate the problems of the previous system.

---

[1] http://advice.cio.com/remi/two_reasons_why_it_projects_continue_to_fail

Speaking from years of personal experience, I have been involved with very few system implementations that could be categorized as unqualified successes. This begs the obvious questions:

- Why do so many system implementations to fail so spectacularly?
- What can be done to increase the chances that organizations' use of new technologies will be successful?

In a nutshell, those two questions drive this book, divided into the following five parts:

- Deciding to Take the Plunge
- System Selection
- The System Implementation
- The Brave New World of Post-Production Life
- Maximizing the Chance of Success

Fantasy World: The Theoretical System Implementation

At the onset of a project, senior management usually believes that their organizations will implement and activate new systems as follows:

- The system is selected.
- The system is implemented, during which time all issues are found and promptly addressed.
- The system is activated.
- Consultants remain on site for a few weeks of "post-production" support, ensuring end-user knowledge transfer.
- IT and functional end-users can independently maintain the new system after consultants leave.

Based on this expected sequence of events, executives approve these massive projects. Unbeknownst to them, however, the process of implementing and activating a system is almost never this easy. After over a decade in the field, I have *never* come across a system implementation that has gone this smoothly.

This book does not attempt to list all of the possible causes for every type of system failure. There are too many variables: type of system, industry, size of organization, budget, timeline, dates, and so on. Rather, this book delves into the "usual suspects," to borrow a phrase from one of my very favorite films. To the extent that each implementation is different—if not unique, the levels of any particular issue can and do vary on each project. For example, consider data issues: One organization may have pristine data in its legacy system[2] while a second may have wildly divergent data. Still, a third may have very minor data issues.

This book focuses on the most commonly encountered issues on system implementations.

The Anatomy of a Typical System Failure

While the specifics vary quite a bit based on industry, type, and scope of the new system, many enterprise resource planning[3] (ERP) and other system failures have similar root causes, issues, costs, and ultimately, consequences. The similarities do not end there. Organizations also tend to experience these problems and disappointments whether they purchase and implement a system or if they build a system internally or via an independent service provider[4] (ISV).

Table 1.1 represents a typical step-by-step failure of a fictitious system, Bonham Software. The client in this example is Page and Plant (P&P).

---

[2] A legacy system is defined as "an old computer system or application program that continues to be used because the user (typically an organization) does not want to replace or redesign it." (Source: Wikipedia)

[3] Enterprise resource planning (ERP) is an enterprise-wide information system designed to coordinate all the resources, information, and activities needed to complete business processes such as order fulfillment or billing. An ERP system supports most of the business systems that are maintained in a single database, the data needed for a variety of business functions such as Manufacturing, Supply Chain Management, Financials, Projects, Human Resources and Customer Relationship Management. (Source: Wikipedia)

[4] Independent software vendor (ISV) is a business term for companies specializing in making or selling software, designed for mass marketing or for niche markets. Such markets may be diverse including software for real estate brokers, scheduling for healthcare personnel, barcode scanning, stock maintenance and even child care management software. (Source: Wikipedia)

Table 1.1: The Typical System Failure

Task	Notes
System Selection	
The senior management of P&P decides that it needs to buy or build a new enterprise system.	
Vendor selection begins. Formal RFIs (requests for information) and RFPs (requests for proposals) are sent to major vendors or ISVs.	
Vendors or ISVs send formal responses, hoping to make the final cut.	
P&P personnel evaluate vendor/ISV responses. Decisions about "next steps" are made and communicated to these organizations.	
Vendors and ISVs formally present to key people or constituents at P&P.	
P&P personnel evaluate presentations and references provided by vendors and/or ISVs.	
P&P narrows down its selection to two vendors or ISVs based on perceived functionality, cost, time to implement, references, track record in the industry, and so on.	
P&P selects Bonham Software as its future enterprise-wide system. For the sake of simplicity, assume that Bonham wins the consulting business as well.	Typically, Bonham will also attempt to win the consulting business. Many times, however, vendors such as Bonham recommend certified partners for the work in the event P&P deems Bonham too expensive or Bonham does not have the resources to complete the implementation.
System Implementation	
The implementation of Bonham Software formally begins.	
Unanticipated data and conversion issues manifest themselves, causing significant project delays. The climate becomes adversarial within among key internal and external players.	The project begins to fall behind.

Task	Notes
Testing is consequently delayed and additional "parallel" tests are added to see if fixes have resolved identified issues.	Delays mount.
Delays and "rework" typically feed into employees' previously approved vacation time or key deadlines (month-end, quarter-end, year-end closing, W-2 printing, and the like). The net result is that delays of two weeks can quickly become two months.	These delays should not be taken lightly, as key players may be unable or unwilling to move their vacations.
Because of certain hard deadlines such as January 1st or the beginning of a new quarter, P&P devotes less attention and fewer resources to properly document current and future business processes.	The downstream impact of this can be enormous, especially if a key resource leaves the organization without sufficiently documenting or training others in how to conduct a key business process.
Functionality and features promised for Phase I of the implementation are pushed to later dates.	
Data challenges cause issues with interfaces to vendors. Vendor delays in returning test files only exacerbate the problem, as they typically have a multitude of clients and cannot focus exclusively on P&P.	Interfaces may include health coverage for employees, direct deposit for employee checks, employment verification, etc. These must work upon going live; there's no room for error here.
A "go/no-go" meeting is held at which point key players determine if they are ready to proceed with system activation.	Despite the objections of several key players, P&P forges ahead, ostensibly aware of the risks.
P&P activates its new system.	Unfound and unsuspected functional, data, training, and interface issues manifest themselves causing emergency "patchwork" or corrections.
Post-Production Support	
P&P end-users are unprepared for issues that may arise. They still have much room for improvement for basic transactions, error correction, reporting, and so on.	
Bonham consultants plan to remain at P&P for two weeks to ensure a smooth transition and to address any system issues. Ultimately, Bonham's stay lasts months afterward (at considerable additional expense to P&P).	

Types of Failure

Not all failures are created equal and there certainly are *degrees* of failure. There are four major types of failures, one of which may not become apparent until months after a new system has been activated. This book will classify each case study in terms of the following failure scale:

- The Unmitigated Disaster
- The Big Failure
- The Mild Failure
- The Forthcoming Failure

The Unmitigated Disaster

The most egregious failure occurs when an organization spends millions of dollars implementing a system and misses deadlines repeatedly. It ultimately junks the new system for a different one altogether or reverts to the legacy system. Relationships between consultancies and clients are often severed. Lawsuits in such cases are not completely out of the question. Fortunately, these abominations are atypical.

The Big Failure

These types of failures are less severe but more common. Perhaps an organization initially budgets $2M and one year on an implementation and ultimately spends $4M over the course of three years, getting much less functionality than expected in the process.

The Mild Failure

Very often, a system failure is so mild that one can hesitate to even call it a failure, especially relative to the two types just mentioned. By comparison, these are rousing successes! For the sake of consistency, however, this book uses the term "failure." An example of the Mild Failure is the company that initially budgets $2M and a year on an implementation and ultimately spends $2.2M over the course of fifteen months, getting slightly less functionality than expected in the process.

The Forthcoming Failure

Sometimes a system failure is not immediately apparent. At first, this notion may seem perplexing. If an organization has met its goals with respect to both its budget and deadline, then how can it consider the system a failure?

Budget and deadline are only two criteria for a system failure, as the statistics at the beginning of the chapter illustrate. The answer to this question lies within the data, documentation, processing, and people. Examples of latent failures include the following:

- The implementation team has made a key mistake that will come back to haunt the organization down the road.
- End-users may not completely understand the system and, as a result, make significant errors or revert to "old ways," negating one of the major benefits of the new system.
- The organization is vulnerable to employee attrition on two fronts:
  - End-user documentation is deficient and, if key staff members leave, their replacements will need significant time and/or training to do their jobs.
  - Knowledge is not dispersed; only a few employees understand the system in sufficient breadth and depth.

In other words, these are failures waiting to happen. Organizations are not prepared for shocks to their systems.

A Prime Example of the Forthcoming Failure

I am reminded of an organization—Oates Healthcare—that activated its ERP in 2003 with a fundamental but unknown problem with the way in which it calculated employee overtime. No one identified this issue during setup or testing. Only when an ex-employee filed a lawsuit did the problem come to light, five years *after* Oates had gone live.

For Oates, fixing the problem in the system involved two things, one simple and one very difficult. The first merely entailed changing some flags for the system to begin calculating overtime correctly *from that point forward*. However, checking those flags did not retroactively go back and recalculate overtime for all employees paid incorrectly over the past five years. A breakdown of those errant employee records is presented in Table 1.2:

Table 1.2: Breakdown of Payroll Records Requiring Analysis at Oates Healthcare

Employees paid per year	6,500
Average types of pay per week per employee	6
Weeks per year	52
Checks per year	338,000
Payroll records per year	2,028,000
Years of data requiring analysis	5
Total records (over a five year period)	10,140,000

The enormity of this task—recalculating employee overtime—was beyond the time and skill of the existing end-user (arguably a failure in itself). Even if an internal super-user knew how to do this on over 10,000,000 records, he or she would not have been able to do it. For *ad hoc* analyses, Oates provided its end-users only with Microsoft Excel, a very valuable tool but one not nearly robust enough to handle a task of this magnitude. As a result, Oates hired Bishop Consultants to perform this task at considerable expense.

Had Oates' end-users properly tested the system prior to going live, it may have avoided the lawsuit. To be sure, it would have not have had to spend the time, internal resources, and funds on Bishop to fix the problem. Bishop recalculated employee overtime pay but Oates' end-users were not available during the remediation project. This prohibited Bishop consultants from transferring any knowledge during the error-resolution process.

Ironically, Oates did not learn from its mistakes. Despite the recommendation from Bishop, Oates did not seriously consider adding a more powerful reporting tool for end-users to conduct similar kinds of analyses (e.g., Crystal Reports, Microsoft Access, or Business Objects). Oates also failed to actively recruit more technical end-users to use these very tools. Should it encounter a similar problem in the future, it will be at the mercy of external consultants such as Bishop once again.

Consequences of a Typical System Failure

The consequences for a failed implementation go beyond mere dollars and cents. Let's return to the P&P example. Bonham Software may forever have a tarnished reputation within the organization among both end-users and employees who actually do not even use the system on a regular basis. Bonham may always be known as "that system that screwed up payroll." Data could be lost or altered in such a way that it will be impossible to retrieve. Due to lack of training or documentation, employees' jobs may actually become *more* difficult than they were with P&P's legacy system.

For Bonham Software, as a company, the project was a disaster. Bonham now has a tarnished reputation in the industry resulting from this highly publicized failure. It may have difficulty collecting the hundreds of thousands in accounts receivable from P&P and lose key consultants. P&P may refuse to provide a reference for its new partner.

As stated before, many types of issues typically haunt system implementations. While each of the case studies detailed in the book differs in terms of the way in which the organizations employed technology and even in the technologies themselves, there is considerable overlap among the issues encountered.

The Expectations Gap

Table 1.1 illustrates that system implementations typically leave many parties disappointed in the ultimate outcomes. Senior management expects the new system to be implemented smoothly, on time, and within the planned budget. Client end-users expect to learn how to properly use the new system's functionality and be self-sufficient when consultants leave. Consultancies expect strong client references. These expectations are often unmet, many times by significant degree.

Disappointments often give way to disasters. A less-than-inconsequential percentage of these projects have their plugs pulled in mid-implementation. Organizations sometimes go live when they are wholly unprepared to do so. Issues abound and the benefits and cost savings once promised by the vendor and consultancy may be significantly less pronounced than what clients ultimately see. In retrospect, after system activation many clients opine that the new system is a far cry from what they expected when senior management signed the original contracts.

Risks for Mature Organizations

While this book focuses organizations implementing new systems, the content applies to the maintenance, enhancement, and support of existing systems as well. Mature systems can fail in several ways. First, successfully-activated systems often begin show signs of future problems. Second, a Mild Failure could easily become either a Big Failure or, in extreme cases, an Unmitigated Disaster. In other words, just because a new system goes live on time and under budget does *not* mean that an organization is out of the woods. There is still significant risk. Systems can and often do begin to experience major difficulties after even successful activation, attributable to:

- Key employee turnover
- System upgrades and the decommissioning of older versions of the application
- The introduction of additional functionality within a system
- Changes to business processes
- Acquisition of a company and the integration of additional legacy systems
- Unwise expansion

A Balanced Approach: Theory, Case Studies, and Examples

Throughout this book, theory and practice are given equal weight with respect new systems. Consider system testing for a moment. The book does not simply espouse the virtues of system testing; to do so would be facile. After all, all consultants and implementation teams intend to run proper parallel tests.[5] How should the importance of—and frequent missteps associated with—testing be illustrated? By drawing upon extensive examples and detailed case studies, the book manifests the *essential* questions related to compromised testing. These include:

- What causes system testing to produce unexpected results?
- What are the effects of failed testing on the project's timeline, budget, and ultimate outcome?
- Most important, what specifically can an organization do from the beginning—and during—a project to promote accurate, timely, and comprehensive testing?

The examples and case studies in this book stem from actual system implementations but, for reasons of confidentiality, the names of the organizations, consultancies, and individuals have been changed. Specific names are not nearly as important as the lessons

---

[5] Parallel testing is the process of feeding test data into two systems—the modified system and an alternative system (possibly the original system)—and comparing results. Source: www.astrainfotech.com.

they provide. As we will see, many ostensibly different organizations face similar—if not identical—challenges implementing systems.

It's commonly said that one learns more from failures than from successes. To that end, this book's case studies and examples will examine in great detail system implementations that failed, identifying the specific individuals, decisions, and events responsible for the outcomes. This book contains eight detailed case studies:

Table 1.3: List of Case Studies in Book

Case Study	Chapter	Description	Result
Costanza	9	A Flexible Client and a True Consulting Partner	Averted Failure
Lifeson	11	Replicating the Old in the New	Unmitigated Disaster
Portnoy	11	A Square Peg and a Round Hole	Unmitigated Disaster
Elton	13	The Stubborn Client	Big Failure
Julian Marketing Partners	15	Building its Own System	Mild Failure
Wilson	15	Good Design but Lack of Resources	Big Failure
Petrucci	18	Trying to Boil the Ocean	Big Failure
Tate	22	Adding on to a Poor Foundation	Forthcoming Failure; Became Unmitigated Disaster

Who Should Read this Book?

This book has no one intended audience. As a full-time independent consultant, I wish that I had known many of the things in this book when I started with systems back in the mid-1990s. (Maybe I wouldn't have gone into the field, but that's a separate matter!) Many current and aspiring consultants would benefit from the advice dispensed in this book, both on a general level as well as in terms of any specific projects on which they may be working.

Beyond consultants, this is a book for end-users at all levels within an organization. First, CIOs thinking about implementing a major new system could learn a few things about vendors and consulting companies *before* they plunk down hundreds of thousands of dollars. Second, many organizations are already somewhere in the middle of such a project. The subject matter, if applied properly and in a timely manner, may help these organizations avoid many of the outcomes detailed in the case studies and examples. Regardless of the stage of the implementation, the practical tips have the potential to right the ship. Understanding the causes of system failures should help organizations avoid them.

Summary

The reasons typically vary but the outcomes of many system activations are sadly the same. Many differ only to the degree to which they have disappointed or outright failed. Rare is the implementation that meets its deadline at or under budget and gives end-users the functionality promised from day one.

Part One: Deciding to Take the Plunge

This section focuses on an organization's decision to retire its legacy system. It starts with the reasons that many organizations are loathe to even consider an undertaking of this magnitude. Many ultimately reach a tipping point and decide that the benefits of the new system finally outweigh their costs—i.e., that the status quo is unsustainable.

Humanity is acquiring all the right technology for all the wrong reasons.

-R. Buckminster Fuller

CHAPTER 2: WHY ORGANIZATIONS MAINTAIN LEGACY SYSTEMS

Introduction

Many legacy systems have long outlived their usefulness. It's not uncommon that a mature organization purchased and implemented its accounting, inventory, or payroll system well before the advents of Internet, email, and other automation and communication tools. To say that a system is antiquated, however, is not to say that it will be retired anytime soon. Many systems remain active for years beyond their utility. The quote at the beginning of this chapter holds quite a bit of meaning for many seasoned executives at mature organizations. Before we explore the reasons for making the jump, let's delve into the eight most common reasons that these dinosaurs are still around. Many of these reasons are completely reasonable. They are:

- Living in Oblivion
- If it Ain't Broke Don't fix it
- The Cost of Action
- All Functions are not Created Equal
- Fear of the Unknown
- Fear of the Known: Horror Stories and Risk Aversion
- Insufficient Time and People
- Change Agents and Employee Turnover

Living in Oblivion

Many organizations maintain their legacy systems for very a simple reason: Certain executives honestly—and incorrectly—believe that their organizations already have at their disposal systems that allow end-users to do their jobs efficiently and effectively.

For example, at one large organization in the late 1990s, a Senior VP of HR remarked that her company's systems were actually wonderful, as they produced very nice-looking, "actionable" reports. She did not know, however, that many end-users needed to cobble together those reports from disparate sources of data over the course of several weeks.

Executives may lack knowledge of their systems' limitations because of true ignorance or denial. Regardless of the reason, the net effect is the same: senior management at these organizations is very unlikely to even consider a superior system because no one with the necessary power will push for it. Not only has the need for a new system not been identified, *the contrary belief exists*. For the idea of new system to gain traction, someone or some event has to convince senior management of each of the following:

- The current system is deficient and cannot meet the organization's current or future business needs.
- Systems currently exist in the market that would meet the organization's current or future business needs.
- The benefits and savings of a new system more than justify the time, cost, and effort involved in purchasing and implementing it.
- Such a system can be successfully implemented in the organization.

Collectively, this is usually a tall order. Many executives mistakenly believe that their business needs are unique. They may stumble on any one of the points above. If that happens, then any momentum for a new system would die right then and there. However, let's delve a bit deeper into some of the dynamics within an organization to explore the case that needs to be made for a new system.

Consider Eric, the head of HR at a fictitious company with deficient systems. Eric understands that many companies have very similar business needs and processes—annual open enrollment, government reporting, etc. He is open to investing the financial and political capital necessary for a new system to become a reality. Before taking that leap, however, he takes a step back. Eric knows that certain pockets of the organization represent considerable political obstacles. Sofia, the head of IT, and Eva, the head of finance, quickly come to his mind. Eric knows that it is premature for him to make his case for a new system. With that in mind, he does the following:

- Based on the quality of the data in the legacy systems, Eric starts a massive data cleanup project within the organization.
- He recruits technology-savvy staff in the last year. He knows that the new system will require more "data" work than has traditionally been the norm for his staff.

In short, Eric knows that these two important steps will help him make the case a new system and lay the groundwork for a successful system implementation. For these reasons, Eric is a very wise man. It is much better for him to take interim steps *before* suggesting that management spends any money on a new system.

When the time is right to broach the subject of a new system, Eric has already essentially negated two potentially lethal arguments from Sofia and Eva. By cleaning up his department's data and hiring more technical personnel, he has robbed his opponents of some fairly potent ammunition. Sofia and Eva may still object for many reasons, not the least of which is cost. However, at least they cannot claim that HR and payroll data is too inconsistent to be successfully loaded into a new system. Further, they will not be able to argue that Eric's staff—which would undoubtedly play a key role—does not have the technical skills to handle a new system. Eric is getting his ducks in a row and will make the push when the time is right.

The case studies and examples in this book will show how infrequently executives display Eric's kind of wisdom and foresight.

If It Ain't Broke Don't Fix It

Using a very similar line of reasoning, many decision makers have framed the argument for a new system in terms of the lowest common denominator. In other words, the criterion for a new system is not whether the legacy system has the latest bells and whistles. Rather, the current system has to be broken or will imminently break. For instance, "Why do I need a new payroll system?" the director of finance may ask. "We are paying employees correctly now. Am I going to spend all of this money to pay them more correctly?"

This mentality is certainly prevalent in many organizations, particularly in mature ones run by "lifers." Truth be told, this is a very tough challenge to overcome for the change agent. It is difficult for anyone to make the case for change if senior management perceives no upside and the affected area is a cost center, such as HR.

The Cost of Action

While this chapter provides detail about the specific costs of implementing a new system, suffice it to say for now that they are substantial in any economic climate, much less a recession. Even the organization that recognizes the need for a better system may very well concede that it is not the organization's top priority. Organizations only have so many dollars to spend. Quite simply, even a system universally recognized as deficient may not make the cut come budget time.

A progressive executive can argue (much like a vendor) that the new system will pay for itself over a number of years. Reduced administrative or personnel costs, coupled with increased access to vital information and analytics, may sway reluctant senior management. Lamentably, the short-term costs are often too high to justify murky, long-term benefits.

All Functions are Not Created Equal
Functions of a business that have historically been regarded as revenue generating tend to have, on average, superior systems. If an organization's sales system is inadequate or cumbersome, then the bottom line suffers. Rest assured, financial systems that make reporting difficult or inaccurate will receive quick attention from a CFO. The data-mining opportunities from a superior system may yield increased revenue and profits.

On the other end of the spectrum, many back office[6] departments such as HR have yet to make the jump to strategic partner and their systems typically reflect that. Consider payroll systems. Businesses do not realize any competitive advantage from paying employees. Key employees do not remain with an employer because of paychecks. In all likelihood, an organization will replace its Human Resource Information System (HRIS) only if it believes that it can dramatically cut administrative costs related to HR, benefits, and payroll, with two exceptions:

---

[6] A back office is a part of most corporations where tasks dedicated to running the company itself take place. The term comes from the building layout of early companies where the front office would contain the sales and other customer-facing staff and the back office would be those manufacturing or developing the products or involved in administration but without being seen by customers. Although the operations of a back office are usually not thought of, they are a major contributor to a business. Examples of back-office tasks include IT departments that keep the phones and computers running (operations architecture), accounting, and human resources. These tasks are often supported by back-office systems: secure e-commerce software that processes company information (e.g. a database). A back-office system will keep a record of the company's sales and purchase transactions, and update the inventory as needed. Invoices, receipts, and reports can also be produced by the back-office. (Source: Wikipedia)

- Support for the current system will soon expire
- Support for the current system will become prohibitively expensive

Fear of the Unknown

Let's consider Roma Industries, a company considering the purchase and implementation of Oracle applications throughout the enterprise. Roma's finance director, Richard, has twenty years of experience with the Roma's legacy system and knows it cold. While Richard admits that the legacy system is clunky, he knows how to enter journal entries, run profit and loss statements (P&L's), and extract and manipulate data. While he may publicly object to Oracle for financial considerations, his real objection is that he has neither the time nor the desire to learn a new system while performing his day job.

Richard will not cop this, however. He uses a different approach: What if Oracle turns out to be no better than the current system? Sure, Oracle's demo looked impressive and the system *may* make life easier at Roma. However, what if Roma does not realize the benefits promised by Oracle's salespeople? Roma could not easily "un-ring" this bell. In other words, organizations that decide to implement new systems stand little chance for turning back. If Roma's implementation was not successful, it will not implement another system for many years, save for exceptional circumstances. Roma will revert to its legacy system and have to swallow the costs of the new software.

The required financial commitment and political capital of a new system are just two of the reasons that virtually guarantee that an organization will get just one bite at the apple.

Fear of the Known: Horror Stories and Risk Aversion

Many ERP implementations fail disastrously and publicly. As a result, many organizations on the fence about implementing a new system are reluctant to repeat the mistakes of their counterparts. These projects almost always have high profiles within organizations and disasters have resulted in involuntary turnover of senior management.

One of the most memorable horror stories occurred a few years back with The Hershey Company.[7] Its implementation of a new SAP supply chain system caused significant delays in production during its two busiest times of the year (Halloween and Christmas). Things got ugly and lawyers got involved. It is understandable that executives do not want to expose their organizations to that kind of risk.

Along with horror stories, many organizations are risk-averse with respect to tinkering with their back office systems. On some level, they may believe that new systems can reduce costs and provide superior reporting, two arguments typically cited by vendor salespeople. Senior managers may still not want to risk missing payroll, losing track of inventory, or being unable to run key financial reports. Perhaps they have seen first-hand how problematic, costly, and time- and resource-intensive these projects can become. Many are aware of other dirty little secrets:

- Vendor and consultant promises often go unfulfilled.
- Many end-users do not take advantage of the new system's increased capabilities.

As a result, many senior executives may believe that, for all of the bells and whistles of a new system, there is relatively limited actual upside. If payroll and inventory are accurate now, the best case scenario is that they will still be accurate in the new system. The worst case scenario is absolute chaos, enough to scare them from retiring their legacy systems.

Insufficient Time and People

Consider OSI Medical Instruments, a company with the requisite budget and desire to retire its mainframe-based accounting system. Senior management is dying to enter the 21st century. What would give it pause? For one, OSI may not have the human bandwidth necessary to implement the new system. The new system may result in a catastrophe. Perhaps some key employees have recently left, so OSI is scrambling to make due in the interim.

---

[7] http://www.financialdirector.co.uk/financial-director/news/2048644/ erp-disasters-bet-company-lose

Senior management at even properly staffed organizations should think long and hard about implementing a new system. Such a project is no small endeavor for any organization and daily end-user workloads will increase substantially, often for six months to a year. A perfectly legitimate question is, "Do our employees have the time to devote to this project and make it successful?" The answer may very well be "no."

Change Agents and Executive Turnover

With senior-level turnover at an all time high,[8] newly anointed executives may well have different priorities than their predecessors. Very rarely will new senior VPs and COOs bring the same visions as their predecessors. Given the amount of money involved in a new system implementation, a new CIO may want to review any major IT initiative upon being hired. As this CIO gets the lay of the land, she may well decide that the current system may not be ideal but the organization certainly should spend its limited dollars elsewhere with better bang for the buck.

Finances aside, politics in organizations also drives the need for new systems. For instance, Keaton Financial hires Mallory as its new VP of HR. Mallory comes from a progressive company with a powerful HRIS. She is full of energy and wants to immediately improve Keaton's systems, taking the function into the new millennium. Upon entering her new role, she encounters antiquated systems, poor data, and resistant internal forces. After two years of fighting uphill, she leaves Keaton for a similar role with a like-minded, progressive organization. The momentum that Mallory generated for a new system will probably leave with her.

Summary

For a number of reasons, organizations often face significant hurdles in even recognizing the basic need for new systems. People, political, technical, financial, and data issues often prevent organizations from retiring legacy systems. However, most organizations eventually reach an inflection point: the perceived advantages of new systems finally justify their costs.

---

[8] http://www.strategy-business.com/press/16635507/20306

If you think there's a solution, you're part of the problem.

-George Carlin

CHAPTER 3: WHY ORGANIZATIONS IMPLEMENT NEW SYSTEMS

For a number of reasons, even the most risk-averse organization has incentives to retire its legacy system. For one, the amount of risk associated with maintaining antiquated technologies increases over time. Also, as system functionality increases, the perceived—and, in fact, real—benefits that an organization can expect to realize from new technologies also increase.

Let's look at COS Entertainment, a company that originally implemented its legacy system in 1980. In 1998, COS management looked at new systems. COS determined that the costs and functionality of new systems did not justify retiring its legacy system. However, new systems have matured and added functionality (to be discussed later in this book). As such, COS revisited the possibility of implementing a new system in 2008. The costs of the legacy system have increased while its benefits have decreased, demonstrated by the figure below.

Figure 3.1: Relative Costs and Benefits of Legacy Systems over Time

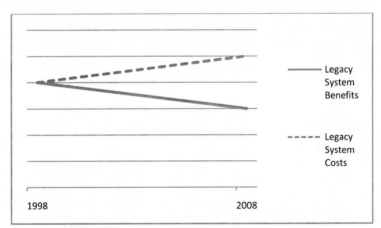

Many organizations ultimately reach an inflection point at which they must seriously consider replacing their disparate legacy systems with a single, unified, integrated alternative. The expected benefits of these new systems, more often than not, must exceed their expected costs by a wide margin. In the COS example, note that the company was not ready to implement a new system at the precise moment at which the costs of its legacy system exceeded its benefits.

Executives cannot look at their legacy systems in isolation and ask, "Does our current system work for our organization?" That question is too simplistic. Rather, systems must be considered within the context of their feasible alternatives. **Senior managers can always upgrade but should first ask a fundamental question: "Does our organization currently possess the human and financial resources and political wherewithal to successfully implement a new system?"**

To answer the financial aspect of this question, let's first look at the costs that organizations can expect for a new system. While not a definitive list, Table 3.1 represents expected costs that a relatively large organization can expect to incur during a new system implementation.

Table 3.1: Ballpark Costs of Implementing a New Tier 1 or Tier 2 System

Item	Cost - Lower End	Cost - Upper End
Purchase of Vendor Software License	$200,000	$500,000
Annual Support	$44,000	$110,000
External Consultants	$300,000	$1,000,000
Internal Resources' Time	$300,000	$1,000,000
Totals	$844,000	$2,610,000

Note that Chapter 5 will examine software tiers in more detail. Also note that additional implementation-related costs may include:

- Recruiting, hiring, and training personnel with skills required by the new system.
- Modifying previously functioning interfaces to and from different vendors.
- Training current employees on how to use the new system.
- Unforeseen costs stemming from typical activation issues— e.g., correcting employee paychecks, underpaying or overpaying vendors, and so on.

If the organization cannot stomach these costs, the political climate is not right, or the resources are not available, then it would be best served by waiting until those obstacles can be overcome. Unless there is some overarching business imperative, the organization should stop immediately.

So, let's return to the question of the costs and benefits of a new system. Is there a sufficient margin between the two such that the organization can make the case for change? For many reasons, particularly in mature organizations, the gap between costs and benefits typically needs to be fairly significant. Very rarely will senior management pull the trigger when expected benefits marginally exceed costs. COS was no exception to this rule.

Let's consider a number of other factors that drive the new systems. The goal here is to understand organizational decisions to retire legacy systems and move to more contemporary—and superior— alternatives. While there is certainly some overlap among the following reasons, they are listed as follows:

- The Costs of Inertia
- Accounting Advantages/Capitalization
- Organizational Growth
- Business Imperative
- Desire for Consolidation and Simplicity
- Cost-Effectiveness
- System Envy
- Acquisition

The Costs of Inertia

At some point, an organization may no longer have the option of maintaining its legacy system. In other words, a mature organization with no burning desire to purchase or build a new system may be forced into doing so because:

- It becomes prohibitively expensive for the organization to maintain its legacy system.
- The vendor of the legacy system is going out of business.
- Relatively few individuals actively support the legacy system.

For whatever reason, sometimes organizations just don't have a choice. Whether they like it or not, they have to depart from the past and embark on a costly and time-consuming journey.

Accounting Advantages/Capitalization

Many organizations can realize certain tax advantages by virtue of implementing a new system. Certain IT costs can be capitalized, impacting the overall net cost of the project.[9] While this alone is typically not the main driver for a new system, it is a nice side benefit for the bean counters and helps make the case for change.

Organizational Growth

Perhaps a company has run a small system that has served it well while it had 400 employees. However, after four years of massive growth, the company is no longer small. It requires a much more powerful system, equipped with a more robust database or "back end" to meet its business needs. In this case, the company can easily justify the costs of the new system.

Business Imperative

Back in the late 1990s, many organizations implemented new systems because legacy systems faced Y2K[10] risks. While Y2K is not a concern today, there are instances in which an organization has a compelling need to pursue a new system. These organizations may be able to continue using their legacy systems but would have to significantly tweak them to support recent regulatory or business developments. A good example of this is the 2002 passage of the

---

[9] Capital expenditures (CAPEX or capex) are expenditures creating future benefits. A capital expenditure is incurred when a business spends money either to buy fixed assets or to add to the value of an existing fixed asset with a useful life that extends beyond the taxable year. Capex are used by a company to acquire or upgrade physical assets such as equipment, property, or industrial buildings. In accounting, a capital expenditure is added to an asset account ("capitalized"), thus increasing the asset's basis (the cost or value of an asset as adjusted for tax purposes). Capex is commonly found on the Cash Flow Statement as "Investment in Plant Property and Equipment" or something similar in the Investing subsection. (Source: Wikipedia)

[10] The Year 2000 problem (also known as the Y2K problem, the millennium bug, the Y2K bug, or simply Y2K) was a notable computer bug resulting from the practice in early computer program design of representing the year with two digits. This caused some date-related processing to operate incorrectly for dates and times on and after January 1, 2000, and on other critical dates that were billed as "event horizons." This fear was fueled by the attendant press coverage and other media speculation, as well as corporate and government reports. People recognized that long-working systems could break down when the "...97, 98, 99..." ascending numbering assumption suddenly became invalid. Companies and organizations worldwide checked and upgraded their computer systems. (Source: Wikipedia)

Sarbanes Oxley Act.[11] From a systems standpoint, SOX compromised the utility of many older financial systems conceived well before the accounting scandals of the early 2000s, such as Enron and Tyco. Legacy systems could not handle SOX requirements for enhanced audit capability.

Desire for Consolidation and Simplicity

Many organizations added disparate parts to their core legacy systems over the years. As a result, many were left with an eye-chart of disconnected systems that typically operated in isolation, contained redundant or inconsistent data, or required excessive maintenance. Widespread frustration from the end-user community over the inability to pull basic and accurate data is sometimes sufficient for an organization to "blow up" the mess that has accumulated and move to a single, integrated system.

Cost-Effectiveness

Even the organization that can survive under its existing legacy system may opt to take the plunge. While certain businesses can continue with the status quo, at some point critical mass may be reached. In other words, there comes a time at which it is more cost-effective to adopt a new system. A perfect example of this is the company that pays an outsourced service provider such as ADP[12] to print employee checks. While ADP offers different pricing models, most of its clients tend to pay for each employee transaction. In other words,

---

[11] The Sarbanes-Oxley Act of 2002 (Pub.L. 107-204, 116 Stat. 745, enacted July 30, 2002), also known as the Public Company Accounting Reform and Investor Protection Act of 2002 and commonly called SOX or Sarbox, is a United States federal law enacted on July 30, 2002, in response to a number of major corporate and accounting scandals including those affecting Enron, Tyco International, Adelphia, Peregrine Systems and WorldCom. These scandals, which cost investors billions of dollars when the share prices of the affected companies collapsed, shook public confidence in the nation's securities markets. Named after sponsors Senator Paul Sarbanes (D-MD) and Representative Michael G. Oxley (R-OH), the Act was approved by the House by a vote of 334-90 and by the Senate 99-0. (Source: Wikipedia)

[12] Automatic Data Processing, Inc. (NASDAQ: ADP) ADP, is a global provider of integrated-computing and business-outsourcing solutions. ADP has nearly $8 billion in revenues and approximately 585,000 clients. ADP offers a range of HR, payroll, tax, and benefits administration solutions. ADP is headquartered in Roseland, NJ, USA. (Source: Wikipedia)

larger organizations that need to print thousands of employee checks receive larger bills from ADP than do smaller organizations.

Let's say that a company (Bonds Construction) with 1,000 employees paid biweekly pays ADP $2 per check, equating to $52,000 per annum. (This amount does not include ADP's creation of custom reports, typically costing clients about $175 per hour.) Now, if Bonds' population grows to 2,000, the annual fee doubles to $104,000. That amount may start to look excessive in comparison to what the company could expect to spend if it processed its own payroll internally. The annual cost of employing a full-time payroll manager (say $50,000 per year) may prompt Bonds to cut its own checks.

Similarly, consider Rutherford Music, an organization paying three separate support and licensing fees each year to different vendors, each of which is $50,000 per year. Rutherford management may not feel that $150,000 per year in maintenance is cost-efficient. GL, Payroll, and HR systems are stitched together by interfaces making the system very cumbersome. Rutherford figures that it can save considerably on annual maintenance costs by implementing an integrated system.

System Envy

Keeping up with the Joneses is not confined to cars and houses. The existing or newly hired VP or COO of Portis, Inc. may come down with "system envy" and decide that he wants to have the "cool" functionality of a new system. Portis' existing systems may be cost-effective and even sufficient for end-users. However, Portis' current systems lack the "wow" factor—i.e., the bells and whistles of other applications.

Acquisition

Sometimes a system can be cost-effective, well-functioning, and integrated but still is replaced. Typically, this takes place during an acquisition. For example, Theismann Apparel acquires Rypien Clothing. Theismann runs Oracle applications while Rypien runs Lawson for the same functions. Theismann has a desire to keep all transactions in one central place and minimize support costs. As a result, Theismann converts Rypien data into Oracle applications.

Summary

This chapter explained the reasons that organizations implement new systems. Different organizations have different reasons, although money is almost always one of the most important considerations. Let's move to the next fundamental question: Will the new system be bought, built, or rented?

It is better to know all the questions than some of the answers.

-James Thurber

CHAPTER 4: THE MAKE, BUY, OR RENT DECISION
Introduction

Having made the decision to retire its legacy system, the next step that an organization needs to take is to address the classic "make or buy" question: Is the organization going to build its own system from scratch or purchase a "mature" system that tens, hundreds, or even thousands of organizations currently use? Note that the traditional make or buy decision has been complicated somewhat in recent years by the advent of SaaS[13] (Software as a Service). Vendors like Workday and salesforce.com provide a third option for organizations that want to "rent" software.

The following chart illustrates the three main system options for an organization and the pros and cons of each:

---

[13] Software as a service (SaaS, typically pronounced 'sass') is a model of software deployment where an application is hosted as a service provided to customers across the Internet. By eliminating the need to install and run the application on the customer's own computer, SaaS alleviates the customer's burden of software maintenance, ongoing operation, and support. Conversely, customers relinquish control over software versions or changing requirements; moreover, costs to use the service become a continuous expense rather than a single expense at time of purchase. Using SaaS can conceivably reduce the up-front expense of software purchases, through less costly, on-demand pricing. From the software vendor's standpoint, SaaS has the attraction of providing stronger protection of its intellectual property and establishing an ongoing revenue stream. The SaaS software vendor may host the application on its own web server, or this function may be handled by a third-party application service provider (ASP). This way, end-users may reduce their investment on server hardware too. (Source: Wikipedia)

Table 4.1: Three System Options: Advantages and Disadvantages

Option	Make	Buy	Rent
Advantages	System is custom-built for organization.	An organization is presumably buying a mature (fully tested) system that should be relatively "bug-free."	Quicker "activation" time.
	No need to pay support to vendor.	Other organizations use the system and act as testers, expediting the discovery and resolution of major issues.	Potentially lower cost of ownership (based on number of transactions).
	Full control of upgrades and enhancements	Employees can be hired from the labor force with experience using the system.	Lower IT involvement, as vendor handles upgrades.
Disadvantages	All testing is done by the ISV or client. A client cannot rely on other organizations to serve as de facto testers.	A generic system may not match end-user business requirements out of the box.	Hosted software and data give rise to security concerns in an organization.
	Starting from scratch typically involves a great deal of design work.	Support of the new system typically runs at 20% of the initial license fee.	Vendor may charge a considerable amount for custom reports.
	There is no available pool of workers with experience in this unique system.	Customizations come at the organization's expense; support will not cover modifications under the vendor's default agreement.	Less ability to customize the system.

Considerations

Many factors drive an organization's decision to buy, build, or rent. Some of these factors include the following:

- Size of Organization
- Number of Expected Annual Transactions (a key in "rental" agreements)

- Budget
- Control
- Timeline
- Security Concerns

Size of Organization

As a general rule, a small organization—in terms of employees and revenue—is much less likely to purchase and implement a very large, expensive system than a larger organization. For example, not too many 200-employee companies poised for modest growth can justify a $500,000 outlay for a new system such as SAP. For these organizations, relatively small-scale solutions like Abra, Peachtree, Sage's MAS90, or QuickBooks are probably sufficient for the time being. If not, then the rental option may be appealing for simple cost reasons.

On the other end of the spectrum, a very large, 40,000-employee firm in multiple countries would tend to find it easier to justify the expense of a large system that has been thoroughly tested. In this case, building a system is often just plain silly. For example, pharmaceutical companies should make enterprise-wide systems about as often as network security companies should manufacture their own aspirin. The vast majority of Fortune 500 companies have some type of ERP, even if it's a very old version that has been greatly customized.

Number of Expected Annual Transactions

SaaS agreements tend to be transaction-based. In other words, the organization that enters more sales or pays more employees will receive larger bills from their vendors than will companies with fewer transactions. Thus, a small organization would be more amenable to a "pay as you go" system. At the end of the year, if the organization pays more, then it probably had a stellar year.

A large organization will typically not rent software, at least enterprise-wide. Certain pockets or departments might go this route, perhaps on a trial period. Consider a company that expects to conduct $4M financial or employee transactions at fifty cents per transaction. It is facing $2M in annual expenses, an amount often large enough to sway that organization towards buying its own system.

Budget

Budget is a primary driver of the make, rent, or buy decision. ERP vendors know that it is very expensive and time-consuming for organizations to build comprehensive payroll, GL, and procurement systems from scratch. They also know that many prospective clients' legacy systems have long outlived their usefulness. Major vendors are all competitively priced. One might be a bit more expensive than another on any one deal, but it is fair to assume that comparable vendors' prices will be in the same general ballpark.

Control

Renting or purchasing software from a vendor may restrict a client's ability to tinker with that software. An organization with the desire, knowledge, and resources to customize its system probably wants no part of renting. The organization that builds a system from scratch or "gets under the hood" of a purchased system controls that system. These viable options present their own challenges to be discussed at length in Chapter 16.

Timeline

The organization that needs to go live in a relatively short period of time may be tempted to rent, thinking that it does not have the time or budget to endure a traditional soup-to-nuts implementation. For example, perhaps a start-up has recently received funding and is looking for a "quick fix." The thinking here is that employees are probably too busy to participate in a full-blown implementation. All else being equal, a SaaS solution *may* have a shorter ramp up time than that of a traditional system. As discussed previously, however, there are no guarantees.

Security Concerns

Certain executives are not comfortable with key employee, GL, or sales information lying outside of their control. While companies like salesforce.com and ADP claim to house their "hosted" information in a secure manner (and I certainly cannot claim that they do not), a CIO simply might feel uneasy about not "owning" her company's information.

Building from Scratch

Returning to Table 4.1 for a moment, organizations should think very carefully prior to building an application from scratch or contracting an ISV for that very purpose. While this is certainly not a book about software development, organizations considering this route need to remember a few cardinal rules:

- Issues found later in an application's development cycle are exponentially more time-consuming and expensive to fix than issues found at the beginning of the cycle.
- Unlike somewhat "pre-built" off-the-shelf applications, developers can essentially build anything. Developers do best with pristine development specifications, allowing them to build the specific applications and functionality desired by organizational end-users.

While exceptional circumstances exist, organizations are almost exclusively better served by either buying or renting systems. In their oft-cited management book "In Search of Excellence," Tom Peters and Robert Waterman advise organizations to "stick to their knitting."

Multiple Vendors and the Best of Breed Approach

When deciding on future system architecture, most organizations opt for a single solution (whether buying or renting). A best of breed[14] (BOB) application is considered the best product of its type and is defined as follows:

> Organizations purchase software from different vendors in order to obtain the best-of-breed for each application area; for example, a human resources package from one vendor and an accounting package from another. While ERP vendors provide a wealth of applications for the enterprise and tout their integrated system as the superior solution, every module may not be best of breed. It is difficult to excel in every niche.

BOB systems can be integrated with other systems, including ERPs. For instance, a company may buy and implement PeopleSoft throughout the organization, integrating it with Taleo's Talent Management product. Typically, the business need is strong enough to justify the additional expense required to integrate the BOB application with the rest of the organization's systems. Two case studies detailed in this book focus on organizations that opted to stitch together BOB systems with their ERPs. **More often than not, organizations will not implement core systems and BOB systems concurrently. Clients tend to integrate BOB systems well after they have implemented their core systems and their end-users have had ample time to adjust to them.**

---

[14] http://encyclopedia2.thefreedictionary.com/best-of-breed

Summary

There is no simple answer to the question of whether organizations are best served by renting, buying, or building systems. The factors discussed in this chapter differ for every organization. However, the following general rule remains: Absent a compelling business need, organizations should purchase or rent a tested, proven solution rather than build one from scratch. From a business perspective, the amount of time, money, and effort required to build a new GL, supply chain, or payroll system will dissuade all but the most naïve or stubborn senior managers. As a last resort, an organization determined to create a new back office system—and incurring the related risks—should consider this: these systems result in no real sustainable business advantage.

For smaller organizations, renting may be a more viable option, particularly if the application addresses a relatively common business need (such as accounting, sales, or payroll) and will result in relatively few annual transactions. These organizations do not tend to have the budget for a large, expensive ERP, unless they project massive short-term growth. They generally do not have the resources to "reinvent the wheel" and build their own core systems.

The case for building is perhaps strongest for organizations that have a niche need with no apparent software application on the market, at least for a reasonable cost. While this is not a book on software development, suffice it to say that many "custom" systems suffer from poorly defined design specifications. As such, an ISV or internal developer may need to make certain leaps of faith that turn out to be incorrect. This hinders development and causes delays and cost overruns.

Part Two: System Selection

This section will focus on an organization's selection of partners for their new systems. Vendors and consultancies submit formal proposals in an attempt to aggressively win the business. We will see how many projects start off on the wrong foot.

The salesman knows nothing of what he is selling save that he is charging a great deal too much for it.

-Oscar Wilde

CHAPTER 5: THE SOUNDS OF SALESMEN
Introduction

Tim is the head of HR for Shelby and Associates, a medium-sized accounting firm. As his firm has grown, the hodgepodge of Access databases, Excel spreadsheets, and other disparate sources of employee information has made doing business increasingly difficult. Things such as government reporting, annual open enrollment, and tracking employee turnover had become administrative nightmares. What's more, knowing which employees possessed which skills—a key in a service-oriented firm such as his—required quite a few phone calls. Finally, he had enough. After a few months of interviewing vendors, he selected a new HRIS for his company.

A few weeks after signing the contract with the vendor, Tim was aghast. The vendor initially claimed that certain functionality was included in the new application, such as electronically automating the new hire "on-boarding" process. It turned out that these were, in fact, "enhancements to the standard application requiring customization." In other words, the vendor could build these features into the vanilla product but the time and expense required would not be covered under the initial contract.

Tim could not believe what he was hearing. Already encountering issues so early into the project, he faced the possibility of going back to his senior management and telling him that the project would require more money. He was not too excited with this possibility. Did I mention that he works for an accounting firm?

Unfortunately, this scenario is all too commonplace, as I told him. While possibly a bit of an exaggeration, the *Glengarry Glen Ross*[15]

---

[15] Glengarry Glen Ross is a 1982 play written by David Mamet. The play shows parts of two days in the lives of four desperate Chicago real estate agents who are prepared to engage in any number of unethical, illegal acts—from lies and flattery to bribery, threats, intimidation, and burglary—to sell undesirable real estate to unwilling prospective buyers. The play draws partly on Mamet's experiences of life in a Chicago real estate

mindset of "always be closing" is still quite prevalent in many software companies. Salespeople view making sales as their primary objective while "getting it to work" is typically a job for the consultants. I cannot recall the number of times that end-users have asked me to demonstrate functionality that they erroneously believed was "out of the box" when, in fact, those features were only possible via some type of system modification.

To be completely fair to salespeople, systems are becoming more powerful with "add-on" tools and "extensions" that increase the power of standard system functionality. When a prospective client asks a question about the "out of the box" functionality of a system, the salesperson will typically say, "Yes, the application can do that." That same individual will often neglect to mention the second part of the answer. For the system to do what the client wants, the client would have to purchase—and implement—one or more of the complementary products mentioned below.

Email Notification
Historically, end-users relied largely on phone calls and intra-office mail to do their jobs. Thanks to technology, however, things have dramatically changed. Systems can prompt end-users to approve purchase orders (POs) and automatically send emails to accounts payable. Along the same lines, systems can automatically send important forms to new hires (I-9, W-4, etc.).

Database Triggers and Notifications
Database triggers[16] take place when an "event" is recorded in the database. For example, an HR clerk changes an employee's hire date or an invoice is overdue beyond 60 days in accounts receivable. To the extent that these events can impact a number of things (such as an employee's benefits or a company's financial statements), the trigger prompts end-users to take additional steps within the system.

---

office, where he worked briefly in the late 1960s. The title of the play comes from the names of two of the real estate developments being peddled by the salesmen characters, Glengarry Highlands and Glen Ross Farms. (Source: Wikipedia)

[16] A database trigger is procedural code that is automatically executed in response to certain events on a particular table in a database. Triggers can restrict access to specific data, perform logging, or audit data modifications (Source: Wikipedia).

Reporting Solutions

Vendor software typically contains reporting functionality out of the box in the form of standard or "canned" reports. Tools such as Crystal Reports and Business Objects, however, are much more robust reporting solutions that can handle very complex reporting requirements. A vendor's canned reports usually do not meet all of an individual client's specific business needs.

Form Design Tools

The "front end" of the application, whether web-based or not, can typically be modified to meet client needs. In some cases, the change can be as simple as the name of a field, such as an "employee name" becoming "associate name." In other cases, the change involves significantly altering existing forms or creating entirely new fields and forms.

Software Tiers and Costs

ERPs fall into major categories or tiers. ERPs in the same tiers tend to be more similar than dissimilar, both on technical and functional fronts. Table 5.1 shows each tier, typical clients, and examples of vendors:

Table 5.1: Software Tier Breakdown[17]

Tier	1	2
Description	Software for the large enterprise.	Software for mid-sized clients; market contains the largest number of potential customers.
Types of Clients	Multi-site, multinational corporations. The average Tier 1 customer has revenues in excess of $200M. Client needs licenses for typically of greater than 200 users.	Clients have revenue from $20M to $200M and may have a single site or a few sites. Client needs licenses for 100 to 200 users.
Examples	Prior to the recent M&A activity, the players included JD Edwards, Baan, Oracle, PeopleSoft, and SAP. Now that Oracle has purchased PeopleSoft (which had purchased JD Edwards), the map has left the three primary ERP vendors: SAP, Oracle, and Baan. One could make the argument that Lawson (after its recent Intentia merger) is now a Tier 1 vendor as well.	QAD, Infor's Syteline, Microsoft Navision (Dynamics NAV), ABAS, Glovia, Ultipro, Best's MAS500, and Epicor Vantage.
Tier	3	4
Description	Software designed for single-site customers	Basic accounting and HR systems.
Types of Clients	These clients have revenues under $40M packages and are looking to expand their capabilities.	Clients include small startups or companies with $2M or less in revenue
Examples	Lily's Visual Manufacturing, Intuitive Manufacturing, Microsoft Great Plains (Dynamics GP), DBA Software and Best's MAS200.	Examples include Microsoft Great Plains (Dynamics GP), DBA Software, Best's MAS200, PeachTree, Accpac, and QuickBooks.

---

[17] Modified with permission from ERP and More (site—
http://www.erpandmore.com/2005/10/28/erp-what-tier-are-you-in).

The following table shows approximate costs by tier:

Table 5.2: Approximate First Year Costs by Software Tier

Tier	License Fee	Impl. Fees	Support	Total (first year expenses)
1	$400,000	$400,000	$88,000	$888,000
2	$200,000	$200,000	$44,000	$444,000
3	$100,000	$100,000	$22,000	$222,000
4	$20,000	$20,000	$4,400	$44,400

Note that these are ballpark numbers and do not reflect any one vendor, client, or even proposal. Such numbers may vary considerably.

Finding the Right Tier

Organizations may find themselves "between tiers" from a budgetary standpoint. The organization not prepared to spend roughly $1M on total first-year implementation costs should probably look at an alternative to Tier 1 applications. It should not even send an RFP to vendors such as Oracle, SAP, or Baan. However, at times, the desired budget for a project might cause senior management to consider software from multiple tiers.

Consider Gavin Industries, an entertainment company with 3,000 employees, $10M in revenues, and a $600,000 budget for a new enterprise-wide system. It is considering two alternatives:

- A more powerful and expensive Tier 1 application that it could not afford to fully test because of budget considerations. The license fee would eat up too much of the implementation budget, forcing corners to be cut throughout the implementation.
- A tested, stable, and "less powerful" Tier 2 application that it could utilize safely, properly, and consistently throughout the organization. The license fee would allow for a proper implementation, with slightly less functionality relative to Tier 1 applications.

What should Gavin do? It most certainly should *not* spend $500,000 for the Tier 1 application's licensing and support. Barring exceptional circumstances, the company cannot successfully implement the product for a mere $100,000. The better alternative is to purchase a Tier 2 solution for $200,000 or so and implement it correctly. **Any perceived or real advantages of a Tier 1 application need to be viewed within the context of the organization itself and its ability to support that application. If not tested and used properly, superior functionally from a more costly application does the organization and its end-users much more harm than good. A more complex, powerful, and expensive system only makes sense if the organization and its end-users can properly manage it.** In this case, the second alternative benefits Gavin and its end-users much more so than does the first.

A Useful Analogy

A few years ago, I heard an interesting analogy with regard to some of the main ERPs. Consider some of the major systems with respect to building a house. With Lawson (at the time firmly in the second tier), the house comes almost pre-built and clients need only to paint and decorate it. PeopleSoft comes with a floor plan and general design. With SAP, the client has not even picked out the land yet. Organizations would do well to keep this analogy in mind with respect to ERP purchases, timeframes, and budgets.

A Note on SaaS and Tiers

As discussed in Chapter 4, SaaS-based companies like Workday and salesforce.com offer an intriguing alternative to the traditional ERP model: Rather than purchasing and implementing a system, clients can rent it and pay a per-transaction fee. Because of its variable cost, SaaS applications and companies transcend tiers. In theory, organizations from ten employees to ten thousand (or more) can run this software at an affordable cost. Thus, SaaS applications are theoretically "tier-independent" and can be run by any organization. As for cost, the following table presents approximate first-year costs for the organization using software on a rental basis:

Table 5.3: Approximate First Year Costs for a SaaS Client

Size of Organization	Annual Trans.	Impl. Time (months)	Impl. Costs Per Month	Total Impl. Costs	Per Trans. Cost	Annual Trans. Costs	Total First Year Expenses
Small	1,000	2	$10,000	$20,000	$1.00	$1,000	$21,000
Medium	5,000	3	$15,000	$45,000	$0.90	$4,500	$49,500
Large	20,000	4	$20,000	$80,000	$0.80	$16,000	$96,000
Global	50,000	6	$30,000	$180,000	$0.70	$35,000	$215,000

Note that these numbers represent rough estimates, not tied to any vendor, application, potential client, and/or deal.

System Convergence and the Software Industry

Organizations considering the purchase and implementation of an off-the-shelf product should understand the following: Systems in the same tier tend to have very similar functionality and scalability. For example, an organization cannot compare PeachTree financial software with Oracle Financials. They are apples and coconuts. Compared to PeachTree, Oracle offers far more across the board, as well it should, given the huge disparity in cost. One cannot realistically compare Ultipro with Lawson's HR and Payroll product; the latter simply offers clients a great deal more integration with other products, such as reporting capability, scalability, and the like.

This is not to say that Ultipro or PeachTree are inferior products on some absolute level; they are not. Systems need to be viewed in relative terms and in conjunction with the business requirements that organizations need them to fill. An organization may only have a need for a small, "bare bones" application for ten end-users and may not need to make the requisite financial commitment required with a Tier 1 ERP. A 300-employee domestic publishing house simply would not use items such as multiple currencies in Oracle, for example. Consider a car analogy. One should not compare a $10,000 used station wagon with a top-of-the-line, $250,000 Lamborghini. Yes, both cars will go from point A to point B. However, if the driver requires the ability to go from zero to 60 in under five seconds and is willing to pay for it, then the Lamborghini is way to go.

The software industry has seen a great deal of consolidation in recent years and many products unable to find traction in the market have disappeared altogether. Ultimately, the organization looking at software vendors in the same tier will find that, in general, there are many more similarities than true differences in terms of delivered system functionality. Systems have converged a great deal over the last ten years. An organization would be hard-pressed to find a truly distinct product, although one vendor's individual features may be temporarily unique, at least until its competitors develop and integrate similar features.

A few examples of this convergence among many applications are instructive.

- Lawson's HR/Payroll application had long made use of employee groups to facilitate reporting, benefits administration, employee vacation and sick accruals, etc. A single vacation plan could encompass employees in the different departments, divisions, and employment statuses (full-time, part-time) and apply different accrual rates to those groups. In other words, an organization would not have to set up and maintain ten different plans for ten different groups. PeopleSoft (prior to being acquired by Oracle) realized that this was very useful functionality and, in fact, a potential differentiator at the point of sale. Thus, years ago it added the equivalent of employee groups.
- While researching Oracle's 11i Benefit application a few years back, I was struck by the number of similar batch programs that have Lawson equivalents. To be sure, the names of the programs are different and they access different tables on the back end. Still, the programs had the same fundamental purposes: They facilitate the administration of benefits and update records en masse.

On a more general level, all of the major Tier 1 players (SAP, Oracle/PeopleSoft, and Baan) provide features[18] such as the following:

- Web-based versions of their products—no longer must the client support a traditional client-server configuration
- Forms of "self-service" for employee open enrollment, time entry, and so on
- Batch processing
- Regulatory, compliance, and financial reporting
- Standard reports and *ad hoc* reporting tools (although the latter tend not to be as robust as "add on" products such as Crystal Reports, Business Objects, etc.)

This is a far cry from saying that all systems (even in the same tier) are identical in terms of absolute functionality, scalability, and cost. Very large organizations from different industries with diverse needs and populations run PeopleSoft, SAP, and Baan, as the salespeople

---

[18] Note that many of the names of these features vary and change on a routine basis. Self-service has given way to "portals," for example. Changing the name of the application does *not* change that application's purpose and features.

from each vendor will certainly mention. Senior management at Katz International may use a consultancy during the sales cycle or go about it alone. Regardless, Katz should not take at face value a vendor's claim that it can uniquely meet Katz's needs. Odds are that another system—from the same tier—can largely meet those needs as well. Katz's ultimate decision will hinge on items such as the perceived advantages and cost of the new system.

Type of Industry: Does It Matter?

Without question, there are perceived leaders among vendors in certain industries. As discussed earlier in this chapter, an international manufacturing organization is much more likely to go with SAP than a Tier 2 or 3 solution. Conversely, a single-site hospital is unlikely to have the budget (or, frankly, the need) for much of SAP's functionality; to that end, it would give Lawson a strong look.

Truth be told, however, the perceptions may trump reality, especially within tiers. The hospital mentioned above could absolutely pay its employees and produce financial statements via SAP. Cost aside, Lawson and SAP are more similar than dissimilar. During system selection, then, the overriding question for an organization should not be, "Which is the *best* system?" Rather, executives should ask a similar, contextual question, "Which system is cost-effective *and* allows us to meet our business needs?"

While this might seem obvious, many times, system implementations start off on the wrong foot because of this disconnect. The specific system (and consultancy) selected tend not to be the primary drivers of a system failure. It is more nuanced. Budgets, profit margins, and business and organizational climates come heavily into play. To elaborate, consider the following two organizations, Dickinson Hospital and Harris Apparel.

Table 5.4: Comparison of Dickinson and Harris Clients

	Dickinson Hospital	Harris Apparel
Industry	Healthcare	Retail
Profit Margins	22%	7%
Revenues	10M	10M
Company Founded Year	1982	1996
Annual Financial and Employee Transactions	1.5M	4M
Age of Current Systems	26 years	12 years
Employees	4,500	4,500

These two organizations have decided to purchase and implement a new system and have narrowed their selections to several Tier 1 and 2 ERPs. Which one should each select and why? While there is no one concrete answer to such a simplistic scenario, each should consider the following, *all else being equal*:

- The profit margins of each should drive its decision to some extent. Retail is a much tougher and dynamic business than healthcare, as evinced by the margins and number of annual transactions. For example, Harris probably cannot afford a two-year implementation of a new system for $4M to the same degree that Dickinson can. By virtue of its less frenetic pace, Dickinson could potentially purchase a "bigger" system and implement more functionality out of the box; it has more resources at its disposal in a less frenetic business environment.
- The more hectic business environment will affect Harris' end-users more severely than those at Dickinson. During "holiday hire" in retail (in November and December), for example, HR and payroll end-users will have virtually no time to devote to consultants. Also, because of the lower profit margins, it's a safe bet to assume that Harris is "leaner" in terms of internal resources than Dickinson. As such, Harris *may* need to use more external consultants for the implementation than Dickinson.
- The more dynamic nature of retail also means that Harris' end-users have probably worked there for shorter periods of time than their Dickinson counterparts. Perhaps Harris' current staff has experience with PeopleSoft, for example, and can offer valuable insight during the selection process.

If Harris chooses PeopleSoft, then its in-house expertise will be a considerable asset and the "organizational learning curve" may be less steep.

- Conversely, healthcare tends to be more rigid and bureaucratic relative to retail. It's quite possible that Dickinson end-users will be very reluctant to change their business practices due to a system limitation. To the extent that these limitations are often discovered after a system has been selected and the implementation has begun, Dickinson management should gauge two things: 1) the willingness of its internal staff to be flexible and; 2) the ease and cost of each system under consideration to be customized.
- Finally, Dickinson's older legacy system will prove to be more problematic than Harris' system. As a general rule, older systems typically contain "tougher" data, much of which may be inaccurate, unobtainable for conversion purposes, or both.

In the end, there are very few absolutes for an organization choosing a system. As this book will illustrate, a system failure is *not* exclusively a function of industry. I personally have worked on successful and unsuccessful projects in quite a few industries. In general, however, healthcare and non-profit or government clients tend to be much more prone to failure than clients in retail and telecommunications. Organizations in the latter industries are usually more adept at handling change than those in the former. **As a general rule, the older a company's systems and data, the higher the profit margins, and the less dynamic the industry, the more difficult a system implementation will be. Organizations should keep this in mind from the beginning (selecting a system and a consulting partner, planning a project, assigning timelines and resources, etc.).**

Should an Organization Rent or Buy?

Tables 5.1 and 5.2 contain important information for organizations considering both the traditional purchase as well as the relatively new rental model. The pricing models of a SaaS-based application may be attractive to many organizations, hinging on their expected annual transactions. This begs the question: Is renting better than buying?

The answer is an unequivocal "maybe." The jury is still out on SaaS; it remains to be seen whether it offers inherent time or cost advantages relative to traditional software arrangements. In theory, SaaS implementations and activations may go more smoothly, result in fewer issues, take less time, and cost less than traditional system implementations. The greatest *potential* time and cost savings are realized in the following ways:

- Software—organizations do not need to install, maintain, or upgrade SaaS software; the vendor takes care of all of this.
- Hardware—SaaS software does not need to be tied to enterprise-wide databases and servers.

When deciding on whether to rent or buy, senior management may feel more comfortable using a single vendor if possible. Large software vendors typically can accommodate the entire gamut of their clients' systems needs, but some SaaS solutions may not. For example, the formerly independent Employease, one of the early adopters of the SaaS model, provided human resource and benefit functionality but not payroll. While Employease did have a partnership with ADP to provide that very service prior to being acquired by ADP in 2006[19], its clients had to enter into agreements with multiple vendors. Along those lines, the recently-launched Workday has a similar relationship with ADP to process employee payroll. This is not to say that ADP or Workday provide inferior products, functionality, or support. However, "one-stop shopping" may be inherently more appealing to the organization with a desire to minimize its vendor relationships.

On another note, certain SaaS clients have encountered integration issues with pieces of their system architectures.[20] Consider the hypothetical example of Stone Construction. Stone begins using Workday—in lieu of its legacy system—for annual open enrollment. Stone still needs to send those enrollments via interface to its benefit carriers. To the extent that different organizations use different benefit carriers, Workday does not provide out of the box integration to Aetna and MetLife, two of Stone's benefit providers. Stone may employ an integration company such as Cape Clear to create those bridges via service-oriented architecture[21] (SOA) or web services.[22] Alternatively,

---

[19] http://www.workday.com/partners/partner_directory/adp.php
[20] http://www.informationweek.com/news/services/saas/showArticle.jhtml?articleID =211200952
[21] Service-oriented architecture (SOA) provides methods for systems development and integration where systems group functionality around business processes and package

Stone's IT department may decide to do this internally. Regardless of which route it goes, SaaS does *not* obviate Stone's effort and expenses related to interfaces and complete integration of its systems.

In the end, there is no silver bullet. To continue with the house analogy from earlier in this chapter, regardless of whether the organization has purchased or leased the land, it still needs to know exactly what it wants to build. It still needs to buy the right materials, hire the right contractors, and test the plumbing and electricity before moving in. **Translation: Poorly defined business processes, bad data, lack of training for end-users, and other implementation issues discussed in subsequent chapters will plague any new system implementation, regardless of the type of arrangement that the organization has with its vendor.**

Contract Language and Distant Early Warnings[23]

While most projects derail over the course of a number of months, occasionally a system implementation implodes immediately after contracts are signed. This was the case in Shelby and Associates, mentioned at the beginning of this chapter. While last-minute issues are sometimes inevitable, organizations obviously want to avoid immediate project fractures. The question is, "How?"

Prior to signing any contracts with vendors and consultancies, senior managers should do the following:

- Painstakingly detail each of its organization's business requirements

---

these as interoperable services. SOA also describes IT infrastructure which allows different applications to exchange data with one another as they participate in business processes. Service-orientation aims at a loose coupling of services with operating systems, programming languages and other technologies which underlie applications. (Source: Wikipedia)

[22] A web service is defined as "a software system designed to support interoperable machine-to-machine interaction over a network" (Source: W3C)

[23] The Distant Early Warning Line, also known as the DEW Line or Early Warning Line, was a system of radar stations in the far northern Arctic region of Canada, with additional stations along the North Coast and Aleutian Islands of Alaska, in addition to the Faroe Islands, Greenland, and Iceland. It was set up to detect incoming Soviet bombers during the Cold War, a task which quickly became outdated when intercontinental ballistic missiles became the main delivery system for nuclear weapons. (Source, Wikipedia)

- Ensure that the final vendor/consultancy contract contains specific line items in relation to each system-delivered feature and service

After signing contracts, neither client nor vendor nor consultancy should have any doubt about which features and services will and will not be provided. Clarity minimizes project confusion among the different parties. What's more, detailed contract language eliminates the ability of the vendor or consulting firm to blast a client with expensive change requests. (Note that Chapter 8 extends the discussion of consultancies with respect to types of firms, system selection, and types of arrangements.)

Admittedly, this is easier said than done. Clients—especially of the first-time variety—may lack the time and expertise to write contract language with sufficient granularity to sufficiently protect themselves in the event of a dispute. Vendors and consultancies will typically not help clients in this regard. To address this issue, organizations should seek the assistance of resources with related expertise. A poorly worded or open-ended contract with a vendor or consultancy increases the probability of miscommunication, contentious relations, and, ultimately, system failure.

Ideally, meticulous contract language is superfluous during an implementation. In other words, senior management would not need to revert to the formal agreement often—if at all—because all parties are on the same page. As a result, no one on the client side will have had any disputes with the vendor or consultancy surrounding the services or system functionality that each is obligated to provide. However, remiss is the organization that does not plan for this very realistic contingency. Absent such language, clients are typically left with the following options when a problem of this nature arises:

- Agree to the requests of clients and vendors for additional funds
- Attempt to reach some type of compromise
- Pull the plug on a project altogether
- Threaten to withhold payments to the vendor or consultancy
- Indicate an unwillingness to provide a positive reference after the completion of the project
- A combination of all of the above

These alternatives may or may not produce the desired results. To be certain, they will create—or exacerbate—an adversarial relationship between client and partner. By insisting upon comprehensive contract language, however, organizations can minimize the need to pursue these confrontational options.

Summary

Winston Churchill once said, "Never trust a man without vices." Applied to software vendors, prospective clients would do well to remember that no system is perfect. Whether renting, buying, or building, remember that salespeople get paid to trumpet the virtues of their software, with an emphasis on "soft" (read: malleable) solutions. Yes, software can be built and customized to meet just about any business need. Sometimes this can be done with relative ease, sometimes not.

Vendor selection is a necessary precondition for an organization to embark on a systems implementation. The choice of a vendor is almost irreversible. Organizations should take every step possible to avoid a "suboptimal" decision because the stakes are so high. To that end, the suggestions offered in this chapter should help organizations make better decisions and help at least to get their implementations off on the right foot.

Vendor demonstrations can be outright dazzling but organizations should view them with a grain of salt. Prospective clients will never hear the word "no" from a salesperson in response to a question such as "Can your software do this?" To be sure, the answer to this question is typically not a complete misrepresentation of the truth. After all, anything is possible. For the prospective client, the better question to ask the salesperson "Does your software do this out of the box?" When the salesperson answers in the affirmative, the follow-up question, of course, should be, "Can you please show me how to do that, right now?"

Good design can't fix broken business models.

-Jeffrey Veen

CHAPTER 6: BUSINESS PROCESSES

Introduction

Truth be told, when implementing new systems, many organizations miss a fundamental opportunity to improve or reengineer key business processes.[24] This omission can take place during the initial project planning or soon after, as testing uncovers unanticipated issues. This short but crucial chapter examines why this is the case.

The Chicken and Egg Question

Organizations with deficient business processes tend to have deficient systems, begging the question of which comes first. There is often no simple answer to this question, as most systems have evolved over time. In other words, organizations change and augment their existing systems as business processes change. For example, Carson Dairy added several "band-aid" interfaces and smaller systems to its overall architecture over the last decade. As a result, Carson end-users face delays or lack real-time access to data, situations that senior management certainly did not foresee years ago. The cure may be worse than the disease, but short of "blowing up" its existing system architecture, Carson is stuck with suboptimal systems and processes for the foreseeable future.

The Symbiotic Relationship between Business Processes and Systems

Based on their experience with legacy systems, end-users are used to doing their jobs in a certain way. Lamentably, often organizations do not give sufficient thought as to how they can improve the efficiency of individual jobs and business processes. Within an organization, the initial level of excitement generated by vendors' dog-and-pony shows

---

[24] Reengineering is radical redesign of an organization's processes, especially its business processes. Rather than organizing a firm into functional specialties (like production, accounting, marketing, etc.) and considering the tasks that each function performs; complete processes from materials acquisition, to production, to marketing and distribution should be considered. The firm should be re-engineered into a series of processes. (Source: Wikipedia)

often dissipates during an implementation, as unforeseen problems invariably manifest themselves. It is understandable—but regrettable—that end-users often revert to what they know and may attempt to replicate the old system in the new one. As a result, features that many times sold the product in the first place are postponed to Phase II and may never see the light of day. Project teams sometimes set up new systems to essentially mimic their predecessors.

Organizations often fail to understand that business processes do not exist in a vacuum; they must be viewed against the backdrop of the technology used to enable those processes. Systems and business processes are related in a symbiotic—but not causal—manner. **Organizations with broken systems typically suffer from broken business processes and vice-versa.**

Consider Opeth Produce, a company with a broken payroll process. Paying employees is painfully slow and rife with errors. With that in mind, one of the following *must* be true with regard to Opeth's payroll system:

- The existing payroll system cannot support a better process as currently configured, irrespective of the knowledge of Opeth's end-users.
- Opeth's existing payroll system cannot support a better process, regardless of any potential type of configuration.
- Payroll end-users do not know how to use Opeth's existing system to achieve superior results, including fewer adjustments and manual checks and more accurate government reporting.

So, would a new system improve payroll processing at Opeth? It depends. If Opeth's management is hell-bent on replicating antiquated processing methods in a new system, then the answer is an unequivocal "no." If the payroll department cannot or will not learn how to use the system properly, then the answer is also "no."

Implementing new systems provides organizations with unique opportunities not only to improve their technologies, but also to redefine and improve key business processes. Ultimately, for organizations to consider these new systems successes, the post-legacy environment must ensure that business processes, client end-users, and systems all work together. Often, these three levers fail to support each other, as the following three examples illustrate.

A Broken Annual Process

Fenster Electric is a multinational corporation with employees in forty countries. Each year, it awards employee merit increases, bonuses, and stock options (MIBSO for short). Because of its eye chart of existing systems as well the general level of coordination involved throughout the organization, MIBSO begins in late August of each year, culminating in April of the following year. In other words, Fenster routinely takes more than half the year to handle employee compensation administration. A high level representation of the tasks and dates in this process is presented in Table 6.1:

Table 6.1: Annual Fenster MIBSO Process

Task	Start Date
Initial data validation of current employee populations and salary data	August
HQ sends personnel files to each Fenster site	September
Budgets announced and communicated	October
Site personnel make preliminary MIBSO determinations, send files back to HQ	December
Senior management begins review of initial site figures	January
Senior management finalizes employee MIBSO figures	February
HQ personnel send final files to central processing unit	March
Bonuses and stock options awarded, merit increases applied to employee salaries	April

Fenster is considering implementing a new system. Let's return to the "chicken and egg" question at the beginning of this chapter for a moment. Fenster needs to start with its business process, *not* the system. In other words, senior management needs to first ask if and how it can streamline MIBSO, *not* if a new system can support this wholly inefficient process. In other words, Fenster should not consider employee compensation administration a sacred process with respect to:

- The amount of time required each year
- Each step in the current MIBSO process
- The order in which each step takes place

If Fenster implemented a new system that left its current MIBSO process largely unchanged, then many in the organization may rightfully ask, "What was the point? It still takes us seven months to manage employee compensation." However, if senior management and experienced consultants determine that Fenster—via a new system—can successfully condense the entire MIBSO process to two months, then that new system will produce tangible results and savings.

A Broken Regular Process

Sanchez Financials receives resumes from applicants via both electronic and snail mail. Its recruiters then manually send letters of acknowledgement to candidates, keeping their resumes on file. Sanchez has no central repository of applicant information and, as a result, posts many jobs multiple times when perfectly viable candidates' resumes exist on individual employees' hard drives and in physical folders.

Sanchez's recruiting costs are excessive, and many applicants complain that they are rejected multiple times for the same job or interview repeatedly for that job. Hiring managers complain that their positions take too long to post and to fill, resulting in out-of-control overtime costs to existing employees. Recruiters spend way too much time trying to locate acceptable candidates and rely on memory while their time-to-fill (TTF) statistics are well below industry averages.

Sanchez purchases and implements a new applicant tracking system (ATS) delivering the following functionality:

- The electronic receipt of resumes
- Automatic job agents so that the posted jobs can be "pushed" to interested applicants
- More sophisticated search capability for recruiters
- Tracking of recruiting expenses

In this instance, the new technology allows Sanchez to completely reengineer its recruiting process. Sanchez could now essentially eliminate paper and electronically track all applicant correspondence. Hiring managers could use powerful search criteria to find the best applicants for newly-posted positions. Recruiting costs could plummet. By virtue of reduced recruiting costs and increased benefits, Sanchez's ATS could basically pay for itself over a three-year period.

In order for the ATS to be successful, Sanchez's employees have to realize that their jobs will significantly change. The possessive recruiter who insists that everything go through him will need to get with the program. Lazy hiring managers who expect HR to do their jobs for them need to accept and embrace their new responsibilities. While Sanchez's legacy system did not contain many bells and whistles, its new ATS does. However, that fact alone does not guarantee the results that Sanchez expects. In other words, just because a new system can do all of the wonderful things promised by the vendor does not mean that it will. In this example, the new ATS itself does not guarantee a thing. In order for the benefits of the new ATS to be realized, Sanchez's end-users need to get on board.

The above example was fairly dramatic. A broken recruiting process can be completely reengineered, and few would argue that Sanchez' status quo is optimal in present-day corporate America. However, let's look at a less obvious situation. Consider an organization with an "unbroken" key business process that could be improved.

A Suboptimal Regular Process

Spencer Seafood is implementing a new system but wants to keep paying its vendors or employees every two weeks. In this sense, Spencer's new system needs to reflect the same business processes as its legacy system. Specifically, system rules need to enable biweekly payments. This is not to say that "everything should be the same" or that "the new system should mimic the old across the board." Alternatively stated, Spencer may still be able to make quantum leaps with its new system vis-à-vis:

- Reporting
- Automation
- Audit capability
- Increased data tracking
- Self-service

Although Spencer maintains the same business procedures with its new system, end-users jobs do not have to remain unchanged. Yes, the AP director might still want to pay vendors herself and the payroll manager may be reluctant to turn the new system's payment print program over to a clerk. Consider the specific improvements that Spencer could still realize from its new system:

- Employee time records could be automatically generated, thus dramatically reducing:
  - The need for payroll clerks to manually enter data

- o The number of expected data-entry errors
- Invoices could be automatically matched via batch program
- Access to the data could be democratized; no longer would end-users need to formally request reports from a central IT function
- Benefit automation rules could enable new employee premiums to be calculated once employees change status. Terminated employees' benefits automatically could cease at the end of the month, no longer requiring manual intervention.

Summary

The organization that wants to realize the benefits and cost savings of a new system must be willing to consider reengineering its core business processes. Doing so makes that organization more likely to succeed: The new system may, in fact, do many of the things promised by the vendor. A new system merely provides organizations with *the opportunity* to do things better and more efficiently. Organizations that revert to antiquated methods maximize the likelihood that their new systems will be just as cumbersome as their predecessors.

Complain to one who can help you.

-Yugoslav Proverb

CHAPTER 7: SUPPORT FOR THE NEW SYSTEM

Introduction

Before it goes too far down the road of setup, an organization should decide very early in its planning phase on the type of support that it will require. Doing so allows it to staff the project appropriately. In this context, support does not mean external consultants or partners who will guide the organization through the implementation. They are the focus of the next chapter. Rather, support means assistance with system troubleshooting.

Types of Support

There are at least four main types of support available for organizations that have purchased vendors' systems. These are detailed below, along with a brief description of the advantages, disadvantages, and risks associated with each.

Support from the Vendor

By far, this is the most common and most expensive form of support. Typically, at about 20 to 22 percent of the initial license fee, vendor support allows clients to access the vendor's support site, knowledge base, application and technical troubleshooting, and other online tools. Clients can access patches and other "fixes," as well as open a case if the vanilla—i.e., not modified—application is not working as designed. For example, if a payroll close does not update history and the client has not altered the underlying code in any way, then a support representative will fix—or help the client fix—the issue. However, if that same client modified that payroll close program by "getting under the hood," then that client would not qualify for support under the terms of the agreement. Typically, in this scenario, the vendor will offer to assist the client to the tune of about $200 per hour.

Most companies opt for the standard level of vendor support. It is important for organizations to understand that vendor support does not cover items such as setting up the general ledger, processing payroll, or assisting with the writing of custom reports, even if the vendor also sells the reporting tool. For example, support representatives are not going to sit with clients for three hours figuring out why a custom purchase order report does not work properly. Again, for this type of assistance, the client will have to pay an hourly rate.

Note that the single notion of direct vendor support is giving way to different levels of support. Under this emerging phenomenon, clients can pay more to get more. A basic level of support might entitle clients to 8 am to 6 pm support Monday through Friday. More advanced and costly levels of support might entail 24/7 coverage, on-demand access to live product specialists, and support with system customization.

An organization should know beforehand the specific items that will and will not be covered under its individual support agreement long before going live. Armed with this knowledge, the organization can make intelligent decisions about customizations, setup, reporting, and so on. What's more, the organization can then allocate the right resources throughout the project and after system activation. Clearly, if an organization has activated a new system without appropriate internal resources to properly support that system, then it has significantly increased its chances for failure.

Years after an initial implementation, organizations may consider a support option typically called "sunset support." In this scenario, a client pays the vendor above and beyond its annual support fee for a relatively limited time while it runs a less-than-current version of the vendor's software. Typically, the client will have to work out a separate deal with its account manager. The client usually weighs the cost of remaining on the older version of the software against the cost of upgrading. To the extent that it is far easier for software vendors to support one or two major releases of their products, these agreements tend to be quite costly.

Support from a Vendor-Sanctioned Partner
Because of strategic partnerships or a lack of resources, a vendor may direct clients to other companies for sanctioned support. Alternatively, a client may go this route because the partner charges less than the vendor. This support may be technical, functional, or both. Note that the support is typically for "out of the box" functionality, not for changing the code of the software. There are instances in which a client may purchase "total" support for delivered functionality and system modifications. However, such support tends to be very expensive.

Support from a Unsanctioned Third Party
Typically the least expensive but riskiest option, organizations can

opt for support from a third party not sanctioned by the software vendor. For example, Chicago Bagel Emporium (CBE) runs Lawson version 7.2.4 and is considering third party support for several reasons. First, CBE management may simply think that it can save a considerable amount relative to its annual support contract with Lawson. Second, and arguably more common, CBE may opt for this type of support because Lawson is forcing clients to upgrade from one major release to another—e.g., from version 7 to 8. For whatever reason (current resources or expense of upgrade), CBE wants to remain on version 7.2.4 indefinitely without incurring the aforementioned and typically pricey "sunset" support costs.

Vendors typically discourage clients from purchasing unsanctioned support for a number of reasons, including:

- The supposed lack of expertise of the independent support company
- The need for the client to stay relatively current
- Vendor enhancements to newer version of the software

Regardless of vendors' pleas, some organizations decide to remain on older versions of applications indefinitely and are more than satisfied with their level of support.

Informal Support Mechanisms

Organizations looking for informal support can always go to a place rife with information on just about every major system: the Internet. Many web sites, blogs, and newsletters exist for just about every application. The lone exception is the home-built application, although software developers exchange advice and best practices in many forums as well. Support here is much less structured than it is for organizations that build their own applications, however. For example, the firm that contracts an ISV to build a custom inventory control system in .NET cannot expect Microsoft to troubleshoot that application; the company would have to purchase support, typically from the same ISV.

Aside from the online world, user groups are enormously helpful resources for networking and learning best practices. End-users from different organizations meet to discuss common issues and solutions. This is the perfect place to go to learn first-hand about everything from client experiences with upgrades to the new features of an enhanced application. Other benefits include meeting end-users from other organizations to exchange best practices, reporting tips, or even business cards for future networking.

Summary

The type of support that an organization requires should vary in direct proportion to the complexity of its system, its internal resources, and its business environment. A relatively small, stable, well-staffed organization with a rigorous internal auditing process has different support requirements than a large, dynamic, chaotic one staffed with insufficient internal resources. Higher level (read: more expensive) support does not negate the possibility of an issue manifesting itself. It can, however, expedite its resolution.

Help me help you.

-Tom Cruise, Jerry MacGuire

CHAPTER 8: SELECTING CONSULTANTS
Introduction
A friend of mine once compared the relationship between the client and the consultancy to a marriage. My friend is a fellow consultant with many years of experience. In his view, clients "court" prospective consultancies after selecting a system and ultimately decide to "walk down the aisle" with one of them. Things tend to go well at first but cracks inevitably appear in the armor. Either the two work through the issues (remaining married), or one, usually the client, seeks a divorce.

Beyond this notion of matrimony, organizations may employ consultants in a variety of ways as they march down uncharted paths. In this chapter, we explore an organization's basic need for consultants throughout an implementation, the types of consulting companies and arrangements available, the pros and cons of each, and several general warnings.

Pre-System Selection
While hardly the norm, there are instances in which an organization will use a consultancy to assist in selecting the system (i.e., pre-implementation), and I personally have been involved in such engagements. Under this arrangement, the client engages a consulting partner that may or may not actually implement the systems currently under consideration. Consultancies may be hired to accomplish any of the following tasks:

- Assist a client in articulating the needs of the business.
- Assist a client in preparing requests for proposals (RFPs) and/or requests for information (RFIs).
- Evaluate vendor proposals.
- Interview vendors and participate in vendor sales demonstrations.
- Refine the pool of vendors.
- Ultimately, assist the organization in making its final decision.
- Negotiate license fees and consulting rates.

Sometimes, an organization that seeks guidance from a consultancy (before deciding on a new system) already has a relationship with that consultancy. Obviously, the organization is placing a great deal of trust in its partner to help it select the "right" system. While the decision is ultimately the client's, the consultancy is in a position of considerable power. For example, if Synchronicity Consulting specializes in PeopleSoft implementations, then it is probably predisposed towards recommending PeopleSoft to its clients, regardless of whether that system is the best fit. There are two reasons for this. First, Synchronicity probably wants the business. Second, Synchronicity probably knows from personal experience that PeopleSoft can work for its clients. SAP or Lawson may work as well, if not better than PeopleSoft, but Synchronicity cannot vouch for those systems. As a result, it may very well recommend PeopleSoft without fully considering other systems.

If an organization elects to use a consultancy to assist with system selection, then it would be well advised to ensure that its partner has no inherent biases towards one system or another. As discussed in Chapter 5, there are many similarities among "off the shelf" systems, particularly those in the same tier. While some true differences exist among systems within the same tier, organizations that use a consultancy for system selection should adhere to the "all or nothing" principle. Clients should utilize partners with experience either with a number of different systems or none of the above.

Implementation Consulting

After selecting its system, an organization needs to address the extent to which it needs external consultants to implement that system. Truth be told, consultants are *not* absolutely essential for a new system to be implemented. However, by definition, experienced consultants have "been there and done that." Organizations considering implementing systems with minimal assistance from external consultants should do so only if they have sufficient internal resources that have participated in similar—if not identical—projects. To the extent that most organizations cannot meet this criterion, they should opt to use external consultants. Alternatively stated, for good reason most organizations use external consultants to lead or at least assist with system implementations. The next question is, "Which types of consulting partner should be used?"

A company's selection of a vendor will, to some extent, drive its selection of a consultancy. Remember that not all consulting organizations do the same thing. Indeed, a client's options run the gamut from small, boutique consultancies that specialize in the software selected to large firms, such as IBM, that can do anything under the sun.

While not all consultants are equally knowledgeable, experienced ones have been in the trenches before and are in the best position to assess the requisite tradeoffs that clients will invariably have to make during the implementation. Fundamentally, consultants should be able to tell their clients honestly whether desired system outputs justify their inputs. Of course, clients need to ask that question first, not just plow ahead with some preconceived notion of what they want. Clients often fail to ask their consultants this question or listen to the answer, often resulting in issues, delays, and budget overruns.

Sometimes a client is familiar with the work of a particular consultant. Consider Satch Services, a company that hires Merchant Consulting to lead its implementation. Satch management is particularly impressed with a consultant named Gary, a rock star with strong procurement and GL experience. Satch feels that Gary is the perfect match for its project. Merchant cannot realistically guarantee *which* of its consultants will work on a project. While Merchant can attempt to accommodate Satch's request, a consultant's individual circumstances (work and/or personal) may make that impossible. Translation: Unless specifically outlined in the contract, Satch management should not ink the deal with Merchant expecting to work with Gary. Ideally, Merchant employs other strong consultants besides Gary.

Type of Consulting Engagements: Fixed Bid vs. Time and Materials (T&M)

Some organizations ask consultancies for a fixed bid contract. In general terms, this is an estimated cost, based on plans and specifications that will also be the actual cost of the job.[25] With respect to systems implementations, a fixed bid contract specifies a flat amount of money to be paid to a consultancy for configuring and testing a system within the client's timeframe and budget.

---

[25] http://www.answers.com

A fixed bid is fundamentally different than a T&M contract. Under a T&M arrangement, an organization agrees to pay, say, $175 per hour per consultant, plus expenses, throughout the duration of the project. While there is no minimum or maximum on the amount of money that the organization will pay the consultancy, a T&M deal is rarely a blank check. The consulting firm typically proposes some type of timeframe to allow the client to estimate total consulting expenditures.

This begs the question, "Which is best?" Of course, it depends. On a fixed bid contract, the consultancy has the incentive to finish the work as quickly as possible because it still has to pay its consultants' salaries. Ideally, the sooner that a consultancy can activate a client's system, the sooner that it can deploy the same consultants on a new assignment. On a T&M contract, however, the consultancy may have the opposite incentive: to extend the length of time that its people are on site for as long as possible because each hour of time results in additional revenue.

On a fixed bid, organizations should expect resistance from a consultancy's project manager (PM) over any type of "enhancement." Implementation team members will hear the term "scope creep"[26] quite a bit from consultancies, as they are incentivized to finish projects as quickly as possible. Conversely, clients will rarely hear about scope creep from consultancies on T&M projects. Their partners have strong financial incentives to maximize the duration of any given project.

Two Warnings

The vast majority of organizations implementing a new system choose a consulting partner at least in an advisory capacity, if not for the entire project. There are a few reasons for this. First, rarely does the organization have the internal expertise in the product(s) being implemented. Second, end-users have their day jobs and cannot focus exclusively the implementation; the consultancy is devoted to the success of this project and, in theory, can help ensure that its clients meet their goals. Third, and sometimes most important, is the political consideration. If the project should start to derail, consultants are the

---

[26] Scope creep is defined as uncontrolled changes in a project's scope. This phenomenon can occur when the scope of a project is not properly defined, documented, or controlled. It is generally considered a negative occurrence that is to be avoided. (Source: Wikipedia)

easiest to blame. By hiring experts who promise a smooth ride during the sales cycle, organizations can hold external consultants accountable for issues, irrespective of whether they are the true cause.

With that in mind, clients would be well-advised to heed the following advice.

Consultant Temperament: Be Aware of the Path of Least Resistance

All too often, organizations select only the consultancies that appear to be the most malleable and obedient. This is an enormous mistake. It is not that companies should choose partners that are rigid, irritable, and outright rude. External consultants will be around for a considerable period of time (typically about a year from start to finish, depending on the project). Certainly, poor personal relations among team members do not move things in a positive direction.

Organizations should hire consultants who insist on doing their jobs throughout the duration of the project: being the product experts. There are limits to the malleability of systems, despite what salespeople tell clients. The consultant who steers the reluctant client toward a particular configuration or business decision is not necessarily being difficult. Especially if the client selected a consultancy with experienced personnel, the consultant probably knows the negative outcomes of the other decision.

Cost: Be Aware of the Lowest Number

Consider Vernon Manufacturing, a company that has decided to implement an ERP. Let's look at responses to an RFP from two different consulting companies: CMU Consulting and Cornell Partners. Both are alleged experts in implementing the ERP. Note that both bids are for Time and Materials:

Table 8.1: Comparison of Two Consultancies' Responses to Vernon's RFP

Resource	CMU Consulting	Cornell Partners
Consultants Required	4	3
Hourly Rate	$175	$175
Hours/Week	40	40
Weeks on Site	32	28
Total Cost	$896,000	$588,000

At first glance, Cornell Partners may appear to be the "better" consultancy. Cornell seems to be able to do the work at a considerably lower rate compared to CMU. However, Vernon is quite foolish if it stops right there and signs with Cornell Partners. Some consultancies try to "lowball" clients with initial bids containing some interesting fine print. The contracts of some deals contain language similar to the following:

> The Vernon proposal reflects all current business requirements and future configuration, reporting, customization, and interface needs. Any deviation from the above will be considered "out of scope" and will constitute a formal change request, not covered by the initial project budget. Those deviations will be performed at the normal rate of $175 per hour.

The translation is that the number submitted from Cornell ($588,000) is *not* comprehensive. Changes will be billed separately. Note that CMU's bid contained no such language.

If Vernon selects Cornell, then it should be absolutely certain that it has properly and completely defined its reporting requirements, interfaces, and so on. Note that this is exceptionally difficult to do prior to an implementation. Vernon's failure to do so—and lack of understanding of the initial contract—will likely result both in contentious conversations with Cornell about "scope creep" and the client spending money not included in its initial budget.

Let's assume that Vernon selects Cornell. Throughout the project, Cornell's PM tells Vernon senior management that the client's constant barrage of "change requests" is adding up. Cornell and Vernon personnel have many spirited debates about the work and its cost. From Cornell's standpoint, Vernon personnel did not adequately define all of its organization's business requirements prior to beginning the engagement. By charging more for the additional work required, Cornell is simply following the contract. The bickering between consultancy and client has left the project running considerably behind schedule and over budget. Cornell's revised costs are listed in Table 8.2 below along with CMU's original estimates:

Table 8.2: Comparison of Two Consultancies' Actual Costs

Resource	CMU Consulting	Cornell Partners
Consultants Required	4	5
Hourly Rate	$175	$175
Hours/Week	40	50
Weeks on Site	32	32
Total Cost	$896,000	$1,400,000

As evinced from the table, CMU's initial bid was both accurate and lower in absolute terms. In other words, the ostensibly less expensive consulting firm turned out to cost significantly more money. Organizations considering multiple consulting proposals should ask themselves the following questions:

- What is covered/not covered by the contract?
- Are the business requirements sufficiently defined so that a strictly-scoped T&M contract is viable?
- Is the organization postponing a long-term headache for short-term savings?

Clients should ask these questions as early as possible, certainly before any contract is signed with a consulting partner. Many projects have become quite adversarial over contract language.

Which type of contract is best?

Generally speaking, T&M contracts tend to have fewer issues than do fixed bids. Rare is the overall positive experience for clients that hired a consulting company on a very low, fixed bid arrangement. Some consultancies sell deals intentionally on the low side in order to increase project revenue via change requests. This often promotes an adversarial work environment, contentious relations between client and consultants, and system failures.

Types of Consulting Arrangements

Given how much consultants cost, many clients might question the need to have a team of three or more highly paid hourly resources on staff for forty hours per week. To be sure, there is more than one way to deploy consultants in a cost-effective manner. As a general rule, the quality and number of required external resources varies indirectly with the quality and number of available and experienced internal resources:

Figure 8.1: Tradeoff between Internal and External Resources during a System Implementation

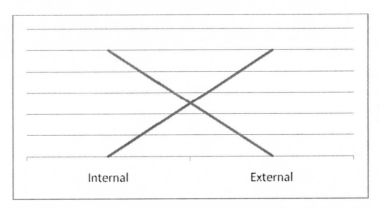

Internal   External

In other words, an organization with extensive internal resources and expertise needs *fewer* external consultants.[27] Of course, those internal resources still have to do their day jobs in order for the organization to conduct business. For example, a payroll manager cannot set up, test, and document the new payroll system at the expense of paying current employees. By the same token, the head of IT cannot configure security for the new ERP while neglecting to fight the fires of the current system. This rule can alternatively be stated as follows: **If an organization wants to minimize the number of external consultants on an implementation, it must ensure that the end-users on its implementation team: 1) are devoted regularly and significantly to the implementation of that new system; and 2) have sufficient expertise in that system.**

---

[27] Fewer does not mean zero. Organizations cannot expect to successfully implement major systems exclusively with consultants or end-users. While not necessarily advisable, note that organizations may be able to handle upgrades and enhancements in a "consultant-free" manner.

The organization that extensively employs external consultants still needs its internal resources to be heavily involved in the implementation from the very beginning until the end of the project. Organizations that do not staff their implementations sufficiently—i.e., in a manner conducive to making key end-users available throughout the project—essentially guarantee a bevy of issues, including:

- Lack of knowledge transfer from consultant to client
- Increased project costs stemming from consultants remaining months after the organization goes live

Minimal consultant input and resources does not mean zero. On just about every major system implementation, organizations need to utilize external application experts, technical resources adept at installing the application, and seasoned project managers who have dealt with many of the issues likely to face the client. To that end, clients' consulting options include:

- Traditional Consulting
- Milestone Consulting
- Multiple Consulting Partners
- Rapid Deployment
- Creative Arrangements

Traditional Consulting

In a traditional consulting arrangement, a firm deploys a team of full-time individuals at a client site for forty hours per week, typically four days at ten hours per day per consultant. Consultancies typically prefer this arrangement for a number of reasons. First and foremost, traditional consulting maximizes billable time and revenue. Second, and there is more than a bit of truth to this, consultants on the ground can better steer clients in the right direction throughout the project, manage issues, and ensure an overall smoother implementation than if they were not present.

On the downside, traditional consulting tends to be the most expensive option for clients. Also, many organizations face end-user availability issues. Client end-users are often overworked and too busy to spend time with consultants. Remember, end-users on implementation teams have day jobs while consultants exclusively implement the new system. While consultants can work independently, at certain points, client input is imperative. Consultants on site are billing regardless of whether their skills are being used efficiently or not.

In the rare event that a project is running ahead of schedule, rare is the consulting company that attempts to move dates up or suggests that its consultants do not need to be on site for several weeks.

Milestone Consulting

Under this arrangement, a client employs a consulting firm to check in with them on a regular basis to ensure that the project is both meeting its individual goals and, from a broader perspective, remains on track. A client will often utilize a hybrid consultant—equal parts project manager, techie, and application expert —to visit on site every two weeks or so.

Benefits of this approach include keeping costs to a minimum. Also, to the extent that the consultant's arrival is known well in advance, end-users can focus on their day jobs during the week knowing that they will devote certain days to the new system, coinciding with the arrival of the consultant. In theory, this can be more efficient.

This method should be used judiciously, as it is rife with potential disadvantages. For one, there may be no one keeping an eye on the implementation on a daily basis, allowing goals and dates to fall by the wayside. Issues may not be broached in time to address them without impacting a go-live date. Also, the implementation's flow may suffer. Projects that constantly start and stop often lose momentum. Projects with more interruptions have a greater chance of failure and milestone-based approaches tend to have this limitation.

Multiple Consulting Partners

Most of the time, organizations choose a single consultancy for its implementation. However, it is not completely unprecedented for a client to hire several consultancies concurrently. For example, let's say that Keel Event Management hires RTB Consultants and FBN Consultants at the same time for the same implementation. Keel senior management believes that it can split responsibilities between its two partners.

The obvious question here is, "Why?" Perhaps Keel believes that RTB and FBN bring different areas of expertise to the table. Perhaps it believes that RTB and FBN can "keep each other honest." Perhaps neither RTB nor FBN is large enough to supply the required resources.

Speaking from years of personal experience, this arrangement is almost always a very bad idea. At least one of the following outcomes is very likely to occur from this type of arrangement:

- RTB and FBN will each neglect to perform an important task based on the honest belief that each thought that the other was responsible for it.
- RTB and FBN will each work on the same task in the belief that each thought that it was responsible for it.
- RTB and FBN will each use the project to try to win more work from Keel, undercutting the other in the process.
- RTB and FBN will view the work completed by the other as inferior and attempt to discredit it.
- Even in the unlikely event that RTB and FBN can table any kind of rivalry, the coordination of their work adds administrative costs and delays to the project (and increases the chances for miscommunication).
- In the end, Keel will suffer from the inter-company conflict.

If a client does not believe that a single consulting company can meet its needs, then it should simply find one that can, with one exception: The client has significant legal or audit-related reasons for one consultancy to audit the other. Absent this, separating responsibilities is almost always a recipe for failure. In this case, the whole is much less than the sum of the parts.

Rapid Deployment

In recent years, some consultancies and vendors have proposed an alternative to the traditional consulting arrangement. They offer budget-conscious clients a rapid implementation designed to take anywhere from three-to-six months from-soup-to-nuts. In return for the reduced consulting time and expense, clients relinquish some traditional decision making concerning application flexibility and setup.

For example, rather than spend a month determining with end-users which GL accounts or benefit plans to configure, consultants arrive on site with these items essentially decided in advance. This does not mean that consultants force clients to erroneously use a petty cash account or start enrolling employees in a 403(b) plan that does not exist. Rather, consultants will quickly configure the client's system with predesigned templates. If the system configuration and business process cannot coexist, then the client will have to change its practice to conform to the new system.

Results of rapid deployment have been mixed. On the positive side, some clients have realized considerable savings, particularly on consulting fees. Efficiency also increases, as end-users cannot debate which codes the organization will use or how it will conduct a major business process; the consulting company essentially makes these decisions for the client. Obviously, this approach will not work across the board, as a change in business process may be too severe for a client to stomach. Alternatively, the delivered functionality of the vanilla system may result in significant reporting or security gaps.

Creative Arrangements

Clients may pose alternate arrangements to minimize consultant cost during the project. Assuming that an organization has sufficient internal expertise, it may wish to have consultants assist only with the setup or testing of the application. A client may wish to independently handle items such as custom report writing.

This approach can potentially minimize consulting time costs. Also, much like the milestone approach, client end-users can theoretically schedule their work to maximize knowledge transfer while consultants are on site.

While costs may be minimized, client risk may very well increase with creative approaches. Consultants not involved in the setup of an application, for example, might point out issues in the middle of an implementation that end-users should have flagged at the beginning. The impact on testing may be significant enough that the go-live date is jeopardized. Some consultancies may be reluctant to take on projects such as these, citing a lack of total ownership. Boutique firms—discussed later in this chapter—are often afraid of bad business and may consider these types of arrangements excessively risky. After all, how can a client expect a consultancy to routinely jump into an implementation at critical points and hit the ground running? What if individual consultants must rotate in and out due to scheduling issues?

This last question is perhaps the most pragmatic and compelling argument against approaches predicated on occasional consultant visits. Consulting firms make money by deploying their people on a full-time basis, not two days per week. Thus, the client that entrusts an excellent consultant with a key role during system implementation will, in all likelihood, not be able to secure that consultant's services on an intermittent basis. The risk is that new consultants will have to routinely review project-related documentation before being brought up to speed. At critical points of a project, the time required for this assimilation simply does not exist. Also, all consultants do not have the same skills, even if they have comparable backgrounds and certifications. Clients that opt to have consultants visit infrequently run the risk that the new consultant is not as knowledgeable as his or her predecessors.

Which is Best?

There are too many factors to determine the best type of consulting arrangement for a client. Certainly, there are potential drawbacks in all approaches. To be sure, most organizations do not have the expertise that consultancies can provide. As such, organizations benefit from knowledgeable, on-site consultants who ensure that the project stays on course, issues are reported and resolved and individual objectives are met.

Types of Consultancies

Organizations have at least four different options with respect to types of consultancies. Clients that do not have the requisite internal bandwidth and expertise to independently undertake a massive implementation can employ the following consulting partners:

- The vendor
- Large firms
- Boutique firms
- Independents

Let's explore each in some detail.

The Vendor

Organizations buying Oracle can certainly hire Oracle consultants—that is, full-time employees of the vendor that implement the system for a living. From a billing and accountability standpoint, things *may* be simpler for the organization that opts to go this route.

First-time clients often do not understand, however, that the consultants implementing the system did not design it. In other words, clients discovering Oracle "bugs" cannot expect Oracle consultants to magically fix them. Now, there are instances in which (during upgrades, specifically) some vendors may provide their own consultants with superior documentation relative to that which they would provide to partners and clients.

A vendor's consultants may not be willing to call a spade a spade. Translation: it is typically tough for a client to expect a vendor's employees to admit to the shortcoming of a product. Also, from a cost perspective, vendor consultants are typically the most expensive of the lot. This does not mean that they are necessarily better than the other groups discussed in this chapter. Vendors can justify above-average rates for their consultants through name and brand recognition.

Most major vendors have partnerships with large and boutique firms. Vendors that do not have enough available consultants to staff a project will commonly reach out to these partners and rent consultants, marking them up accordingly. In other words, a client might sign with Oracle only to have a consultant from another firm (an Oracle partner) working on the actual implementation.

Large Firms

Firms such as IBM and Deloitte and Touche (D&T) have hundreds if not thousands of consultants supporting just about every ERP. Their businesses each have multiple revenue streams; they hedge their bets by playing in multiple sandboxes. Compared to boutique firms, a relatively small percentage of the total revenue from these consulting firms emanates from any one system.

Large firms offer the auspices of credibility, often at rates upwards of $200 per hour per consultant. Aside from cost, name and brand recognition are high for these firms. Like vendors, large firms also "rent" additional consultants for projects as needed. Also similar to vendors, large firms tend to employ a range of consultants, from the highly experienced to the neophyte, often staffing large projects with a combination of both so that new hires gain valuable experience. Right, wrong, or indifferent, it is not uncommon for these firms to deploy consultants currently "on the bench" for engagements for which they might not be a pure fit. For example, a large firm may send to a client implementing Oracle Financials a Lawson Financials consultant, particularly for a "low visibility" assignment. Remember from Chapter 5 that these systems are very similar. If a consultant can write reports or run scripts from one system, then he should be able to do it from another.

Like vendors, large firms rarely turn down "bad" business. If these firms do not have the requisite consultants to staff any one project, then they either hire more or enter into subcontracting agreements with independents or partners. A project that appears to be problematic will usually not dissuade the large firm from pursuing it, regardless of probable pitfalls. Remember that ERP practices in large firms typically constitute a very small portion of overall revenue; the partner or salesperson in that firm that passes up a sale—regardless of any red flags—is probably going to be reprimanded or asked to leave the firm. As we will see in the Portnoy case study in Chapter 11, large firms often ignore substantial risks under the guise of "pleasing the client." This mentality often leads to system failures.

Boutique Firms

Unlike their large brethren, boutique firms specialize in the system that the client is implementing. These firms do not offer a vast array of services or cover the same range of projects as their larger counterparts. Boutiques' main selling point is their often exclusive focus on the system itself. They tend to employ only very experienced, knowledgeable consultants, not newly minted ones. Boutique firms are apt to contract seasoned independents as needed because their business models tend to be very sensitive to the sales cycle. They simply cannot afford to have full-time consultants "on the bench" for long periods of time. They have nowhere to put them. Unlike their larger counterparts, boutiques do not employ as many consultants, both in terms of sheer numbers as well as variety of applications and technologies. For these reasons, boutiques do not place available consultants currently on engagements for which they are not suitable.

Boutique firms typically work with only a few clients concurrently and are very averse to failures. They tend not to be "chop shops" in the eyes of their own consultants and clients. These firms sometimes do what larger firms consider unthinkable: turn down "bad" business. Management at boutiques knows red flags when they see them and often do not want to risk sullying their companies' reputations with botched implementations. Established boutique firms tend to have very high client retention rates.

During the sales cycle, both boutique and large firms often trumpet their ability to bring certified consultants to the table. To be sure, all else being equal, a certified consultant is better than an uncertified consultant. However, vendors often play games with the certification process for partners, and I personally have met more than a few consultants—while technically not certified—who knew twice as much as their certified counterparts. Translation: Certified does not mean "better."

Independents

Finally, organizations can go the independent route either by contacting known independents directly or by using a recruiting agency to find them. If an organization uses an agency, then that agency typically marks up independents anywhere from 30 to 60 percent.

Like the other consulting options, independents have their pros and cons. On the cost side, independents tend to cost significantly less for a number of reasons. They almost never maintain a proper business office, since they actively try to minimize overhead. This allows independents to charge rates typically 40 percent lower than those of established firms. Even with a reasonable markup by an agency, the final cost is often considerably lower. On the downside, independents do not have the same name recognition and network of a larger company. If an implementation implodes, an executive will have to defend the ostensibly risky decision to hire a single, independent vendor.

As a general rule, independents tend to be a very knowledgeable bunch. Most have "graduated" from larger organizations and like the autonomy of working for themselves, choosing the projects that make the most sense for them. Ironically, many organizations use independents whether they know it or not. As stated before, often vendors and consulting firms will augment their staff with independents as business and staffing needs mandate.

Let's consider a detailed example of an organization in need of staff augmentation. Pratt University is in the midst of its PeopleSoft implementation. Pratt's consulting partner—LLD—just lost its lead procurement consultant and does not have a suitable replacement immediately available. Other LLD consultants are engaged at Pratt at the rate of $175 per hour. Pratt turns to a recruiting agency (Townshend Recruiters) to augment its staff while LLD attempts to backfill the position. Townshend finds two suitable consultants:

First up is Joe the Independent, to borrow from the 2008 presidential campaign. Joe has over twelve years of experience as a consultant in PeopleSoft procurement and financials. Aside from being a certified functional consultant, he knows how to make some basic technical tweaks and has extensive reporting knowledge in a number of mainstream reporting tools. His rate is $120 per hour.

Next is Rena, an independent relatively new to PeopleSoft. She has three years of experience and is much less technically savvy than Joe. Her rate reflects her comparative lack of experience: $80 per hour.

Townshend marks up independents 50 percent, making Joe's hypothetical rate to Pratt $180 per hour and Rena's rate $120 per hour. Townshend knows that rate will be an issue with Pratt and asks Joe to "be flexible" and move into Rena's ballpark. In all likelihood, Joe will not drop his rate by one-third. Townshend needs to understand (as does Pratt, for that matter) the additional costs associated with being independent, detailed in Table 8.3.

Table 8.3: Estimated Annual Revenue and Costs of an Independent Consultant*

Hourly Rate	$100
Hours worked per year	1,500
Total gross revenue	$150,000
Extra Social Security taxes because independent is often an employee and an employer, based on 2008 $102,000 wage limit.	$6,324
Annual medical insurance (based on full family coverage)	$8,000
Annual Errors and Omission Insurance	$2,000
Total Revenue (pre-federal, state, and local taxes)	$125,370

The costs in Table 8.3 do *not* factor in the additional risks that independents like Joe and Rena incur, including billing issues and the potential difficulty of finding work. Independents are not on a company's payroll like the LLD consultants in this example. Joe faces the very real risks of both not finding work and not being paid by a company that owes him for wages and expenses. In total, Joe must deal with much more risk and significantly higher expenses (see grayed items in Table 8.3) than regular W-2 consultants, both of which justify his higher hourly rate. Reward should be proportional to risk.

One of the many positives of being independent is that Joe can write off more business expenses than a W-2 employee. In other words, Table 8.3 does *not* reflect net income for an independent. The following point is critical: Joe needs a compensating wage differential to justify being independent. If Joe could only make, for example, $60 per hour (roughly $100,000 per year) as an independent, then he would be taking unnecessary risks. Joe can very easily earn this much as a full-time employee of a consulting company, given his vast experience.

Let's return to the Pratt example. Townshend submits the profiles and final rates of Joe and Rena to Pratt, whose senior management strongly prefers Joe over Rena but balks at Joe's rate. Townshend attempts to negotiate Joe down but he will move to only $110 per hour. Townshend agrees to reduce its markup as well so that Joe's revised rate is $150 per hour, an amount acceptable to Pratt.

In this scenario, everybody wins:

- Pratt gets an experienced consultant who can hit the ground running. The delay to the project is minimized, especially if Joe can work effectively with other LLD staff.
- Townshend makes $40 per hour on Joe's work for the duration of the project.
- While Joe's risks and costs are substantial, locking down a long term assignment for $110 per hour is probably a smart business decision.

The bottom line with independents is that organizations get what they pay for. An independent's rate is a direct reflection of the experience that he or she brings to the table. The organization that opts for the less expensive independent should not expect the same level of performance that it would receive from a more seasoned—and expensive—one.

Which Consulting Option is Best?

The "best" consulting partner is a direct function of the individual consultants placed on a given project. To that extent, senior management often overrates the name recognition or larger consulting firms. Paramount considerations are the experience, knowledge, and quality of the consultants on the project, regardless of the name on the organization's stationery. Firms of *all* sizes have run unsuccessful implementations. A client that hires a large, well-known firm in no way guarantees the successful activation of its system. In fact, a smaller firm may provide a better chance to succeed.

In the end, an organization should not make the mistake of assuming that all consultancies and individual consultants are equal, nor should it choose a partner solely on the basis of cost. The skills of consultants from a more expensive firm may, in fact, be worth a premium.

As stated earlier in this chapter, cost is simply one of the many factors for organizations to consider when choosing a consulting partner. This next section discusses the questions that organizations and consulting firms should ask each other before signing contracts.

Questions for the Client

Ideally, organizations perform comprehensive due diligence throughout the selection and implementation of their systems. Senior management should look at the organization itself, potential project team members, and the vendor and its software. Investigating and interviewing potential consultancies and their individual consultants should simply represent a continuation of this process.

After the organization identifies suitable consultancies, it should seek to fully understand the candidates' consulting philosophy and previous outcomes. The organization's objective should not be to find the most malleable partner that will accede to each and every one of its demands. That is a recipe for failure, as several case studies will demonstrate. Disagreement between client and consultancy is inevitable and even natural throughout a project. Organizations would be wise not to simply find a partner that it can "bully" into agreeing with poor decisions.

Aside from this general tip, some of the fundamental questions that an organization needs to ask potential consulting partners include:

- Are the long-term benefits from working with this company worth the costs?
- Does our potential partner have a history of satisfied clients?
- Will our potential partner challenge us if we start to veer down the wrong path?
- Is our potential partner equipped with sufficient resources (relative to the internal ones) to handle this project?

Questions for the Consultancy

Taking steps to ensure a healthy, productive relationship with proposed partners is *not* the exclusive domain of the client. In a similar vein, consulting companies should also ask certain questions prior to accepting a new client, including:

- Are the long-term benefits from working with this organization during its system implementation worth the risks and costs?
- Is this potential client hell-bent on a setup that cannot be successful?
- Will this potential client let us do our jobs?
- Does the client have sufficient internal resources devoted to this project?
- Will the client provide the requisite sign-off at key points?

Foolish is the consulting firm that attempts to win business at any cost. Consultancies risk their reputations with each project. While no consulting firm can guarantee a successful implementation, experienced salespeople and consultants know red flags when they see them. By carefully screening prospective clients before signing papers, the best consultancies consistently minimize the chance of a highly publicized meltdown and maximize the chance of a productive, healthy, mutually beneficial relationship for all concerned.

Q&A with Mark Hayes of JAT Consulting

Few professionals have a more complete point of view on implementing new systems than my friend, Mark Hayes. Mark is a seasoned consultant and project manager involved in technical, functional, and project management aspects of large implementations. Mark is also typically involved in the sales cycle for his company, JAT Consulting, a boutique firm specializing in Lawson and Kronos for which he is a vice president. Mark took the time to discuss many facets of system selections.

PS: What are the two or three main reasons that clients decide to implement new systems?

MH: There are a number of reasons for clients to implement new systems. First, they are compelled to change systems because they are changing hardware platforms, moving off a mainframe platform or changing between UNIX and a Windows-based platform. Running multiple platforms is costly for clients because they need technical experience in each one. Consolidating platforms can represent significant savings for an organization.

Second, they are consolidating to an ERP package that can meet the needs of multiple areas within the organization. Companies running separate financial packages, HR packages, and supply chain packages from different vendors will look to consolidate. Ideally, they can support just one new complete package able to meet the needs of multiple areas within the organization. Cost savings will typically drive this decision. The technology base will be the same, support contracts will cost less, and internal support can be consolidated.

Third, acquisitions will typically require an organization to migrate to the system and platform of the parent company.

PS: What would you say are the three most important criteria that clients should use in choosing a consulting partner?

MH: First, internal experience with the vendor is crucial. New management or key employees with positive experience with a particular vendor hold a great deal of water.

Second, functionality is critical at the higher end of the market but less so with the smaller clients. At the higher end of the market, more users and more business requirements mean that new systems need to essentially work out of the box (read: without extensive customizations). Smaller organizations have a willingness to work around product deficiencies to realize a cost savings. Excessive features are often even seen as a detriment in the sales cycle due to the perception that the system will be more operationally complex.

The third factor is business relationships and comfort with the vendor during the sales cycle. It is critical to make prospective clients feel comfortable. You have to be able to communicate that you understand the business requirements and have the necessary skills to provide the solution. The client needs to trust the vendor to deliver on promised services.

PS: How often does a deal come down to cost? Do you find that clients get what they pay for?

The deal comes down to cost about twenty percent of the time. When I estimate a project, I make all attempts to accurately gauge the actual effort to perform the required services. I will not underestimate a project in an attempt to get business (with a change request plan to augment my low estimate). Therefore, when I lose a business to cost, one of the following has happened:

First, another vendor has intentionally bid low. While I may have lost this business this time, this is the type of client from which I probably will gain future business. That organization is likely to have a bad experience with its vendor.

Second, I overestimated the project. If I have done proper due diligence and have understood the prospect's business requirements, then this should rarely happen.

Third, my rate is higher than that of my competition. While I will routinely make minor rate adjustments while negotiating in good faith with a client, I rarely attempt to match rates that are outside of my profit margin.

PS: Do clients get what they pay for?

MH: The answer is somewhat nebulous. The client always gets what I propose. In rare instances where my consultant is not performing up to par, the problem is almost always addressed to the client's satisfaction.

Sometimes a consultant is put into a position where delivering services is hindered by lack of client availability, slow decision making, poor systems design, or incomplete prerequisites. In these instances, it is important for me to bring these factors to the client's attention immediately.

PS: Talk to me about the importance of client references during the sales cycle.

MH: Clients universally want references. In fact, clients frequently ask for references that are within their same vertical, company size, state, platform, and release level. I sometimes think that clients miss the mark on this. By asking for such detailed prior experience, they may be eliminating some of the best consultants from consideration. A great consultant with no healthcare experience will do a better job implementing a system at a healthcare client than an average consultant with healthcare experience.

PS: How often are you able to successfully talk clients out of bad setup or design decisions?

MH: If the desired design is truly bad and decision makers have their minds made up, then I will not pursue the business. I have recommended that clients not move forward on a project on which I was about to bid because the project did not make good business sense. Bad business decisions typically result in failed over-budget projects and, ultimately, bad references.

PS: Let's talk about "bad business." What are some examples of red flags?

MH: I occasionally run into a prospective piece of business that is not worth the risk of pursuing. An ineffectual project manager is one of those flags. Lack of consensus among the project team in regard to system direction is another.

PS: Can you comment on some of the root causes of some less-than-successful projects?

MH: Budgetary and calendar goals are one and the same: If you don't hit the implementation date, then the budget will increase. So, this is really about hitting the date. I recognize that there are instances in which increasing the number of consultants on a project can result in meeting the date while, at the same time, result in budget overruns.

One of the biggest causes for project failure is the process that organizations use to determine the go-live date. Many clients start the process by picking the live date and backing into the effort that must take place to meet that go-live date. Organizations should first to determine a reasonable start date and calculate the end date based upon effort and dependencies.

Poorly defined client business requirements often drive cost overruns. If a client discovers that it needs twenty interfaces and reports to go-live rather than the ten originally estimated, then the project will go over budget. Clients not understanding their own current business processes is something that happens far too often. Many of these items can be caught up front by a business-savvy consultant. If a client RFP omits a routine implementation task, then the consultant should bring it to the attention of the client.

Scope control is another major reason for project failure. Scope overruns are largely a failure of the project manager. In order for a project to be successful, it must have a defined scope that cannot change mid-project. Critical scope items not included result from poorly defined business requirements. Increases in project scope—especially non-critical items— reflect the inability of the PM to say "no" the client.

Summary

Consulting firms run the gamut in terms of size, philosophies, quality, and cost. Some relatively inexpensive consultants bring a tremendous amount of knowledge and number of tools to the table. Unfortunately, other consultants do not give clients the same bang for their buck. While no consultant should have *carte blanche*, clients would do well to listen carefully to the consultants' recommendations. Organizations that doubt the expertise of their partners should probably not have hired them in the first place.

Part Three: The System Implementation

The next section will delve extensively into the inner workings and the key players within an organization during a typical implementation. The objective is to analyze the root cause of many system-related problems. Along with a discussion of the different implementation strategies, phases, and issues, case studies will be used extensively to illustrate how and where projects have been derailed.

There's a difference between knowing the path and walking the path.

-Lawrence Fishburne as Morpheus, *The Matrix*

CHAPTER 9: IMPLEMENTATION STRATEGIES AND PHASES

Introduction

This chapter focuses on key decisions that organizations make surrounding the implementation that will, to be blunt, make or break their projects. The right implementation strategy is like accurate driving directions: while a driver could still hit traffic or suffer an accident on the way to a destination, wrong directions virtually guarantee that he will not arrive on time. In the worst case scenario, the organization that picks an unsuitable strategy has virtually no chance meeting its time and budgetary objectives. Let's focus on high-level implementation strategies before turning to the specific phases of an implementation.

Implementation Strategies

Arguably, the fundamental decision that an organization needs to make prior to beginning is one of strategy. Particularly at large, multi-site clients, senior management needs to determine the order in which modules are going to be implemented at each entity. Organizations have multiple options, ranging from little victories to the whole kit and caboodle.

For this section, consider the example of Byrne Healthcare. The organization consists of five relatively autonomous individual hospitals, each of which runs its own system. Fed up with excessive maintenance costs and an inability to run simple, enterprise-wide reports, Byrne management purchases an ERP and intends to implement it throughout the organization.

The Full-Blown Implementation

Byrne can implement all modules at all hospitals concurrently. This "full-blown" approach is depicted in Table 9.1.

Table 9.1: Full-Blown Implementation for a Multi-Site Organization

Hospital	HR	Payroll	GL	Procurement
Victoria	Phase I	Phase I	Phase I	Phase I
Winfield	Phase I	Phase I	Phase I	Phase I
Mattingly	Phase I	Phase I	Phase I	Phase I
Gamble	Phase I	Phase I	Phase I	Phase I
Jackson	Phase I	Phase I	Phase I	Phase I

Advantages of this approach include:

- Byrne will not have to build interfaces built from the new system's payroll and HR systems to the hospitals' GL systems.
- Byrne will not have to continue paying maintenance on existing legacy systems.

Disadvantages of this approach include:

- Very little learning can be applied across hospitals.
- Lessons cannot be applied to other hospitals.
- In the short-term, the project will be more expensive and consultant-intensive than a gradual implementation.
- A project of this scope has more room for failure; "problem" hospitals can cause the whole project to suffer, resulting in the entire organization missing key dates.

The Staggered or Phased Implementation

Another approach is typically called the staggered or phased implementation. This approach has two variations, best illustrated by an example.

Phased Approach, Version 1

In Version 1, all of Byrne's sites implement the system in the same modules in the same phases.

Table 9.2: Phased Approach for a Multi-Site Organization, Version 1

Hospital	HR	Payroll	GL	Procurement
Victoria	Phase I	Phase I	Phase II	Phase III
Winfield	Phase I	Phase I	Phase II	Phase III
Mattingly	Phase I	Phase I	Phase II	Phase III
Gamble	Phase I	Phase I	Phase II	Phase III
Jackson	Phase I	Phase I	Phase II	Phase III

Advantages of this approach include:

- In the short-term, the gradual approach is less consultant-intensive than a full-blown implementation.
- HR and payroll are "out of the way," and all HR and payroll headaches are dealt with at one point.
- Internal resources may be able to implement Phase II and IIII hospitals with less involvement from external consultants—if sufficient knowledge transfer has taken place.
- A project of this scope has less room for failure than the full-blown implementation; "problem" areas in an organization can cause the whole project to suffer and, potentially, to miss key dates.

Disadvantages of this approach include:

- Relatively little learning can be applied across hospitals because Byrne implements HR and payroll concurrently throughout each hospital.
- Byrne will have to build interfaces from the new payroll and HR system to individual hospitals' GL systems. Byrne will have to maintain those interfaces until it activates its new GL system in Phase II.
- Byrne will have to continue to pay maintenance on existing legacy systems until all hospitals are live.

Phased Approach, Version 2

In Version 2, different sites at Byrne implement the system in different phases, as shown below:

Table 9.3: Phased Approach for a Multi-Site Organization, Version 2

Hospital	HR	Payroll	GL	Procurement
Victoria	Phase I	Phase I	Phase I	Phase I
Winfield	Phase II	Phase II	Phase II	Phase II
Mattingly	Phase II	Phase II	Phase II	Phase II
Gamble	Phase III	Phase III	Phase III	Phase III
Jackson	Phase III	Phase III	Phase III	Phase III

Advantages of this approach include:

- In the short-term, the gradual approach costs less than a full-blown implementation.
- Lessons can be applied from other implementations at other hospitals. For example, the Winfield implementation should go smoother than the Victoria one. These lessons can potentially reduce project-wide costs over the long-term.
- A project of this scope has less room for failure than the full-blown implementation. "Problem" hospitals *cannot* cause the whole project to suffer and potentially miss key dates.

Disadvantages of this approach include:

- Byrne will have to continue to pay maintenance on existing legacy systems until all hospitals are live.
- Byrne will have to build interfaces from the new payroll and HR system to individual hospitals' GL systems. Byrne will have to maintain those interfaces until it activates the new GL system in Phase II.

Phased Approach, Version 2a

Note that an organization need not have entities at multiple sites in order to go the staggered route. While logistically a single-site employee does not face the same challenges as its multi-site counterpart, a perfectly valid model for such an organization is presented in Table 9.4.

Table 9.4: Phased Approach for a Single-Site Organization

Organization	HR	Payroll	GL	Procurement
Garnett, Inc.	Phase I	Phase I	Phase II	Phase III

In other words, an organization certainly does not have to implement all modules concurrently simply because it is comprised of one entity.

Which Strategy is Best?

There is no one "correct" strategy for an organization with regard to a systems implementation. Cost is certainly a factor, in terms of external consultants, temporary interfaces, and legacy system maintenance. Size of the organization is a major consideration. For the single-site organization, it is tough to argue that only certain departments should have HR and payroll implemented while others should not. Organizations should certainly know and assess the risks associated with each alternative. If internal political or financial conditions do not permit a "full-blown" effort, then the organization should go with a phased approach. It's probably better to win a series of small battles, building momentum in the process, than to risk losing one spectacular war.

Implementation Phases

After an organization has recognized the need to implement a new system and has selected a partner to assist with the implementation, it is ready for the next step: starting the actual transition from legacy system to new system. The number and severity of potential pitfalls can corrupt even the most carefully conceived project plans.

While consultancies typically have slightly different methodologies, most follow the following phases for implementing a new system:

- Project Planning
- Application Exploration
- System Design
- System Testing
- System Activation

Understanding the objectives and constraints of each phase—by itself and in relation to the other phases—is imperative. The phases provide the framework for understanding the entire implementation; every task in an implementation has its natural place and phase.

Moreover, the issues brought to light in each individual case study become clearer when viewed against this backdrop.

Project Planning

When thinking of project planning, I am often reminded of a quote from *Thirteen Days*, a movie about the Cuban Missile Crisis and also one of my favorites. When confronted with the knowledge that the Soviets had placed intercontinental ballistic missiles in Cuba, President Kennedy—played by Bruce Greenwood—says, "First we gotta figure out what we're gonna do before we figure out how we're gonna do it." Well said. Each project begins with some sort of planning.

Phase Objectives

Planning a project of the magnitude, duration, and cost of a new system implementation is no small endeavor. Internal and external resources need to be mapped both to overall goals and to the individual tasks needed to accomplish these goals. Aside from extensive resource coordination, plans need to encompass dates and task dependencies. Whether using Microsoft Project, Excel, or some other project management tool, the first objective of the planning phase is to produce a comprehensive and realistic project plan. This is the single, unifying document that aggregates each person, task, and goal. The plan should easily produce project status reports. Further, delays should allow for the deadlines for dependent tasks to be automatically adjusted.

Ideally, the creation of a project plan should involve quite a bit more than mechanically applying dates, tasks, and resources to a predefined template. Remember that no two implementations are identical in terms of system design, challenges, resources, data, and so on. Without accurate task, phase, and project end dates, the road map to go live is meaningless. Absent a good project plan, it is hard to imagine a multi-million dollar project having a remote chance of being successful.

Project plans should not remain untouched and unaltered throughout the implementation. On the contrary, they need to be living documents, reflecting issues discovered and subsequent changes required. The final version of a project plan often bears little resemblance to the initial one. Resources, tasks, and dates are added and changed, often on a weekly basis. However meticulous the planning, issues invariably manifest themselves during a project, requiring modifications to the original plan.

How Long Should Project Planning Take?

Planning a six month (or longer) project takes time. Even the experienced PM who starts with a template will have to spend a great deal of time customizing it to meet the client's needs, resources, and objectives. Initially, project planning should take at least a month in order for a decent prototype to be presented to senior management. Good prototypes include high level milestones, discrete tasks, and the resources assigned to those tasks.

Application Exploration (AE)

In this phase, end-users and consultants sit down in front of the computer and literally explore the application, typically loaded with test data. AE typically takes place in a training data area in which end-users can perform dummy setup and processing without fear of "breaking anything." Note that end-users do not need to make final or even preliminary decisions with regard to setup, processing, and reporting, although this should be in the minds of all involved. The point of AE is for end-users to become more familiar with the new system and the different options available to them. This knowledge, in turn, will enable them to ask better questions and make better decisions for the next phase—System Design).

Typically, external consultants guide clients through AE. After all, it is very difficult for an end-user with no experience in the new system to explore it effectively without extensive help or input, even if that person attended training. During AE, consultants should foster an atmosphere conducive to learning and building end-user confidence. Consultants should answer questions as needed and provide tips on items such as navigation. Nothing frustrates client end-users more than not being able to get around in a system, especially when they will routinely have to work with that system during and after the implementation.

Phase Objectives

The specific objectives of AE are as follows:

- To begin the process of knowledge transfer between client and consultant
- To identify any gaps between what the delivered application can do and the client's business requirements
- To explore the different setup and configuration options available to the client and the pros and cons of each

Finally, foolish is the client or consultancy that minimizes the importance of AE. I once worked with a project manager who told a client that AE could be combined with System Design—to make up for delays caused by her own negligence. This was not a wise course of action and the client soon requested that her management remove her from the project.

How Long Should AE Take?

AE can begin before project planning is complete; it is not necessary to have the project plan finalized for end-users to play with a system in a test data area. Typically, after a month of AE, client end-users (especially those who went to training) are experienced enough with the system that they can contribute in a meaningful manner and begin to think about decisions related to system design.

Note that AE should primarily focus on items included in Phase I of an implementation. If employee self-service, for example, is clearly out of scope for the first phase, then client end-users should not spend very much time learning it. There will be time for that in later phases. While AE should focus primarily on items targeted for the upcoming phase of the implementation, Phase II items should not be completely ignored. Configuring the system with the knowledge that it will need to be substantially changed after go-live is ill advised. Here, consultants must lead the way.

System Design

Based on the results of AE, the organization and its end-users should be ready to move on to System Design. In this phase, end-users configure the system to meet their business needs. Specific examples include the setup of the following:

- Organizational structure
- GL accounts, accounting units, and other GL/financial setup
- Benefit plans, payroll structure, employee status codes, and other HR-related setup
- Item master, vendors, and other procurement items
- System security

At this critical point, consultant input is invaluable. With respect to the new system, end-users who have been exposed to the application for several months (at most) do not know what they do not know. **End-users insisting on a sub-optimal or cumbersome setup are creating problems down the road that can adversely affect the entire project.**

Consultants should guide system design. Ultimately, the system configuration should be in line with "best practices" lest the client be left with a system that it cannot easily support.

Phase Objectives

The specific objectives of system design are as follows:

- To create an initial security matrix
- To establish the specific framework of the new system
- To continue the knowledge transfer started in AE
- To finalize and document the client's desired system setup/configuration

Security Design

Security is an important part of the design of a new system. It is quite typical for an organization to use a security matrix that details the rights, roles, and permissions assigned to each user upon logging in. This matrix typically comes in the form of an Excel spreadsheet representing the security setup in the new system.

When creating the initial security matrix, consultants usually start with a template from a previous assignment. It is generally unnecessary to start with a blank spreadsheet because, more than likely, another client's security matrix can serve as a very useful starting point. To be sure, the matrix will need to be refined based on the unique roles of client end-user. However, it's unlikely that the head of AP will need to run payroll batch processing programs or the IT manager will need to pay vendors.

Specifically, the matrix outlines the following:

- The names of the different security roles or classes
- The specific reports and forms of each security role or class
- The assignment of specific role(s) to each system end user
- Limitations assigned to each end-user (e.g., the head of HR can view information on all employees but a "line" HR person can see data only on the people whom she supports)

An example of a simple security matrix is provided below:

Table 9.5: Sample Security Matrix

User	Job Title	Security Class/Role	Form(s) and Reports	Notes
Alex	Head of AP	AP Super-user	All AP forms and GL setup forms	
Geddy	IT Manager	Administrator	All	Should not be able to see payroll data
Neil	Payroll Manager	Payroll Admin	All payroll forms and reports	Should not be able to change employee data
Mike	Procurement Analyst	Procurement Admin	All procurement forms and reports	
Kayla	Payroll Clerk	Payroll Clerk	Time record entry	Can only enter payroll data; cannot run reports
Jordan	Benefits Manager	Benefit Admin	All benefit setup and reports	
Marlene	HR Manager, Eastern Division	HR User Sales	All HR-related forms and reports for the Eastern Division	Should be able to change employee data for Eastern employees
Selena	VP of HR	HR User Read-Only	All HR-related forms and reports for the entire company	Read-only access; should not be able to change employee data

How Long Should System Design Take?

If end-users participated to the extent necessary during AE, then System Design should go relatively smoothly. AE and System Design are critical phases that serve as the basis for successful testing. As a result, it is preferable for an implementation team to spend a little too much time designing the system—within reason—than too little time. Remember that system configuration errors should manifest themselves in the next phase: Perfection is *not* required at this point. Additional codes and rules can be added as needed and the team will certainly need to make tweaks. However, at the completion of this phase, it is common for the consultancy to ask the client formally for sign-off on the system configuration.

Let's return to the house analogy. After System Design, the client has agreed to build a ranch. It may later decide on a different color of paint or to move the furniture. However, it realistically cannot, after testing, blow up the foundation and design a duplex, expecting to meet its go-live date and budget.

System Testing

Before delving too deeply into testing, consider a few definitions of major types of testing:

- User Acceptance Testing (UAT)[28] – End-users attempt to enter transactions into the system by using scripts provided by consultant.
- System Integration Testing (SIT) – End-users test entire processes from soup to nuts, not specific scenarios.
- Unit Testing – End-users test specific scenarios, not entire business processes from soup to nuts.
- Stress Testing – End-users "pound" the system to see if expected levels of traffic can be handled; testing may include entire business processes, individual scenarios, and extensive reporting.
- Parallel Testing – End-users test an entire process (e.g., running a complete biweekly payroll, month-end GL closing, etc.) in an attempt to replicate the results of the current (or previously closed) period in the legacy system.

While consultants may participate in testing to some extent, client end-users should drive the vast majority of testing. Doing so maximizes knowledge transfer and readies the end-users for "real life" under the new system.

System testing—in the generic sense of the term—is both a cause and an effect of implementation issues. On the "cause" side, end-users' lack of system knowledge may be causing them issues, such as their inability to match invoices incorrectly. In turn, this causes GL balancing issues. On the "effect" side, poor setup decisions should come to light

---

[28] UAT may also be called Conference Room Pilot (CRP).

during the testing process. Consider the payroll manager who tries to report on hours paid and discovers that the current system configuration does not separate hours to her satisfaction.

Phase Objectives

The main objectives of system testing include:

- To discover any design, data, processing, or application/system issues
- To refine the system configuration/setup as required
- To test any customizations and custom reports
- To continue the knowledge transfer process and make end-users comfortable with their roles after the new system is activated
- To identify any resource issues that may occur in the future—e.g., training needs or extra personnel
- To identify any business process issues that may occur in the future
- To refine the initial security matrix to reflect changes discovered or required by testing

How Long Should System Testing Take?

The time required to complete system testing is hardest to quantify relative to other phases. The short answer is, "As long as is necessary." If the previous phases have been successful, then testing should go relatively smoothly. This is rarely the case, however. Typically, project delays stemming from the issues uncovered (or not uncovered) in previous phases significantly delay and complicate testing. Because of these issues, it is not uncommon for testing to take twice as long as initially anticipated.

System Activation/"Go Live"

Assuming that the new system has been properly configured, tested, fixed, and approved by the necessary players, it is ready to be activated in a production environment. The organization's legacy system will no longer be its system of record. After a brief down period—typically called "cutover", end-users will enter real-world transactions into the new system.

Phase Objectives

The main objectives of this phase are:

- To activate the system
- To formally and permanently retire the legacy system

How Long Should System Activation Take?

This is typically the shortest—but most important—part of the implementation. If testing was successful in identifying all of the issues, then system activation should be a mere formality that can be safely accomplished over a weekend. As is often the case, however, system testing did not manifest all of the issues—and the resolutions to some known issues are still pending. In such a case, activation may be a gut-wrenching process that takes twice as long as expected, endangering mission-critical items: everything from employee paychecks to financial reporting to company sales.

Note that a legacy system may remain as a source of historical information within an organization after it goes live with the new system. For example, data conversion and extraction may not have provided the desired results, but the organization forged ahead and activated the new system anyway. On occasion, the legacy system may remain for the exclusive purpose of viewing previous transactions and information.

Costanza Medical Case Study: A Flexible Client and a True Consulting Partner

Let's return to project planning for a moment. As discussed previously, project plans conceived at the start of an implementation change, often based on issues discovered in AE and System Design. The following case study illustrates the dynamic nature of project plans and the need for clients to listen to their consultants.

Background

Costanza Medical was in the middle of an implementation of its new system with its partner, Van DeLay Consulting. Van DeLay judiciously gathered Costanza's business requirements before even bidding on the work and submitted a simple T&E bid. Van DeLay's PM, Rosalinda, was impressed with senior management at Costanza, who seemed to be very pragmatic. Costanza purchased the standard level of vendor support, covering basic software patches and access to the vendor's support site.

A Potential Showstopper

The implementation progressed reasonably well. Costanza's end-users devoted significant time to training, AE, system design, and testing. End-users and consultants began configuring the application after very successful AE sessions. With respect to payroll, end-users set up the following pay codes:

Table 9.6: Pay Codes at Costanza Medical

PAY CODE	DESCRIPTION
REG	Regular pay
OT1	Overtime pay
HOL	Holiday pay
VAC	Vacation
FMLA	FMLA unpaid leave
BON	Employee Bonus

End-users continued designing the system and proceeded to the testing phase. At this point, the implementation team discovered a major issue:

Many nurses at Costanza are paid hourly. Consider Kramer, a registered nurse who makes $20 per hour. Out of the box, the HRIS calculates Kramer's rate of pay at $20 per hour. For overtime (time-and-half), the ERP correctly calculates the rate of pay at $30 per hour for all hours over 80 in a two week period and all hours over eight in a day. However, Costanza has overpaid its employees for years because its legacy system could not calculate overtime correctly; it feared lawsuits and employee morale issues stemming from a perceived pay cut by a large group of employees. Costanza wanted to explore the merits of customizing the ERP's overtime calculation program such that it would pay employees in a manner consistent with the "old" way.

The team reported the issue to Rosalinda who knew that this customization would not be a small endeavor. A former application expert, she knew that customizations were much more involved than merely using a system's desired codes, functionality, and reports to meet a client's business needs. In other words, a change in the software's code—specifically in this case, to its overtime calculation—is fundamentally different than adding pay codes to track types of employee pay not identified during system design, such as sick pay.

Rosalinda had created the project plan and knew that it contained neither the time nor the budget for a major system customization. In this case, the customization would have severely compromised Costanza's desired go-live date and budget. Still, the decision rested in the hands of Costanza management; she could only provide the issue's context. Rosalinda immediately met with senior management to discuss the issue. In the meeting, she pointed out the following:

- Tweaking software code may cause something else to break in the future.
- Customizations are risky moves rarely sanctioned by the vendor. Translation: The basic level vendor support does not cover customizations.
- Upgrades and patches may well compromise or even reverse the customization.

Rosalinda advised Costanza management that it should proceed with the customization only if it possessed the internal resources to support that customization. Since it did not, Costanza would need to upgrade its vendor support agreement—at considerable cost—to cover customizations. Costanza management wanted to avoid these outcomes and asked Rosalinda to provide alternatives. She presented the following options:

Table 9.7: Gap Resolution Options at Costanza Medical

Option	Cost and Date Impacts	Change in Business Process
1. Proceed with the customization and revise the project's dates and budget accordingly.	High	None
2. Get creative, perhaps by exporting time records from the application, modifying them via a tool such as Microsoft Access, and importing them back into the system.	Low	None
3. Change the business process to conform to the ERP's delivered functionality.	Low	High

Costanza selected option two and the project remained on track. Within a day, a Van DeLay consultant created and fully documented a custom process by which Costanza end-users would extract payroll data from the system, run it through a custom Microsoft Access application, and import it with employee overtime already calculated. In other words, Costanza could circumvent running the system's overtime calculation altogether, without changing its business process or customizing the software's code.

Outcomes

In the words of American author and journalist Anna Quindlen, "A man who builds his own pedestal had better use strong cement." On a less existential level, Rosalinda knew that her client did not have the financial and internal means to successfully go the customization route. She did not look at the customization as a means to extend the project for Van DeLay; she remained committed to ensuring that Costanza met its date. To that end, she listed the options available to Costanza, detailing the pros and cons of each. Rosalinda helped Costanza make the best decision for its business. Ultimately, Costanza went live on time and within its initial budget. Costanza now uses Van DeLay exclusively as a consulting company and provides it with glowing references.

Summary

A great deal of time and effort is spent from the very beginning stages of a project (planning) until the very end (system activation). In the middle are major objectives, deadlines, and often hundreds of individual tasks, any one of which—if not performed correctly—may have a detrimental impact on the entire project. This chapter provided the objectives, timelines, and tasks required in each phase. Beyond implementation phases, the chapter analyzed the pros and cons of the different implementation strategies, from phased or partial implementations to full-blown ones.

With strategies and phases made clear, the next section will delve deeper, elaborating on the different roles and responsibilities during these phases.

The leader follows in front.

-Spanish Proverb

CHAPTER 10: THE GROUP RESPONSIBILITY MATRIX

Introduction

Having described the phases of the implementation, the focus of the book will now shift to the individual roles within those phases. This short chapter emphasizes which resources are most involved at each stage of the project.

Table 10.1 shows the required levels of involvement by key players during each phase of a *typical* implementation.

Table 10.1 – Group Responsibility Matrix (GRM)

Person/Group	Project Planning	Application Exploration	System Design	System Testing	System Activation
Senior Management	High	Low	Low	Low	High
Project Manager(s)	High	Medium	Low	Low	High
Functional client resources	Low/ Medium	High	High	High	High
Technical client resources	Medium	Low/ Medium	Medium	High	High
External Consultants	Low	High	High	High	High

A Guide, Not Gospel

The GRM is a generic and high-level document, unlike a formal and detailed project plan consisting of many tasks and goals. Because all projects differ, they require different levels of participation at different points from different end-users and groups. For example, a project that uses extensive external consultants and resources may rely relatively less heavily on internal resources.

For each person or group in the GRM, daily or weekly involvement might vary at any given point. For example, a gap found during testing by the functional team between vanilla system functionality and a business process may require the immediate intervention of senior management, as was the case in the Costanza case study discussed in the previous chapter.

Also note that every person and group is included in Table 10.1. For example, clients typically purchase vendor support—discussed at length in Chapter 7—at significant cost. Based on the types of issues found, clients may not need support at all throughout the implementation. Alternatively, clients may need extensive support at critical points as issues are discovered. However, to the extent that mature software works relatively well out of the box, especially when configured by seasoned consultants, the discovery and reporting of true "bugs" does not tend to be a regular occurrence.

Communication

Senior management and PMs should communicate and emphasize the group responsibility matrix to each person and group early and often. Clients face many dangers if key end-users are not involved at key points. In a similar vein, key individuals need to have the requisite time and knowledge at key points to make optimal contributions.

Consider a payroll manager (James) who works at LaBrie Industries. James does not participate in AE and has had virtually no input into the setup of the new payroll system due to his own time constraints or poor project planning. James is too busy fighting fires with current payroll to be bothered about future payroll issues. As a result, he misses key opportunities learn both the new system and to contribute to its setup. The PM fails to recognize the importance of this issue. Under the pressure of deadlines and lacking sufficient documentation on LaBrie's business processes, external consultants make critical assumptions about the required payroll setup. Two months later, in the middle of a parallel payroll test, James finally has time to look at reports and test the system (using the provided scripts). James finds issues with the setup that require major rework and, potentially, some customizations to the ERP. The net result is that the project is delayed by six weeks.

Involvement, Collaboration, and Backup

Low participation does not mean zero participation in the group responsibility matrix. For example, a PM is probably not a functional or technical expert in the new system. For example, she will not be the one deciding whether the client requires ten benefit plans or two in the new system. However, the PM should certainly be aware of the outcomes of these decisions because they absolutely affect upcoming phases as well as the overall system activation date.

Collaboration at all levels is imperative throughout the implementation. As previously discussed, system design is an extremely important phase. As such, it requires input from—and the approval of—senior leadership. It is tough to argue that the decision to spend hundreds of thousands of dollars (at a minimum) on the purchase and implementation of a new enterprise-wide system should be made independent of senior management. Executives should ensure that their organizations make the best decisions.

The type of involvement is critical. Folks in the corner offices should not mandate how to configure the system before consultants have even arrived on site. A poor system setup can essentially doom a project from the beginning, no matter how many hours worked by employees and consultants. Unfortunately, sometimes executives make irreversible configuration decisions in a vacuum, not reaching out sufficiently to internal subject matter experts or external resources beforehand. Decisions of this importance need to be made in collaboration with both consultants and the end-users who will have to live by these very decisions.

Organizations should also ensure that they have lined up backup or contingency plans in the event of employee departures. Let's return to the LaBrie example. Kevin the IT manager has a scheduled two-week trip to Europe starting May 1. Management approved his trip at the very beginning of the implementation. April arrives and the project has been delayed six weeks because of the setup changes mandated by testing. The project is off course and the stress testing—that Kevin needs to lead—must begin on April 28, *not* on March 14. Kevin needs to know this as soon as possible so he can arrange for appropriate backup. Telling him on April 27 does not allow him ample time to make arrangements, and as a result, the project delays could well be exacerbated.

Potential Red Flags

The very process of reviewing and approving the GRM allows organizations to *potentially* identify any red flags prior to beginning the implementation in earnest. For example, Collins Publishing intends to implement a new system with neither a full-time PM nor consultant from its partner, Thompson Consulting. Collins' management believes that it can complete the project almost exclusively on its own, with a Thompson consultant *occasionally* on site every few weeks. In a nutshell, Collins simply does not appreciate the gravity of the task confronting it.

By placing Collins' proposed resources in the GRM, Thompson should be able to illustrate to its client's management that the project is not sufficiently staffed. As such, it has a low chance of success. The GRM should immediately manifest practical questions, including:

- Who will oversee the work?
- Without a full-time functional consultant on site, how can Collins' end-users successfully learn the new system, much less participate in its configuration and testing?
- Given the fact that Collins' end-users will be wearing two hats throughout the implementation, how can management realistically expect the project to meet its objectives and hit its dates?

While Collins and Thompson may uncover the same staffing issues by creating a comprehensive project plan, the GRM is much simpler. What's more, why bother developing a 400 line project plan based on wholly insufficient resources?

Summary

The last two chapters have outlined the implementation phases and the roles that team members are supposed to play. Specifically, the next several chapters will explain how plans go awry, poor decisions are made, issues are missed, and systems ultimately fail.

Issues are separated into the following categories:

- Setup Issues
- Testing Issues
- People Issues
- Reporting and Interface Issues
- Documentation Issues

How does a project get to be a year late? One day at a time.

-Frederick P. Brooks

CHAPTER 11: SETUP ISSUES
Introduction
The intelligent configuration of a system is crucial to its overall success. For an implementation that relies heavily on external consultants, clients would do well to let consultants guide them through the process. This is not to say that consultants should march into an organization and force the wrong system configuration on clients. Organizational business practices may vary quite a bit from one client to another, even for those in the same industries. For example, hospitals may pay their nurses differently, although one would hope that all pay practices abide by relevant legislation.

Consultants should not merely take orders from clients. Rather, consultants should ask their clients questions about what they currently do and what they would like to do in the new system. Most of the time, a new system can handle client business requirements with the right system configuration, processing, and error handling without a single customization to the new system. During AE, consultants continue learning about their clients' business practices. At the same time, client end-users should learn about the new application—with consultants leading the way. Team members should document and report to the PM any and all gaps discovered between the system and business needs. The ideal relationship between client and consultant is symbiotic: By working together extensively and effectively, the "right" system configuration for an organization can be established, setting the stage for successful testing and, ultimately, system activation.

Of course, this is not always the case. The two case studies in this chapter focus on poor design decisions that plagued two projects from the beginning. It is instructive to note that, in both cases, external consultants did not recommend the system configurations. Client senior management made these decisions independent of the input from the product experts hired, allegedly for their expertise.

Portnoy Case Study: A Square Peg and a Round Hole
Let's turn to the next case study. Portnoy Healthcare is a very large, multi-site healthcare organization. Portnoy wanted to integrate a

number of new systems via interfaces into its already complex existing systems framework.

Portnoy is particularly instructive as a case study because its setup essentially guaranteed the failure of a new system from day one. Its senior management demanded a very complicated system configuration, approved long before the first consultant ever showed up on site. Portnoy manifests a number of different challenges and issues endemic, to some extent, to many new system implementations (e.g., knowledge transfer, data integrity, etc). However, by and large, most of Portnoy's issues are atypical: Rare is the organization these days that attempts to build a set of disparate systems. Most organizations aim for simplicity, transparency, and integration with respect to their systems.

While the focus of this case study is system configuration, Portnoy is also a prime example of the following:

- A consultancy not knowing the definition of "bad business"
- An organization believing that its business processes were unique and thus warranted a unique, complicated system setup
- An organization not having the personnel to support the monster that it chose to create

Background
Portnoy Healthcare consisted of ten different hospitals. Over the course of a number of years, Portnoy acquired a number of individual hospitals without imposing strict system and data standards on these new acquisitions. Therefore, each hospital maintained a great deal of autonomy vis-à-vis maintaining its own systems. What's more, some sites outsourced their payroll, and some ran payroll internally.

Rather than fully implement an "off the shelf" system to meet its needs, Portnoy senior management decided to create a monster. It attempted to stitch together a number of disparate legacy systems via a third party ETL[29] tool and keep them all in sync. The overall system—and

---

[29]ETL is a process by which data is Extracted, Transformed, and Loaded into a data warehouse. The process involves extracting data from outside sources, transforming it to fit business needs (which can include quality levels), and ultimately loading it into the end target: the data warehouse. (Source: Wikipedia)

related ETL tools—would allow for disparate rules at each hospital. Note that, in the long-term, Portnoy intended to eliminate its legacy systems.

Portnoy senior executives listened to proposals from different consultancies, expressing their desire for a unique setup because of its "unique business needs." Portnoy's fundamental question to potential partners was, "Can your firm stitch together these different systems and make them talk to each other?" Consultancies should have responded not in the affirmative but with two questions for their own:

- Why does Portnoy need to do this?
- Do Portnoy have the internal resources and expertise to support what it wants to create?

As discussed in Chapter 5, the majority of salespeople at large consultancies do not want to appear difficult and risk losing business. As a result, Portnoy faced little resistance during the sales cycle. It found that most consultancies neither asked these kinds of questions nor emphasized their importance.

Lee Consulting ultimately won the business, largely because of its name recognition. During the sales cycle, Lee salespeople strongly emphasized that it had the talent to build the amalgam of systems desired by Portnoy. Lee did not fully advise the client of the many difficulties that it would undoubtedly face by undertaking such an endeavor. If it had, then Lee may not have won the business in the first place.

Lee was a very large consulting organization. Within it, the ERP group represented a very small percentage of total company revenue. The salespeople at Lee saw a multi-million dollar carrot and opted to ignore the risks associated with chasing it. Surely, Lee had overcome more formidable client challenges than the one posed by Portnoy. Note that it is very likely that smaller, boutique firms—such as the ones described in Chapter 8—would surely have walked away from this deal upon learning about what Portnoy wanted to build.

Lee and Portnoy mapped out the specifics of the system architecture. In theory, the systems were supposed to look and work like this:

Figure 11.1: Portnoy Proposed System Architecture

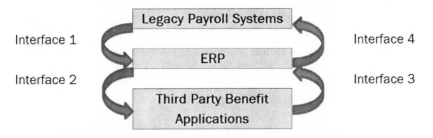

- **Interface 1** – Basic employee demographic, payroll, and benefit data are transmitted via an ETL tool from different client legacy payroll systems into a Third Party Benefit Application (TPBA).
- **Interface 2** – Benefit information is transmitted from the ERP to the TPBA.
- **Interface 3** – Data is transmitted from TPBA to the ERP. In theory, this would ensure that the information in both systems is in synch.
- **Interface 4** – Benefit elections are returned to the legacy payroll systems, thus ensuring that employee deductions are accurate and employees are covered under health, dental, and other plans.

Note that each interface was actually a group of interfaces. In order to load employee benefits from the legacy systems into the ERP, for example, each of the following types of information needed to be loaded separately: employee, employee dependent, employee benefit, and employee dependent benefit. What's more, one error would cascade through the chain. For example, if the system rejected an employee due to an invalid social security number, then her benefits, dependents, and dependents' benefits would also kick out.

Portnoy management wanted to go live in October, coinciding with its annual enrollment. While the project began in January of that year, the convoluted configuration in Figure 11.1 immediately challenged the feasibility of that date. Any remotely intelligent IT professional could argue that the architecture of this new set of systems was not sound. Further, that same individual may ask why any rational consultancy would even attempt to do this.

Implementation Issues

To be certain, many implementations face last-minute, unexpected data issues and crises. A post mortem on such implementations can typically point to a few key points at which the project derailed. This project, on the other hand, had no viable chance of succeeding from the start; the system architecture virtually ensured that this project would never hit its financial and calendar objectives. Specifically, implementation problems included:

- Each application (legacy systems, ERP, and TPBA) had its own business rules that, out of the box, did not mesh with other the systems' business rules. All rules had to be created and maintained in external tables to interact with each other. These tables were technical in nature and, as such, were not available to functional users. Any change to the system would require IT involvement, thus making the system forever tied to IT for even the most basic of system edits.
- The ERP vendor had already released a relatively mature— and quite respectable—benefit enrollment application. The application would have eliminated the need for Portnoy to continue using both the legacy systems as well as the third party benefit applications. While this web app was certainly not "best of breed," using it would have simplified the project tremendously.
- The ERP did not conduct any transactions; it simply housed transactions sent over via interfaces one and three. In laymen's terms, the ERP just "got in the way."
- No one consultant from Lee had ever worked with all of Portnoy's different systems, much less the ETL tool required to make these systems talk to each other.
- Portnoy's PM insistence on constant retesting magnified project delays.
- Integration issues aside, from a cost perspective, Portnoy had to pay license and support fees to each vendor.

As Table 11.1 demonstrates, Portnoy's system configuration led to nine possible categories of potential issues with this setup—three types of issues in three different systems:

Table 11.1: Types of Potential Issues during Portnoy Implementation

System	Setup	Data	Interface
Legacy Systems	x	x	x
ERP	x	x	x
TPBA	x	x	x

People Issues

The project lost momentum in early January, as Lee's sole functional ERP consultant (Bonnie) abruptly left the organization, leaving an enormous vacuum. Lee eventually filled the position five weeks later. Because Bonnie had not completed the ERP's setup before leaving, much of the interface development ceased during that period.

On the client side, issues abounded. Because the project was extremely technical in nature, most of the work required the sign-off of Portnoy's "technical architect" as well as the input of a few client-side functional end-users who were, quite frankly, out of their element. While they could appreciate the complexity of the different applications and interfaces, they did not have the skills to manage them independently, once the consultants were scheduled to leave. This situation fostered dependence on Lee's consultants, thus making Portnoy's PM justifiably weary. After all, how could the project be successful on any terms if it basically guaranteed that expensive consultants would be there indefinitely? Also, what would happen if one of the consultants left? Consultant attrition is not exactly uncommon, as everyone saw back in January.

On the functional side, Portnoy also did not possess the necessary internal resources to address setup issues in the ERP. Remember that a benefit election from the TPBA had to pass through the ERP in order to make it all the way back to the payroll systems.

A perfect example of this occurred when Lee's chief functional consultant moved on to another project. Despite his copious documentation and attempts at knowledge transfer to Portnoy personnel, interfaces failed because Portnoy end-users could not properly change codes within the ERP. A new or modified business rule could bring down the whole house of cards. Lee's consultant had to be contacted to fix the problem remotely. This was particularly scary given that the ERP passed so few types of data to and from the other systems via interfaces.

Beyond the core implementation team, the level of system expertise at Portnoy's local hospitals was wholly deficient. As a whole, end-users did not understand what was expected of them or, in fact, the point of the whole project. Most became frustrated and could not or would not follow testing scripts, causing even more delays.

Tensions intensified throughout the project between employees from Portnoy and Lee. Testing revealed many errors stemming from the different and overlapping systems. From the perspective of Portnoy end-users, their partner was one of the purported experts in the field. Portnoy, as an organization, was paying millions of dollars for this project to meet specific deadlines routinely not being met. Lee employees expressed frustration over their management's blind acceptance of Portnoy's complicated setup; the different systems and interfaces were *not* meant to work in the fashion desired by the client.

When Portnoy end-users were summoned to the corporate headquarters for integrated testing, additional people issues arose. Portnoy's employees resented being taken away from their day jobs. They had pressing issues to address and were distracted from testing the system.

Lastly, more problems stemmed from the presence of an internal auditor throughout the project. He would trust only reports that came from "the system." To the extent Portnoy was implementing three different systems, there was no one single standard report that could possibly capture all of the transactions sent up and down the food chain. While a Lee consultant created and ran such reports using Microsoft Access, the auditor chose not to trust these reports because they had the potential for human error. His questions about data integrity, however legitimate, served as a major bottleneck throughout the entire project.

Outcomes

The project went live well after the initial date and well past the initial budget of $3.5M. Portnoy's PM involuntarily left the organization well before system activation. Portnoy's senior management client claimed that they did not know the extent to which the integration issues would prove problematic and wanted blood. Lee lost the Portnoy account and now has a less-than-stellar reputation in the ERP world. Portnoy brought in a new consultancy that essentially blew up the old system configuration and recommended that the vanilla application be implemented at each hospital individually, with the legacy systems replaced altogether, not simply integrated into the rest of the systems.

Aside from a horribly-conceived setup, Portnoy's disastrous system failure ultimately resulted from the inability of its senior management to enforce system or data standardization across the entire organization. End-users at each hospital were used to having their own sandboxes; they were not accustomed to working and playing with other children. In the end, the executives who mandated this setup did not give the project a remote chance of being successful on any term. As a result, Portnoy can be rated on the failure scale as an Unmitigated Disaster.

Lifeson Case Study: Replicating the Old in the New

The following case study manifests what happens when an organization rips out the guts of a new system to have it mimic its predecessor. It proves that nothing good can come from such an endeavor.

Background

With over 50,000 employees across the globe, Lifeson is a large manufacturer lacked a central repository of information on its employees. Simple questions such as "How many employees work here?" took weeks to answer. By the time that the number was calculated, it was doubtless incorrect. Also, relatively straightforward administrative processes, such as awarding employee bonuses and stock options, took nearly six months, thus crippling any attempt by the HR department to function as a truly strategic partner. How could it? It was too tied up in basic administration and did not have meaningful employee data, much less the means to analyze it.

From a systems perspective, Lifeson was a mess. For years, Lifeson management created disparate "band-aid" systems for very specific purposes. The following facts put its internal systems architecture into context:

- Lifeson maintained over fifteen different homegrown HR and payroll applications.
- Even within the narrow area of employee compensation, data was dispersed. One system housed annual merit increases while others contained bonuses and stock options separately. Foreign Service National and employee payroll data were stored in two totally disconnected systems.
- Many individual employees kept separate spreadsheets and stand-alone databases containing information on employee skills, training courses, and other useful information.

- Within the main legacy system, end-users processed three out of every five HR and payroll transactions retroactively. In other words, Lifeson administrative personnel failed sixty percent of the time.

Reporting was less-than-ideal, as one can imagine. With so much data stored in so many different systems, report requests were routed to a central IT function. Also, as one would expect, end-users often would have to resubmit report requests multiple times because the reports contained fields that did not match the initial requests. Even when the IT folks got it right, the data were at best inconsistent and, at worst, incomplete and inaccurate.

In the late-1990s, Lifeson finally decided to implement an ERP, at first, globally, then domestically, in a phased approach. At least it didn't attempt to do it all at once, a massive undertaking on all terms. Lifeson selected a boutique firm with both technical and functional expertise: Jordan Consultants.

Implementation Issues

The implementation started internationally. Lifeson wanted to bring the US up on the ERP after other parts of the globe were already live. In retrospect, this approach allowed many of the US internal players—against the project from the get-go—to delay making important decisions and face the reality of the new system. Many of them hoped that the project would never gain traction so they would not have to deal with it after the international phases were completed.

Key Missteps

As a result of the campaign of misinformation, the naysayers and "change blockers" were able, at least partially, to sabotage the ERP from the start. Rather than change business processes and retire systems that had well outlived their usefulness, Lifeson had Jordan dramatically customize the ERP, leaving it basically another system in the company's labyrinth. In other words, Jordan inserted additional code, screens, and batch jobs specifically to retrieve data from—and send data to—Lifeson's existing array of HR and compensation systems. The ERP would house certain data but would not actually create or alter it; it would simply be one big storage facility that would typically be out of synch with the other systems. Not exactly the best way to guarantee a positive ROI!

Aside from failing to deal with obstinate managers, Lifeson's top brass made a number of other critical errors in the planning phase of the project. Lifeson failed to create a central authority or committee within the company with its requisite "teeth" for holding the regions accountable to some type of data standard. For the most part, each region of the globe marched to the beat of its own drummer. This gave additional ammunition to management vehemently opposed to the ERP. As they saw it, if things were already spiraling out of control internationally, why should Lifeson extend the project to the US?

A Campaign of Misinformation Leads to Successful Internal Sabotage

To say that everyone was "on board" with the new system at Lifeson could not be further from the truth. A few heavy hitters saw the ERP as a means to "blow up" the eye chart of internal systems that evolved over the years. These people were few and far between; internal resistance to the project could not be understated. Specifically, two key directors at Lifeson (Dennis and Steve) fought tooth and nail to prevent the project from gaining any traction. The very idea of this system threatened their existence. Many opponents were sacred cows (under the status quo), rich with institutional knowledge on how many of the company's proprietary systems really worked. In their eyes, the ERP system threatened their livelihoods.

At key senior meetings, Dennis and Steve would misrepresent the functionality of the new ERP. For example, Dennis once claimed during a senior management meeting that the new ERP could not update multiple salaries concurrently, unlike "his" system. Never mind the fact that he was flat-out wrong; the other executives in the room were hardly ERP super users and could not comment on the veracity of his claim. One entry-level employee did mention that the ERP could, in fact, perform this task quite easily. His protestations, lamentably, fell on deaf ears.

The amount of disinformation surrounding the system was astounding. In a different meeting, Steve openly expressed his anger over spending over three million dollars "on a system that can't run a (expletive deleted) report." He actually believed that a system that many other large, multinational organizations successfully ran could not provide basic information and that Lifeson's internal systems were vastly superior.

That the implementation was occurring in three regions concurrently—but not in the US—posed its own set of problems. Jordan consultants were too geographically dispersed to alter the general direction of the project or any specific decisions, not that they had the power to do either. For Jordan, the Lifeson account was a huge win.

Given the aforementioned obstinacy of folks like Dennis and Steve, the Jordan PM treaded very carefully around Lifeson, knowing full well that the company could pull the plug at any point and find more obedient consultants at a moment's notice.

When the implementation finally did turn to the US, the project had a less-than-stellar reputation internally. Along with budgetary issues, Lifeson decided not to implement the ERP's core modules. Rather, in lieu of buying a new training system, senior executives made the unwise decision to implement the ERP's training module *without having core employee information in that very system.* This is analogous to having a branch of a tree without the trunk. The system would store some employee classes and certifications but would not store essential employee data such as job codes, departments, addresses, salaries, and key employment dates.

Outcomes

After spending over $5M, Lifeson eventually scrapped the ERP altogether. Steve and Dennis won; broken internal processes remained in place for years. A few years later, Steve and Dennis were shown the door and Lifeson opted to implement a completely different system. As of this writing, that project is still ongoing.

Much like the Portnoy case study, Lifeson shows that systems initially meant to simplify processing can easily be corrupted by senior executives with an agenda and an honest belief that their business needs are different than those of other organizations. This belief is almost always unfounded but try telling that to a senior director who has never worked anywhere else and is five years removed from his pension. A project of this scope needs many things to be successful. First and foremost, however, senior leadership needs, in the words of the US Marine Corp: "Lead, follow, or get out of the way."

Lifeson can be rated on the failure scale as an Unmitigated Disaster

Comparison of the Two Case Studies

The following table illustrates the similarities between the organizations examined in the two previous case studies:

Table 11.2: Comparison of Portnoy and Lifeson Implementation Issues

Issue	Portnoy	Lifeson
Unsustainable Setup	x	x
Excessive Integration	x	x
Customized ERP		x
Unnecessary Maintenance of Legacy Systems	x	x
Phased Approach	x	x
Lack of Standardization of Data	x	x
Lack of Standardization of Business Practices	x	x

Both organizations attempted to integrate new systems into their spaghetti architectures.[30] The vast majority of the problems associated with each implementation and, ultimately, system failure can be traced directly back to management and setup issues. The senior management at each organization believed that its business needs were unique and, as such, required a complicated and costly setup. This assumption is almost always a big mistake.

Summary

The poorly designed system has virtually no chance of succeeding in either the short-term or the long-term, as evinced by the Portnoy and Lifeson case studies. Excessive interfaces and creative system configurations may reflect a fundamental unwillingness of the organization to embrace the future. Perhaps they reflect a mistaken belief of senior management that their organizations and business needs are unique. Regardless of why, this is a recipe for failure.

---

[30] A spaghetti architecture is one in which inter-application interactions are complex, numerous, and tightly coupled. This can result from bad planning and design either at the application or architecture level, or (more commonly) as an inevitable result of normal long-term incremental maintenance. Frequently such a situation is accepted by IT because "that's the way things are designed," "things work," and because it is perceived that there is no business value in re-architecting. Unfortunately in some cases architecting can also be viewed as threatening by those staff responsible for maintaining the existing systems (whether IT owners or business sponsors). (Source: www.ccpace.com/Resources/documents/Spaghetti_Architecture.pdf)

The next chapter focuses on testing and will show that even a system configured in a straightforward manner can run into formidable challenges.

On two occasions I have been asked,—"Pray, Mr. Babbage, if you put into the machine wrong figures, will the right answers come out?" I am not able rightly to comprehend the kind of confusion of ideas that could provoke such a question.

-Charles Babbage

CHAPTER 12: TESTING ISSUES

Introduction

After an implementation team has designed the system, it proceeds to coordinated testing to flush out any issues, continue knowledge transfer, and simulate real life for end-users once the system is activated. Assuming that the application has been set up correctly (or at least in a manner that seems acceptable at first), testing the configuration should identify any issues with respect to:

- Data
- Security
- Software

Data Issues: Snakes in the Woodwork

Mr. Babbage's quote at the beginning of this chapter can be restated as GIGO: garbage in, garbage out. To be sure, ERPs have advanced to the point at which they can easily receive data converted from legacy systems. Implementation teams typically understate the enormity of this task. Vendors often imply to clients that it's quite simple to load all sorts of data into their products. In practice, however, there are three main challenges involved in this process.

Getting at the Legacy Data

Often times, a company's legacy data is difficult to retrieve from a "back-end" perspective. Older databases were not designed to facilitate data extraction. As a result, powerful and commonly used tools such as SQL[31] queries may not do the trick. The relational databases of today allow for the easy extraction of any and all data from SQL Server,

---

[31]SQL (Structured Query Language) is a database computer language designed for the retrieval and management of data in relational database management systems (RDBMS), database schema creation and modification, and database object access control management. (Source: Wikipedia)

Oracle, and the like. The same cannot always be said for thirty-year-old mainframes. The short answer to the question regarding the ease of data extraction is, "It depends."

Often client end-users or technical consultants can easily extract the data required to load into the new system. Getting at the data is only half of the battle, however. Lest a client think that it is home free, it should consider very carefully the format of that data. Is the data gobbledygook or is it in a usable format? By usable format, everything does not need to be properly aligned or even remotely pretty. Whether comma-delimited, tab-delimited, or fixed-width, technical consultants and end-users can convert data consistently formatted into a "conversion-friendly" format on a regular basis.

In any event, before an implementation team can even think about using vendor-supplied conversion programs to get legacy data into its new system, it needs to profoundly understand its data before testing commences. After all, true parallel tests should contain converted legacy data. Shortchanging this aspect significantly increases a project's risk of delays and budget issues.

An example will illustrate this point. The IT Director at Montclair Bank (Neil) was able to parse weekly payroll data from its legacy system through a complex set of Microsoft Access-based routines. Using over sixty individual steps, he was able to produce incredibly accurate results (greater than 98 percent), both in terms of substance and style. Neil would make those files available for the payroll end-users to validate.

Montclair's resource constraints and the sheer number of conversion files made it likely that end-users would miss a conversion issue. Payroll validated a fair number of employees but missed a major issue: Employees at the end of the page of extracted data had hours totaled not just for themselves but for their entire departments. For example, an employee at the end of the page was converted into the new system with 500 hours worked for that week. As it turned out, Neil was able to easily fix this issue but someone had to spot them first. Lamentably, Montclair end-users did not discover this problem until it was in the middle of going live with the new system. Obviously, this was a less than optimal time.

Readers resistant to new systems may claim one little victory. How good can a system be if it lets something like that happen? Those more technically-savvy and new to conversion programs may be asking two questions, "Why would a presumably superior system have no system edit against this field? Why is there no edit in the vendor's conversion program that would limit to 168 (or some other number) the number of hours that an employee can work in a week?"

There are very valid reasons for a lack of what may appear to be commonsense edits in many systems and, more specifically, conversion programs. For one, not every organization decides to load detail-level information; it's not at all uncommon for an organization just to load summary historical information (quarterly or annual totals). In terms of the data being loaded, the number of hours in a "week" may be 500 because that week coincided with the end of a quarter. Remember, client end-users use generic conversion programs, not something specifically written for their organizations and related business rules. If they attempt to load "bad" data, the conversion programs may not kick out questionable values.

Clients should not lose faith in conversion programs. They have many edits that minimize the chance of bad data being loaded. Remember, many of these systems and their attendant conversion programs have been around for many years. They catch quite a few things, such as:

- GL transactions in which debits do not equal credits.
- Employee checks with net pay not equal to gross pay minus employee deductions.
- An employee benefit cannot be added before the plan went into effect.

The bottom line is that off-the-shelf products cannot catch every conceivable type of data-oriented error. Although consultants can certainly provide tools, the onus is on client end-users to validate the data.

Quality of the Legacy Data

Let's say that IT has been able to extract, manipulate, and present to functional end-users the data from the legacy system *en masse*. Let's also concede that the data extract is perfect and that every field from the legacy system has been accurately captured. Marlene, the benefit manager, looks at employee benefit contribution amounts in a spreadsheet and is baffled.

Table 12.1: Employee Deduction Amounts in Legacy System

EMPLOYEE	ENROLL DATE	BEN PLAN CODE	COV OPT	DEDUCTION AMOUNT
123	1/1/2008	HEALTH1	SINGLE	40
456	1/1/2008	HEALTH1	SINGLE	40
789	1/1/2008	HEALTH1	SINGLE	120

If the per-pay-period deduction for the health plan is $40 for single coverage, then why is employee 789 having $120 deducted? IT tells Marlene that employee contributions were derived from the amount that employees most recently had deducted from their pay checks. Marlene looks at payroll history and homes in on the true issue.

In the legacy system, Marlene finds that employee 789 took an unpaid leave of absence with benefits continuing. Upon returning, employee 789 had the deduction taken out three times in the same pay period; employee 789 was paying the company back. Marlene goes back to IT and tells them to modify the conversion routine so that all employees enrolled in the same plan with the same coverage option should have the same amount deducted *for future paychecks.*

In the example in Table 12.1, the fix was relatively straightforward. Any decent technical resource can write a rule to set employee deduction equal to $40 if the coverage option is single. In this case, IT understands the issue and makes the requisite changes. Let's consider another, more complicated example.

In the following example, an employee's deduction was entered incorrectly by a payroll clerk. Rather than attempt to correct this with "one-time" deductions, the clerk changed the amount of the deduction several times over a number of weeks to try to "make the employee whole." As a result, the deduction amounts stored in the legacy system are very inconsistent.

Extracting the information, IT provides Marlene with the deduction history for this employee but cannot make this call. IT is not responsible for determining the employee's level of coverage and deduction amount; it can only assist functional end-users in making these determinations. Table 12.2 presents the data for employee 678.

Table 12.2: Employee 678 Historical Deduction Amounts

EMPLOYEE	CHECK DATE	DEDUCTION CODE	BEN PLAN CODE	COV OPT	DEDUCTION AMOUNT
678	1/1/2008	ABC	HEALTH1	1	40
678	1/8/2008	ABC	HEALTH1	1	20
678	1/15/2008	ABC	HEALTH1	1	20
678	1/22/2008	DEF	HEALTH2	2	80
678	1/29/2008	DEF	HEALTH2	2	80
678	2/5/2008	ABC	HEALTH1	1	40

The obvious question is what should the employee's level of coverage and deduction amounts be? Short of asking the employee, this can be a difficult question to answer. Because of "garbage" being entered (and the legacy system allowing it to happen), this issue may take some time to resolve. Typically, these issues tend to be isolated but not unique. A 20,000-employee organization will need a considerable amount of data "clean up" to load correct data into the new system.

Mapping the Legacy Data: Bridging Old to New

Data may well need to be mapped or translated from old values to new values. Typical names for these critical tables include translation ("XLAT") tables or crosswalks. A typical example might include the following for employee deductions:

Table 12.3: Tax Code Mapping Table

COMPANY	LEGACY DEDUCTION CODE	DESCRIPTION	NEW DEDUCTION CODE
100	1111	Federal Income Tax	T000
100	1112	Social Security - Employer	T001
100	1113	Social Security - Employer	T003

Table 12.3 simply indicates that employees who had federal income taxes taken by deduction code 1111 will now have the same taxes taken in the new system via deduction code T000. The new naming convention might facilitate grouping and reporting from the new system, as all taxes would conceivably be identified by the letter "T."

Note that translation tables are not always required. In this example, the "1111" is absolutely a valid code in the new system; there's no technical requirement that new taxes start with "T." However, implementing a new system typically involves consultants who will bring along "best practices," one of which may be "smart-coding" certain values like deduction codes, vendor groups, and the like.

Regardless of whether an organization decides to map its legacy data to new values, remember one thing: codes that are part of the index[32] of a particular table cannot easily be changed in the database. In other words, after going live, the payroll manager cannot decide that she wants the code to be another value, say "T123." The description of the code "Federal Income Tax" can be changed because it is not part of the index. The short technical answer is that indices—or fields within an individual index—often exist in multiple tables, often as part of the relationships to those tables. Imagine changing a golf course: One cannot simply move the green on a par four dog leg left 200 yards to the right. One would have to completely reconfigure the entire hole. This is no small task.

All data are not created equal. Key fields of many systems include: employee numbers, vendor numbers, the item master, and GL accounts. Client end-users must agree upon these values—from a data mapping perspective—as soon as possible, as they are prerequisites for setup, testing, conversions, and system activation.

Let's look at the example of Planet Appliances, an organization implementing a new HRIS. Planet's implementation team mistakenly does not give much thought to the numbers that the new ERP will assign to employees. In the legacy system, employee numbers equaled their social security numbers. However, Planet initially activated its legacy system back in 1984, long before the privacy concerns of HIPAA[33] carried the weight that they do today.

---

[32] A database index is a data structure that improves the speed of operations on a database table. Indices can be created using one or more columns of a database table, providing the basis for both rapid random lookups and efficient access of ordered records. (Source: Wikipedia)

[33] The Health Insurance Portability and Accountability Act (HIPAA) was enacted by the US Congress in 1996. According to the Centers for Medicare and Medicaid Services (CMS) web site, Title I of HIPAA protects health insurance coverage for workers and their

Thus, the organization creates the following crosswalk:

Table 12.4: Simple Employee Number Mapping Table for Planet Appliances

DIVISION	LEGACY EMPLOYEE NBR	LEGACY EMPLOYEE NBR
100	123-45-789	1234
100	223-45-789	4567
100	333-45-789	7890

This is a very straightforward approach. Planet will now assign employees an arbitrary but unique value that masks the true social security numbers. Of course, Planet may have a hard time determining certain employees' true social security numbers. However, let's assume that end-users can verify that information.

Already considerably delayed, Planet's implementation team discovers the following: Not all pockets of the company used the same employee number conventions. As a result, there is no consistency and the extracted data now look like this:

---

families when they change or lose their jobs. Title II of HIPAA, known as the Administrative Simplification (AS) provisions, requires the establishment of national standards for electronic health care transactions and national identifiers for providers, health insurance plans, and employers. (Source: Wikipedia)

Table 12.5: Employee Number Mapping Table with Issue

DIVISION	DEPT	LEGACY EMPLOYEE NBR	HIRE DATE	NEW EMPLOYEE NBR
100	ADMIN	123-45-789	1/1/1997	1234
100	HR	223-45-789	1/11/1997	4567
100	FINANCE	333-45-789	1/21/1997	7890
100	MARKETING	123-45-789	1/31/1997	1234
200	MARKETING	7897	1/4/1996	7897
200	MARKETING	333-45-789	1/14/1994	7890

In other words, because of HIPAA, in 2006 the marketing department in Division 200 started entering employee numbers unrelated to their social security numbers. While hardly an insurmountable technical challenge, discoveries like this concerning key fields can cause delays. What's more, they can cause key players to publicly—and loudly—question the accuracy of the basic data about to be converted into the new system. For projects to remain on track, influential opponents of the new system do not need additional fodder.

Let's look at another example of data mapping issues. King Motors is implementing an ERP throughout the organization. In preparing for the conversion, IT extracted data from its legacy system and revealed almost 50,000 job codes, many of which were unnecessary and ostensibly duplicates. Data for one job code are presented below:

Table 12.6: King Job Code Legacy Data

COMPANY	OLD JOB CODE	OLD JOB TITLE	NEW JOB CODE	NEW JOB TITLE
100	S1111	Secretary	ADMIN1	Administrative Assistant
100	S1112	Admin Asst	ADMIN1	Administrative Assistant
100	S1113	Administrative Assistant	ADMIN1	Administrative Assistant
100	S1114	Admin. Asst.	ADMIN1	Administrative Assistant
100	S1115	Admin. Asst2.	ADMIN1	Administrative Assistant

COMPANY	OLD JOB CODE	OLD JOB TITLE	NEW JOB CODE	NEW JOB TITLE
100	S11146	Admin. Asst.	ADMIN1	Administrative Assistant
100	S1115	Dept Secretary	ADMIN1	Administrative Assistant
100	S1116	Secretary/Asst	ADMIN1	Administrative Assistant

King has eight different job codes for what appears to be the same job. Obviously, King did not exactly have tight controls on which end-users had the ability to add new job codes. Many end-users did not bother to look at existing values when entering a new employee (or processing a transfer). What's more, the system allowed them to add as many codes as they liked.

From a technical point of view, the fix is easy: Use the mapping table below to convert old values to new as follows:

Table 12.7: King Job Code Mapping Table

COMPANY	OLD JOB CODE	OLD JOB TITLE	NEW JOB CODE	NEW JOB TITLE
100	S1111	Secretary	ADMIN1	Administrative Assistant
100	S1112	Admin Asst	ADMIN1	Administrative Assistant
100	S1113	Administrative Assistant	ADMIN1	Administrative Assistant
100	S1114	Admin. Asst.	ADMIN1	Administrative Assistant
100	S1115	Admin. Asst2.	ADMIN1	Administrative Assistant
100	S11146	Admin. Asst.	ADMIN1	Administrative Assistant
100	S1115	Dept Secretary	ADMIN1	Administrative Assistant
100	S1116	Secretary/Asst	ADMIN1	Administrative Assistant

Here's where the human element muddies things, however. King's senior management argues ceaselessly about titles and job descriptions, not to mention the employees who may be recategorized. Elaine—the secretary in marketing—is about to be given the same title as Jerry, an assistant in HR. Elaine's manager, George, has a fundamental problem with that. (Yes, I am a big Seinfeld fan.) George knows of Elaine's work and believes that she adds more value to the organization than Jerry does. He's going to fight this reclassification tooth and nail.

One may be asking, "Why does this matter? What are the reasons that a job code or title is important from a systems' perspective?" In this example, job code may drive government EEOC[34] reporting, wage analysis, and so on. Also, imagine King spending millions on a system and not being able to answer a simple question, such as, "How many administrative assistants work here anyway?"

Now, add the complexity of different countries, languages, and legal requirements. Is it even possible to have the same title throughout King? ERPs typically have no practical limit on the number of codes that can be added, whether they are GL accounts, job codes, vendors, and so on. However, the following rule is typically a prudent one: Set up as many codes as needed—no more, no fewer.

Even in the unlikely event that the extracted data is squeaky clean, King's implementation team must answer fundamental questions before the data can be loaded into the new system. For the examples mentioned previously, the questions include:

- What are the values of the individual codes that will be set up in the new system?
- Can any codes be retired?
- Which new codes need to be created?

---

[34] The US Equal Employment Opportunity Commission (EEOC) is a federal agency charged with ending employment discrimination. The EEOC investigates discrimination complaints based on an individual's race, color, national origin, religion, sex, age, and disability and also investigates allegations of retaliation (e.g., demotion, discharge, discipline, harassment, etc.) for reporting and/or opposing a discriminatory practice. The EEOC is also tasked with filing suits on behalf of alleged victim(s) of discrimination against employers and as an adjudicatory for claims of discrimination brought against federal agencies. (Source: Wikipedia)

- Which unnecessary codes can be consolidated with other codes?

If all of the legacy codes remain the same, then no mapping needs to take place. This is never the case, however. Remember that no two systems are the same. Codes required for one system may well not be required for the other. Conversely, entirely new codes will be required. The mapping of old to new codes—and the defining of new codes—are imperative for conversion programs to work properly and completely.

To the extent that these codes are end-user driven, IT may ask functional resources to use applications such as Microsoft Access and to provide these maps or "translation tables." IT can then easily use these maps to convert legacy data into a format that the new system will accept.

Loading and Testing Legacy Data: The Inevitability of Errors

Many implementations stumble into issues related to loading data after it has been extracted, mapped, formatted, and represented in a conversion-file-friendly format. Note that systems typically contain database or system tools for advanced users that allow for the "cramming in" of data irrespective of the business rules. No respectable vendor will unilaterally recommend this approach, so this discussion will focus on mainstream data loading methods.

PMs, end-users, and executives would do well to remember two things with regard to data conversion errors. First, to quote software guru James F. Cooper, "Systems are to be appreciated by their general effects, and not by particular exceptions." Translation: If a conversion program accurately loads 99 percent of its records, then focusing on why one percent failed misses the point. Unfortunately, some end-users—particularly those going through their first major system implementation—foolishly believe that they will not encounter any major data problems. They are misguided and naïve, at best.

Second, errors are actually helpful the vast majority of the time. They are essentially communicating information. In this instance, the value that the load program attempted to load did not mesh with the system's current configuration and its rules. The data or the rule needs to be fixed. End-users should not want their new systems to accept data that do not meet the organization's business rules.

Going back to the earlier examples, let's assume an IT would not attempt a trial conversion until all end-users formally approved all of the organization's job codes, deduction codes, pay codes, employee numbers, and GL accounts. This is a crucial error and can significantly affect the timeline and budget of an implementation. It is imperative that organizations "kick the tires" on conversion programs as soon as possible, even if all data values have not been finalized.

From earlier in this chapter, the IT director at Montclair Bank (Neil) understood this point and routinely updated his data cleansing routines. Each revision improved the accuracy of the legacy data as well as the format required by the new system. Thus, when Montclair's end-users changed business rules or entered bad data into its legacy systems, Neil's routines—and the system's conversion programs—would isolate records with potential or actual errors. As a result, end-users could focus on the root causes of the problem and not have to wade through hundreds of thousands of records in an attempt to find the problem records.

Conversion programs yield two types of errors:

- "Kick-outs" due to invalid data or business rule-data conflict
- Valid data accepted by the new system causing errors down the road

An example of the first type includes an invoice with a vendor number of "AAAA." Obviously, this is not a valid integer and any conversion program will reject this value if the data type of the vendor number field is "number." Alternatively, consider a payroll history conversion program in which the system will not load a gross check for $1,000 with total deductions of $300 for a net check of $800. The math just doesn't add up. These errors typically "spit out" in either a separate file or at the end of a conversion program, making it easier for them to be identified and ultimately fixed.

Errors of the second type are arguably more dangerous, as end-users tend to uncover them during testing. Let's say that an organization loads employee payroll history and the basic equation below holds for each employee payment:

Gross Pay – Total Deductions = Net Pay

End-users evaluate the data and confirm that all payments have been successfully loaded. However, months after system activation, the payroll manager notices a problem. Specifically, employees are contributing to their 401(k) plans beyond the federally mandated limit.

How could this be? She looks at an employee's deduction history and sees that payroll history was converted via one deduction code (H401) but the current employee contributions fall into a separate deduction code (401). During the setup, end-users and consultants failed to notice that the two are not currently linked in the system, resulting in a significant number of employees contributing too much to the plan. What's worse, the company matches employee contributions.

Corrections in this scenario involve a number of methods. For one, on the payroll side, these employee deductions need to be "given back." Also, payroll manager must reverse the organization's matching contributions and modify GL history. Outside of the payroll system, corrections may well have to be made with the TPA (third party administrator) that manages the plan. Interfaces have sent out payroll information that needs to be fixed. If the data had been properly loaded, mapped, and tested, then the new payroll system would have recognized the other deduction code and the entire problem would have been avoided.

Conversion programs may catch these types of errors. However, there simply is no conversion program in any system that can possibly check every conceivable type of error. There are too many options and possibilities within the same organization, much less across a multitude of domestic or international organizations. The bottom line is that implementation teams need to test everything.

Manual Entry of Legacy Data: The Final Option
Load programs have advanced quite a bit over the last fifteen years. There are now more ways than ever to bring information into a new system without having to sit for hours at a keyboard. This is not to say, however, that all data can be loaded. Occasionally, the time spent reformatting data for the purposes of automatically loading it is much greater than the time required for end-users to simply key it. End-users must decide if the "squeeze is worth the juice."

The above examples illustrate two key points about systems and data:

- Different systems almost always represent data in different ways.
- The very process of converting data typically manifests significant data quality issues.

Security Issues

The implementation team should test the security matrix extensively to determine that end-users can do what they are supposed to do and see what they are supposed to see. The converse of this is equally important: End-users should test to see that they cannot do what they are not supposed to do and cannot see what they are not supposed to see.

As issues related to security manifest themselves, the implementation team should address them and refine the security matrix. Issues may include the following (derived from the matrix displayed in Table 9.6):

- The payroll manager cannot access a key payroll report.
- A payroll clerk has "read only" system access and cannot modify or enter new time records.
- A line HR manager discovers that she can actually view information on her colleagues in HR.
- Reports that AP end-users now need have been added to their security roles.

Software Issues

During testing, a client might discover an issue not related to system configuration or data entry. The software may not be working as designed. Examples may include:

- Employee taxes are not being taken from pay checks
- Invoices are not matching
- Employee life insurance is not being calculated correctly
- A screen to which a user has access does not appear
- A report "hangs" (i.e., does not finish)

At this moment, a consultant or client end-user should initiate a call to vendor support. The vendor will require the following information to assist in resolving the issue:

- The specific version of the software that the client is running—e.g., not just version 8, but version 8.1.1.1
- The software's operating system
- The version of the database if necessary
- Screen shots of the problem
- Additional screen shots related to setup

- Other items, depending on the nature of the case

The vendor will not help with items such as a customized program or screen in the application, the writing of a custom report, or basic setup. The vendor's basic support only covers true "bugs"—i.e., instances in which the application is not doing what the documentation clearly states that it will do.

Advice for Logging a Call to Support

Vendors usually employ product specialists to assist clients in resolving issues. These experts can resolve an issue much quicker when the end-users provide them with as much information as possible. In other words, logging a ticket described as "benefit plan does not work" is not very descriptive. Rather, the description should detail the specific issue—for example, "employee 401(k) contribution is not permitted." Further, the ticket should contain as much backup documentation as possible.

Also, end-users should demonstrate to support specialists that they have done their homework. To that end, end-users should provide the steps that they have already taken to resolve the issue—for example, verified that an employee is eligible to participate in the 401(k) plan, the plan start date is valid, and so on. Aside from eliminating fruitless options and saving time, such information shows the specialist that the end-users is knowledgeable and cannot be dismissed with a facile explanation of the issue.

The Challenge of Replication

One of the most frustrating things that end-users experience is an inability to replicate a problem. For vendor support to diagnose the issue effectively—and find or create a potential solution, the support representative has to see the issue in action, typically in real time. To this end, the support representative may:

- Try to replicate the problem independently on its own test systems
- "Dial in" to a client's network to view the problem first hand

Intermittent issues are the hardest for the vendor to spot and ultimately fix. End-users encountering issues should take as many screen shots as possible to expedite the resolution of a problem.

Summary

As the great Woody Allen once said, "Eighty percent of success is showing up." The parallel for systems is that a properly designed application stands a much greater chance of withstanding the rigors of testing and the challenges of an implementation. "Creative designs," to be polite, increase the odds of encountering problems before, during, and after an implementation. The organization that wants to reinvent the wheel had better have enough bandwidth, documentation, and backup for when the brakes fail.

So much of what we call management consists in making it difficult for people to work.

-Peter Drucker

CHAPTER 13: PEOPLE ISSUES, ROLES, AND RESPONSIBILITIES

Introduction

Implementation issues are not confined to the data and system realms. On the contrary, many of the problems encountered during a typical implementation stem from people, the roles that they are required to play, political issues, and their comfort zones.

Returning to the Group Responsibility Matrix in Table 10.1, it is time to explore the main implementation roles in greater detail. This chapter focuses on the responsibilities of the following throughout the implementation:

- Project Managers
- External Consultants
- Client End-Users

Project Managers

While PMs steer the ship, good ones rely on their crew members. To continue with the metaphor, a project may be the equivalent of smooth sailing at the beginning. Everyone wants the same thing: smooth sailing—i.e., a successful implementation under budget and on schedule.

PMs should not focus on life at 30,000 feet. While they should *not* micromanage and unnecessarily involve themselves in many of the day-to-day issues, PMs who focus exclusively on high-level objectives are remiss. Rather, PMs need to do the following throughout an implementation:

- Listen to consultants when they bring issues to light
- Proactively approach consultants to ensure that individual objectives are on track
- Broach issues and their impacts to senior management as needed

Let's look at an example of an issue on a project that requires action by the PM, Tony. During the testing phase of an implementation, consultants discover that the integrity of a client's employee hire date (typically critical for HR and payroll systems) is suspect. That date drives items such as employee benefit eligibility, deductions, and vacation/sick plan accruals. Until the date issue is resolved, the team cannot complete a key testing requirement—in this case, the employee conversion from old to new.

Let's be clear about Tony's role here. He is not an HRIS expert and cannot be expected to know the impact of something as ostensibly trivial as employee hire date. What's more, it is not his responsibility to ask about each field on the employee conversion program. As will be discussed later, functional consultants must address this issue with Tony. He then must communicate this issue—and the potential solutions proposed by the team—to senior management as soon as possible. If he does not, then the issue may result in further delays.

How does a good PM recognize such risks and determine what to do about them? Good PMs do not need to know answers to these questions much of the time. Rather, the best PMs solicit and rely upon the expertise of the consultants. After all, they are the subject matter experts (SMEs) in their respective fields. In so doing, PMs minimize project risk. The PM is not, in all likelihood, a GL expert or a procurement guru. It is incumbent on PMs to rely on the people who are.

Is a Consultant PM Truly Necessary?

On certain projects, client management might look for a way to minimize costs. They might question the need for a full-time consultant PM. This may be a mistake. As a general rule, the need for a full-time external PM is a direct function of the following:

- The size and scope of the implementation
- The number and expertise of the client's internal resources

At one extreme, a 50,000-person organization hires an external consultancy to implement a full ERP (from soup to nuts). The consultancy brings ten full-time consultants from all functional and technical areas because the client has limited or no internal expertise and no PM with remotely similar experience on the ERP front. As such, the client would be foolish *not* to employ a full-time PM from the consultancy. Too much coordination exists among the different areas not to have someone with a "global" view. At the other extreme, a small

2,000-person hospital hires one consultant to implement a new module within its existing ERP. It probably can make do without a devoted PM. In fact, the on-site consultant can often serve as the *de facto* PM. In reality, most projects fall somewhere in between these two extremes, making the presence of a full-time PM a murkier matter.

Multiple PMs

On particularly large implementations, such as the one detailed in the upcoming Petrucci case study, it is not uncommon for a client PM and consultant PM to co-manage the project. In this scenario, the client PM is probably implementing the specific system for the first time. Perhaps the client PM has managed a fairly large project or two before at this organization, but never one of this scope. After all, organizations tend to implement ERPs only once in any employee's tenure. As discussed, ERP implementations are expensive, highly visible projects in any organization. With items such as employee self-service, the new system may well touch each and every employee. Client PMs often stake much of their internal political capital and reputations on the success of these projects. As such, they tend to be very reluctant to concede major points of contention. In their view, the vendor promised their organizations certain functionality prior to the beginning of the project. Come hell or high water, their organizations will have it.

This is a key point. Client PMs will have to answer to their senior managers if projects exceed approved budgets, miss key deadlines, and/or do not deliver key functionality. As a result, they have a tendency to push both implementation teams and external consultants, often up to their breaking points.

Unlike their client counterparts, PMs from the consultancy are rarely "first-timers." Ideally, the consultant PM should be a seasoned expert in the field, having managed multiple implementations of the system before. More than expertise or certification (PMP), the consultant PM must challenge a client PM if the demands, timelines, and enhancement requests are unreasonable and put the entire project at risk. In other words, during the course of a project, the level of alignment between the consultant and client PMs may diminish and for good reason. The consultant PM has to keep the client PM in check.

Problem PMs

PMs play a key role on most new system implementations, especially for large organizations. Ideally, they act as a buffer between senior management, consultants, and client end-users in the trenches.

An experienced, qualified PM is essential to the success of the project for both client and consulting company. The ideal PM knows when to escalate an issue, when to call a meeting, and, just as important, when to let the implementation team work. The following four types of PMs should be avoided if at all possible:

- The Yes Man
- The Micromanager
- The Procrastinator
- The Know it All

The Yes Man

Certain PMs fear conflict and will agree to every client demand. These PMs may have a sales background and, as a result, are used to saying "yes." They typically mean well and certainly do not try to sabotage projects. Perhaps Yes Men simply want their clients to be happy with their companies. However, by failing to confront a "client gone wild," Yes Men implicitly or explicitly make promises and commitments that can endanger an entire project.

The Micromanager

Much like Yes Men, Micromanagers mean well and merely want to understand each step in a process or the nature of a complex issue. However, on a project, the PM is *not* supposed to be the product or application expert. During a project's crunch time, consultants often do not have the time to explain each facet of a complex issue to anyone, much less a neophyte, regardless of benevolent intentions. Micromanagers need to let experienced consultants do their jobs. Depending on the timing, a PM may have to live with a high-level explanation of an issue. Should The Micromanager need more detail, he should bring consultants to steering committee meetings or have them write the updates to status reports, providing the requisite level of detail.

On most projects, PMs convene many meetings. While project and team communication is very important, PMs need to let consultants breathe—that is, get the actual work done. No consultant can be effective if she spends most of her time briefing her PM on the status of each issue. PMs need to minimize the number of status meetings, especially as a project reaches critical points.

The Procrastinator

PMs who routinely fail to deliver cause organizations to miss project deadlines. Procrastinators put consultants in the untenable position of having to defend the indefensible in front of clients. Speaking from personal experience, it's a no-win situation for the consultant having to deal with issues caused by Procrastinators to a justifiably angry client. The Procrastinator often ducks clients and does not deliver promised results—project plan, documentation, and status updates. In such a case, clients are likely to lose faith in the consultancy and its individual consultants, whether the latter are contributing to the delays or not.

The Know it All

No PM or consultant can know everything about an application. Some PMs have "graduated from the ranks" of application or technical consultants and might have the ability to answer questions about some system-related issues. While being able to speak intelligently about issues is hardly a liability, PMs who do not engage their teams at key points do a number of inimical things. For one, these PM can alienate their consulting teams and make client end-users less likely to broach issues with them in the future. Second, by routinely not involving the experts, Know it Alls effectively minimize the contribution of those consultants, possibly causing clients to question the need for those consultants in the first place. Unless the consultant was specifically hired in a hybrid role of consultant-PM, that individual should routinely involve the implementation team throughout the project.

External Consultants

Consultants play an absolutely essential role in the typical implementation of a new system from day one until they leave. A point made earlier bears repeating: For an implementation to be successful, consultants must be able to immediately challenge potentially questionable client decisions that could have a substantial impact on the project.

A few examples will help illustrate this point. First, consider an organization that wants to utilize a very complex GL configuration. This setup would require an enormous amount of customization of the system and, in the process, obviating the possibility of using a great deal of system functionality and a number of standard reports. The GL setup, for example, would mean that the "canned" P&L would not accurately break out expenses and revenue in a remotely accurate manner. Of course, the client does not know this; the CFO simply wants to replicate the "old" GL in the new system, come hell or high water.

Second, consider Amy, a payroll manager who wants to change the default method that the new system calculates employee local taxes. She just does not trust the tax assigning functionality of the new system. As a result, she wants to manually assign all federal, state, and local taxes to employees. She knows that the new system can technically support this process without any modifications and her management supports her decision.

The best consultants are the ones who, after listening to the business needs in each of the following cases, advise clients of the resultant problems if the clients continue following these routes. Specifically, in the first case, the desired setup means the following:

- The normal P&L won't work.
- The organization will either have to create a new P&L or modify the standard one.

In the second example, Amy is clearly unaware of the amount of work that will be involved in enabling and disabling taxes when employees work in different states, change residences, and the like.

Remiss is the consultant who is afraid of conflict, even with senior client management. Again, the time, place, and tone of the disagreement are important to ensure buy-in, avoid personal rivalries, and ensure a productive, long-term relationship. The consultant's ultimate objective should not be "to be right," although that might be the outcome. Rather, the consultant should make all attempts to ensure that the client is making the best decision to utilize the new system as efficiently as possible given the business needs, level of IT/end-user support, and so on.

This last point is critical: The consultant can only make the client aware of the work involved and the consequences of their decisions. If client management has budgeted the time and resources for suboptimal decisions, then the consultant has truly done all that she can do. In the previous examples, the CFO who will pay a Crystal developer big bucks to create a custom P&L is well within her rights to do so. If Amy has a dedicated and knowledgeable staff devoted to getting taxes right, her organization can absolutely go the manual route for taxes. Having made the point, the consultant should then move on, whether she agrees with the decision or not.

Aside from exercising "freedom of speech," consultants need to do the following throughout an implementation:

- Transfer knowledge to clients
- Make themselves expendable
- Listen to client issues and broach them as needed to PMs, team members, and senior management.

Consultants have an obligation to transfer knowledge to client end-users on a routine basis. Certainly, there will be times that a consultant is swamped with fixing a complicated issue requiring complete concentration. As a result, he cannot walk an end-user through that issue's resolution at that particular moment. However, as a general rule, consultants should find the time to explain setup, processing, and error resolution techniques to clients in a timely manner.

Only by transferring knowledge can consultants make themselves expendable. Consultants do not transfer knowledge simply by fixing problems and providing answers. Clients can learn a great deal by observing the method by which the consultant resolves an issue. Testing will manifest issues and end-users can learn a great deal by seeing how the new system created an error in a purchase order or employee paycheck. This is not to imply that consultants know all of the answers. The best consultants know which questions to ask and how answer them. To this end, consultants should share knowledge bases, news groups, end-user documentation, application tips, and other "clubs in the bag" with clients with the aim of making them self-sufficient.

The type of knowledge transferred depends on the type of consultant as well as the type of client end-user. For example, consider a consultant proficient in Crystal Reports as well as the financial suite of an ERP. He can extract and present the information in just about any fashion. As he works with IT and functional end-users, he shows them tricks on how to write efficient reports. However, when working with the less-technical head of Accounts Payable, he tables his Crystal knowledge and demonstrates how to set up a vendor and pay an invoice.

Finally, consultants must report issues not only on a routine basis but also as situations warrant and as they arise. Aside from reporting issues, consultants should assess their impacts and propose solutions. The flip side to being left alone by PMs is the implicit assumption that consultants will keep PMs in the loop. Consultants should keep issues at a high level at first, for the PM is typically not an expert in the same field as the consultant.

Client End-Users

Before discussing clients' responsibilities throughout an implementation, it is instructive to break clients into the four categories into which they typically fall (regardless of job title and specific role in an implementation):

- Willing and Able
- Willing But Not Able
- Able But Not Willing
- Neither Willing Nor Able

Note that consultants were not put through the same "willing and able" ringer as clients. *They should be both!* If not, then it's time to get new ones.

Willing And Able (WAA)

At the risk of simplifying, certain people are much better than others in terms of setting up and testing new systems. Some people enjoy the challenges and complexities of learning and implementing a new system more than others. WAAs view the new system as an opportunity to enhance their skill sets and embrace a new technology. WAAs can quickly assimilate new information, make logical jumps, and ask "next step" questions, thinking about the implications of the answers. If only everyone was as enthusiastic as these valuable resources. From a consultant's perspective, it is simply a joy to work with these people.

Close to the pure technology enthusiasts are those that may not love learning new systems but recognize the reality of their situations: Their organizations have made the decision to implement new systems and they have to get on board. These individuals are realists and will do what is necessary for the project to be successful.

From a project management perspective, WAAs do not need a kick in the pants. They tend not only to accomplish their tasks ahead of schedule but to identify potential issues missed by others. I once had the pleasure of working with a finance manager at a small hospital in the northeastern US. For this project, I led the upgrade and implementation of the Lawson Absence Management application for her organization. Her job did not require her to be directly involved with this application. Despite this, she attended training, participated in design sessions as much as her schedule would allow, and broached real and potential issues.

Now, let's move down the "ease of use" ladder.

Willing But Not Able (WBNA)

Not for lack of trying or desire, WBNAs very much want to learn the new system. They can grasp simple and moderately complex system concepts but do not appreciate every consequence of their actions and inactions. In testing, they may become confused and/or panic, sending emails or making calls to others in a frenzied attempt to help. However noble their intentions, they can cause more harm than good, particularly when working with the "Able But Not Willing" and "Neither Willing Nor Able" groups described later in this chapter.

WBNAs can certainly graduate to the WAA group but they will require time, training, and experience. If they possess the desire and have the time, then they may very well make that jump.

I once worked with an HR manager and created a custom reporting tool for him. I documented the tool extensively and showed him repeatedly how it worked. He was able to follow my direction at a high level but was not able to maintain it independently. He certainly tried to keep up but his technical skills were a bit lacking at first.

WBNAs attempt to meet their objectives on a project plan and will quickly ask for help if they need it. To this end, it is also a pleasure to work with them. They attempt to learn as they go, for they know that consultants will not be on site forever and the clock is ticking.

Able But Not Willing (ABNW)

Working with ABNWs can be exceedingly frustrating for everyone on the project. ABNWs have the requisite skills to be vital contributors to implementations if they would only "get on board." ABNWs typically have an axe to grind. Perhaps they are not happy with their roles on the team or are offended that senior management did not involve them in the system selection process. ABNWs are very intelligent and, if turned around, can be a true asset to a project. If left unchecked, however, they will use every opportunity to say "I told you so" upon the discovery of an issue. Many times, the ultimate objective of the ABNW is to delay or sabotage the project. When they interact with WBNAs, ABNWs can be absolute poison, attempting to "turn them to the dark side" every step of the way.

ABNWs will actively blame consultants for a task not being completed or a project delayed. For consultants pressured to meet deadlines, it is usually very difficult to work with ABNWs in a constructive manner.

Neither Willing Nor Able (NWNA)

Like the ABNWs, NWNAs tend to view new systems as too complicated compared to legacy systems. NWNAs may be close to retirement and do not want to devote the required time to learning new systems. Many NWNAs fear new technology and, unless retirement is imminent, may also fear that the new system will threaten their jobs.

NWNAs may claim to be "on board" with the new system but simply too busy to do is the tasks required for a project. Truth be told, the typical NWNA will repeatedly find excuses to not learn the new system. Like ABNWs, when issues arise, NWNAs may also assign blame to consultants. Many times NWNAs just don't want to be bothered with issues and want the new system to go away. As a result of their actions and attitudes, it also can be frustrating to work with NWNAs. Finally, in a sense, NWNAs are less dangerous than ABNWs because NWNAs do not possess the same level of system knowledge, a limitation tends to decrease their credibility with others on the implementation team.

Client Responsibilities

Client responsibilities hinge on a number of factors, including:

- Specific role—e.g., functional vs. technical
- Systems aptitude
- Availability

An end-user's specific role in an implementation is a function of a number of things, including his or her current role in the organization, future role, availability, and individual capabilities. A few examples will clarify this.

Consider Ted, the finance director at Frobisher, Inc. In his current role, he is responsible for setting up and maintaining accounts, running Frobisher's P&L, and investigating and resolving GL-related errors in the legacy system. After Frobisher activates its new system, Ted's role will largely be unchanged. Thus, Frobisher needs Ted to play a key role in configuring the GL in the new system. Ted should be familiar with all GL accounts, sub-accounts, and so on; they will no doubt affect financial reporting. If he does not have the technical aptitude or time to devote to this project, then he needs to alert his management immediately. If the external financial consultant (Gary) is having difficulty making time with Ted, then Gary needs to broach this subject with his PM. After training and AE, if Ted does not possess the systems aptitude to participate in design discussions—and ultimately sign off on the GL setup in the new system, then Gary needs to make that known.

Now consider Gwen, Frobisher's payroll manager. In her current role, Gwen runs payroll but has made it clear that she is going to retire at the end of the year. In this case, Frobisher has hired Ellen to run payroll for the new system when it goes live. Ellen's sole job is learning the new system, setting it up, and testing it. Thus, Gwen's lack of participation in the project is not a major issue.

Sufficient Human Capital

Organizations often will spend hundreds of thousands of dollars or more on a new system, entranced by vendors' slick PowerPoint presentations and demos. Yet, those same organizations many times do not take the requisite steps to ensure that the project can meet its objectives. Specifically, many organizations have the unfortunate tendency to do the following:

- Fail to provide timely training to key end-users
- Tolerate end-users with an axe to grind regarding the new system
- Provide inadequate resources during an implementation

These shortcomings may stem from senior management buying into "the myth of easy implementation" created by the vendor and/or the consultancy. Unfortunately, many organizations do not know what they do not know. More than blaming the organization, however, individual end-users bear much of the responsibility for many of project issues and delays. For most projects, it is simply unfair to exclusively blame external organizations for an implementation gone awry.

Clients with foresight understand the need to hire employees with previous experience in the new system early in the process. A company implementing Lawson Financials, for example, would do well to hire employees who have that experience already. Note that this will not apply if it contracts an ISV to build a new system from scratch.

Aside from skill sets, however, client end-users need to maintain a positive outlook during the implementation. End-users should not let implementation or testing issues discourage them from getting the most out of the new system. Usually, system functionality is not a binary; systems have *levels* of functionality. Features can be enabled at different points. If a module or significant feature of a system does not make the cut for Phase I because of delays, budgets, or lack of successful testing, then the organization should revisit it in Phase II.

PMs and senior managers need to have serious discussions with client naysayers early on. NWNAs are simply cancers on these projects. Carping from a disgruntled employee is the last thing that an end-user enthusiastic to learn the new system needs to hear. NWNAs can do a tremendous amount of damage during a project, causing delays in testing, morale problems, and the like. If these end-users are not going to help make the new system successful, then they need to find either a different role in the organization or a different organization altogether.

This is not to say that a healthy skepticism isn't warranted, especially, during the sales cycle when vendor promises might seem—and often are—mile high. Beyond that, during the implementation, end-users should insist that new GL balances and payroll are accurate. However, outright negativity and, in extreme cases, sabotage can only hinder a project and, ultimately, cause it to fail.

I am reminded of a certain client experience. I worked for a few months at a hospital and became friendly with its HR manager, Pilar. She initially had a less-than-stellar opinion of Lawson. Over the course of my time with her, I was able to show Pilar ways that Lawson could be used to extract and track many types of information—things that she had never known. After a few months, I met Pilar's boss, the VP of HR. Right after meeting me, the VP remarked, "Lawson isn't very good software." I realized then how Pilar came to dislike Lawson: It's hard to like a system if your manager does not exactly share your viewpoint and you have never seen what it can do.

Finally, on a much more positive note, even if key processes remain the same from old to new, end-users would be wise to let go of the old mindset. They should look for ways to improve both their jobs and business processes through the new system. Change might be tough at first because the new system, in all likelihood, does work exactly like the old one. What's more, some of the vendor's lofty promises may fail to materialize. Get past that. The new system probably has some significant benefits for end-users who give it a chance.

Dealing with Problem Clients
If only every client were willing and able, consultants would have much easier jobs, and many projects would come in under budget and

ahead of schedule. Alas, this is almost never the case. Management typically has three major means to redress destructive behavior:

- Carrots
- Sticks
- Outright Removal

Carrots

After understanding the nature of the problem employee's issue(s), management should list the benefits to "getting on board" with the project. They typically include:

- An opportunity to learn an exciting new technology
- An opportunity to be "more strategic" because the new system will decrease administrative burden
- The skills obtained will make that employee more marketable, both internally and externally (should the employee decide to look elsewhere in the future)
- If the increased workload and stress are the source of the employee's behavior, then either a flexible work arrangement (to the extent possible) or bonus might be appropriate

Sticks

Of course, the carrot does not always do the trick. Some end-users resist new systems as part of their *raison d'être.* Typical "sticks" include the following:

- Using the usual management techniques, including verbal and/or written warnings
- Indicating that other employees on the project embracing the new system are increasing their stock within the organization

Outright Removal

To quote from one of my favorite movies, *Cool Hand Luke*: "Some men, you just can't reach." Depending on the phase of the implementation, it may be best to simply cut the cord with a problem employee, particularly early in a project and if that employee plays a key role. While a new hire will have a learning curve, a positive attitude may more than offset the replacement's lack of institutional or system knowledge.

Training

Organizations are wise to hire or place employees with previous system experience into key roles. However, organizations are not going to completely replace their entire AP, purchasing, HR, and payroll staffs. To this end, it behooves that organization to train its existing end-users properly. This training will allow end-users to maximize their contributions to the project. The properly trained end-user is simply better equipped for configuring, testing, diagnosing, and—ultimately—using the new system.

While the above statement may seem obvious, not every organization properly trains its employees on a new system. As is the case in the Wilson Retail case study in Chapter 18, some organizations still believe in "trial by fire" and rely exclusively on "on the job" (OTJ) training.

Types of Classes: Public vs. Private

Organizations have two choices for formal training: public and private classes. Public classes typically take place at vendors' offices or at vendor-approved locations. These classes cost in the neighborhood of $500 per day per student. Many organizations in different stages of an implementation send students to public classes to learn how their systems work in a generic sense. In other words, a payroll manager should not go to a public class intent on learning how to set up and process payroll at *her* company, although she should walk away with ideas to that end from the class. Because payroll personnel from other organizations attend public courses, the instructor will discuss the payroll application in general terms.

For public classes, clients will have to travel to vendor sites, sometimes incurring significant travel costs. To the extent that client end-users are out of the office, they should be able to focus exclusively on the class and the applications being taught. From a technical perspective, vendors should have sufficient computer terminals and training data areas. In other words, clients need no IT involvement to attend a public class.

Private classes are very different, both in terms of costs and content. For one, it's not uncommon for a vendor to charge upwards of $3,000 or more per day for a customized class at the client's site. Vendors know that client end-users will not have to incur travel costs. As for content, instructors will typically customize agendas specifically for each client. In a private payroll class, for example, the payroll manager can ask many specific questions related to her company's payroll setup and processing.

In fact, it may be less expensive for clients to host private classes in which trainers come to them. However, understand that end-users during private classes are in the office. Crises or emergencies can take them away from the class, reducing overall learning. Also, from a technical perspective, the trainer is not going to bring laptops configured with the software and training data areas. The amount of IT involvement is much greater than that of a public class. The organization that brings in an instructor at $3,000 per day should ensure well before that trainer's arrival that its hardware and software are up to snuff. Nothing inhibits a class and frustrates all concerned more than "buggy" software and the lack of a proper training data area. The last thing that a client's management wants from a public class is a disaffected end-user base.

Purpose

Regardless of the type of instruction, training should be a positive experience for all involved. End-users need to soak in the new application, ask practical processing and setup questions, and participate fully. Above all, it is critical for end-users to pay attention and absorb information. As someone who has taught dozens of classes to hundreds of students, all too often end-users use classroom time as an excuse to surf the web, make personal phone calls, or deal with issues related to their day jobs. The end result from these distractions is that end-users are unprepared for AE, system design, and testing.

Timing

While the most organizations recognize the importance and need for end-user training, less consensus exists on when training should take place. Truth be told, there is typically not a single "best" time. At one extreme, training can certainly occur too early. End-users who attend classes six months before projects begin are unlikely to remember very much from those classes. By the same token, end-users should not attend training in the middle of testing. End-users' first exposure to a system should not occur during a parallel test.

Generally speaking, functional end-users probably take courses immediately before Application Exploration, as that phase will reinforce the material covered in class. Technical users need to attend training prior to that because their jobs mandate that they be able to create data areas, set up security, and perform other essential tasks.

Specific Classes

Many times, the audience for each course is fairly obvious. The IT manager should know how to create data areas. The benefits manager should know how to set up benefit plans and enroll employees. However, remember that a new system presents new challenges as well as new opportunities. To this end, end-users should not necessarily be "pigeon-holed." For example, Julie is a bright, willing, and able HR specialist who has expressed a desire to learn Crystal Reports. To the extent that the organization is going to require a number of custom reports, it would be well served to send Julie to a three-day Crystal course. After all, why have all reports written by expensive consultants who, after the implementation finishes, will walk out the door? Perhaps Julie can write some of them.

Elton Case Study: The Stubborn Client

In this case study, we will look at a mid-sized, single-site healthcare organization, Elton Hospital, implementing a new ERP. The project took almost twice as long as anticipated because of the reluctance of key end-users to learn the new system.

Background

Founded over 20 years ago, Elton Hospital employs about 3,500 full-time associates. Elton utilized an antiquated HRIS. As a result, processes such as annual open enrollment were manual and fraught with errors. Elton payroll was split between its legacy system and ADP, resulting in key information being scattered among many sources. What's more, staff maintained many separate spreadsheets and physical files. In 2002, Elton management decided to enter the 21st century and implement a new ERP.

Management had the right idea in mind with regard to setup and resources: It chose to blow away its legacy system—unlike the management in the Portnoy and Lifeson case studies—and implement the entire ERP suite. Management staffed the project appropriately, proposed a reasonable timeline, and hired a boutique consulting company with expertise in the application, particularly in the healthcare industry.

Implementation Challenges and an Unwilling Staff

Team members were trained on the ERP soon after the decision was made to purchase it. Management spent tens of thousands of dollars ensuring that employees had the exposure necessary to make intelligent setup decisions. After training, however, end-users focused almost exclusively on their day-to-day responsibilities. The momentum created by the training largely dissipated, along with much of the knowledge gained.

Elton management chose a full-blown implementation with only one consultant, Charles, who worked on-site four days per week with all functional areas. However, Charles could do only so many things at once. He could not concurrently train end-users, act as *de facto* PM, test the system, and force Elton end-users to make setup decisions. As a result, Elton routinely missed key deadlines.

This is not a slight on Charles. However, he could only do so much. End-users found excuses not to make important setup decisions and incessantly argued about policy decisions. After more than a year of sputtering, Elton brought on an additional resource, Ellis, to assist with the implementation.

Ellis created data validation tools and custom queries to expedite the resolution of issues. True to form, however, Elton management would not give him ODBC access (essentially, a bridge to live data), citing security concerns. Undeterred, Ellis labored on and automated much of the validation tools to the extent possible. Ellis presented end-users with reports that isolated the accuracy of testing, setup decisions, and data entry. He also spent a great deal of time creating an automated report distribution tool.

Many Elton end-users continued to resist going live, claiming not to be comfortable with the system setup and requesting additional time. Both Charlie and Ellis expressed frustration at the inertia. Aside from the consultants, Elton's payroll manager (Georgina) was also exasperated. Issues that affected payroll during testing stemmed from other (read: non-payroll) users' lack of knowledge.

Outcome
In 2004, after more than two years implementing the new system, Elton management decided that enough was enough. It could not continue to keep consultants around at a cost of over $10,000 per week and decided on a go-live date. The project was initially slated for one year but took more than twice that, with related budget consequences. Elton management opted not to use Ellis' report distribution tool because of alleged security concerns, opting instead to print hundreds of reports each week and physically mail them.

Elton can be rated on the failure scale as a Big Failure.

Summary

Even perfectly planned projects can easily go by the wayside with difficult or inadequately skilled team members. Knowledgeable end-users with axes to grind can derail projects from the beginning, especially if not admonished. Staffing a project with willing and able end-users dramatically increases the chances of a successful implementation.

This report, by its very length, defends itself against the risk of being read.

-Winston Churchill

CHAPTER 14: REPORTS AND INTERFACES

Introduction

Functional end-users are typically very familiar with reports and interfaces emanating from their legacy systems. I have met payroll managers who have been looking at the same payroll register or "positive pay" files for twenty years. This chapter details the specific interface and reporting challenges facing organizations implementing new systems.

Reporting Challenges

Organizations that purchase or rent systems will find at their disposal many standard reports in each module. For instance, Lawson contains hundreds of standard reports for benefits, HR, payroll, GL, inventory control, etc. What's more, Lawson is hardly alone in this regard. Even "lower tiered" applications provide many standard reports. I actually use Mind Your Own Business (MYOB) for my business, a Tier 4 application, containing over 150 reports for sales, accounts receivable, payroll, accounts payable, and inventory.

The fundamental reporting challenge for an organization implementing a new system is that some standard reports may not, for a variety of reasons, meet all of an organization's business needs. End-users often require many custom reports but lack the time and resources required to create them. Specific reporting issues and their causes can be broken down into the following categories:

- Traditional Organizational Roles
- Different Systems Represent Data in Different Ways
- Time Constraints
- The Functional-Technical Disconnect
- Insufficient, Incomplete, or Inaccurate Reporting Specifications
- Overreliance on Custom Reports
- Inefficient Reports

Traditional Organizational Roles

Mainframe-based systems did not exactly enable the creation of custom reports. In many IT departments, only one or two end-users historically pulled information from the legacy system to fulfill end-users' reporting requests. Typically, functional end-users submitted formal report requests to IT. A few days later, end-users received responses related to the feasibility of the report requests. Perhaps the information was attainable, perhaps not. One response was very prevalent: IT had some difficultly retrieving that information. After IT created rough drafts, end-users volleyed back and forth with different versions. Often, much is lost in translation and final reports typically took weeks to generate.

As a result of these historical roles, many functional end-users are not comfortable writing reports. This is unfortunate because new systems are poles apart from their predecessors in terms of reporting ease. One need not be a "coder" or "techie" to create powerful reports from a new system. IT no longer has to be the gatekeeper for custom reports. In this sense, ERPs and their ilk are democratizing forces: End-users can easily obtain information via standard and custom reports without the involvement of IT. While vendors make many lofty claims, this one is unequivocally true.

Many end-users do not believe that they have the time, skills, and/or experience to write even simple listings, much less more complicated reports. In many organizations, report writing still tends to be seen as an "IT function." The Wilson case study in Chapter 15 is a perfect example of end-users whose "old school" reports did not change during or after the implementation.

Different Systems Represent Data in Different Ways
Another reporting challenge stems from the fact that old and new systems tend to store similar data in very different ways. Let's look at the fictitious data below from a legacy system's employee deduction table:

Table 14.1: Records in Simple Legacy Deduction Table

Employee	ABC	DEF	XYZ	Total
123	40	20		60
124	40		10	50
125	40			40

Employee data are stored in aggregate (or buckets). From a reporting point of view, deduction totals can be pulled quite simply; no calculations are required. Now, let's look at the way in which data elements are likely to be stored in a relatively new system with transactional tables:

Table 14.2 Records in New System's Transactional Deduction Table

EMPLOYEE	CHECK DATE	DEDUCTION CODE	DEDUCTION AMOUNT
123	1/1/2008	ABC	40
123	1/1/2008	DEF	20
124	1/1/2008	XYZ	10
125	1/8/2008	ABC	40
126	1/8/2008	DEF	40
127	1/8/2008	XYZ	20
128	1/8/2008	ABC	10

While this example may not seem that significant, the implications for reporting are enormous on a number of fronts. First, the number of records is much greater in the new system relative to the old. Second, Table 14.2 requires summaries to be derived; there is no "total ABC" field or "total deduction" field.

Typically standard reports offer a variety of different summary options, requiring no additional work for the client. What's more, in the event that these standard reports do not meet clients' needs, reporting software such as Crystal Reports, Business Objects, Microsoft Access, and Cognos Impromptu can do so much more than calculate simple totals. Using any one of these tools, end-users can calculate these totals. The important point is that, by default, the data are not stored in the same manner to which the client has become accustomed.

It's a fallacy to blame implementation delays exclusively on the differences regarding the storing of data. There is a much more fundamental reporting problem: people. Specifically, end-users are typically too busy to devote the time necessary to learn how to create custom report. Many end-users merely expect developers to continue writing custom reports. Unfortunately, those end-users rarely provide developers with sufficient specifications to create those reports properly.

Time Constraints

Freddie is a payroll manager who runs a biweekly payroll for 3,000 employees. Along with this task, he has to deal with adjustments, quarter-end, year-end, W-2 processing, and other emergencies. During the implementation of a new system, he casually looks at the new system's payroll register. In doing so, however, he neglects to notice that the new register does not provide a key piece of information, rendering the vendor-provided register inadequate. Only at the end of the implementation does he realize this, thus creating more work for developers—taking them away from their previously scheduled activities.

Alternatively, perhaps Freddie requires a report that needs to be run only at the end of a quarter. Developers build this report based on quarterly tables in the ERP, since they contain a fraction of the records found in the weekly or transactional tables. In terms of performance, there's no comparison between tables that have X records and tables that have 5X records. However, upon further review, Freddie changes course and determines that the report needs to be run on demand—i.e., not always at the end of the quarter. The developers have to junk the report and start from scratch.

This last example brings to light a major issue with regard to reporting.

The Functional-Technical Disconnect

During most implementations, client end-users are, by definition, functional. The AP clerk goes about her job, for example, by entering vendor and invoice data into the system. She may very well not know—or care to know—the specific fields and tables that she is updating.

Now, let's turn to the typical report developer. Unlike his functional counterparts, he does not enter data into the system. He only wants to know the fields and tables required by the end-user to build the custom reports. Equipped with that knowledge, he can then build the required report. This begs the question: Is the report truly required? Most report developers do not know if the new system contains a standard report that will meet end-user's needs. How would they know? For one, they are not functional. Second, they are often just as unfamiliar with the new system as the end-user asking the question. What to do?

Ideally, consultants would be able to step in and tell end-users when a custom report is truly required and when it is not. Unfortunately, much like clients, consultants also tend to be either functional or technical; rare is the consultant skilled in both. As a result, many times organizations spend money and resources creating unnecessary custom reports when a standard one will suffice. Also problematic is the creation of inefficient reports that join[35] unnecessary tables—i.e., linking table A to table B to table C when it's more efficient to go simply from A to C.

Insufficient, Incomplete, or Inaccurate Reporting Specifications

Nothing frustrates a developer more than unclear specifications. A developer cannot write a report for an end-user after receiving only a vague reporting request. For example, a benefit manager might want a report of all employees' enrollments in its 401(k) plan. Simple enough, right? The smart developer would respectfully disagree and respond with such questions as the following:

- Since employees can change contribution percentages or cease to participate in the 401(k) plan, does the report need to list enrollments or only current employee enrollments?
- What other fields are required for the report? (Name, social security number, etc.)
- How should the information be grouped and sorted? By department? Employment status type?
- What (if any) subtotals are required? Employee counts?

---

[35] A SQL JOIN clause combines records from two tables in a database. It creates a set that can be saved as a table or used as is. A JOIN is a means for combining fields from two tables by using values common to each. ANSI standard SQL specifies four types of JOINs: INNER, OUTER, LEFT, and RIGHT. In special cases, a table (base table, view, or joined table) can JOIN to itself in a self-join. (Source: Wikipedia)

The list could continue but the general point is this: The better the specifications that end-users provide, the faster and more accurately the developer can write the custom report. I use a questionnaire or specification template for each required report:

- What is the report title? Description?
- What are the name(s) and role(s) of the person(s) who need the report?
- In which format(s) do the reports need to be seen (spreadsheet, PDF, or text file)?
- How often does this report need to be run?
- Does this report need to be archived? When? Where?
- Are there any similar system reports to your knowledge? What are they?
- Does this report need to be scheduled to run for optimal performance, or does it need to be run in real-time?
- How does this report need to be summarized? Grouped? Sorted?
- Does the recipient of this report have any restrictions (by GL, division, company group, etc.)?

While sometimes a challenge, I try to have clients fill out each question before I even start writing a custom report.

Overreliance on Custom Reports

Some end-users are so accustomed to seeing data in a certain way that they insist that the new system do the same. Again, no two systems represent data in the same manner. ERPs and other "off the shelf" systems typically include quite a few standard reports—P&Ls, payroll registers, aging reports, and many more. These reports tend to meet many client needs as is—that is, *without* creating new ones.

A standard report missing a key field might have to be created for the sole purpose of including that field. For example, consider a vendor's standard accounts receivable aging report that does not list a key date on each invoice. That omission may render the report useless.

Alternatively, expect the following standard report to be rewritten: a report calculates employee tenure based on *hire date* but the organization needs that calculation based off of *anniversary date*. Reporting can become very cumbersome and time-consuming for the organization with fussy end-users who focus on minutiae —e.g., that the order of fields on the new reports exactly matches the order on the legacy reports. This tends to frustrate IT, especially when those same end-users show no initiative to learn how to create these reports for themselves.

Inefficient Reports

The performance of a report may be suboptimal even when written correctly—i.e., it returns the right data in the right order and is summarized correctly. For example, a payroll manager requires a custom report that lists employee pay period, month-to-date (MTD), quarter-to-date (QTD), and year-to-date (YTD) employee deductions. The manager submits a detailed spec to IT and a developer is assigned to write the report. The report ultimately takes over four hours to run because the requisite table (listing all employee deductions by pay check) was added four times: once for pay period totals, once for MTD totals, once for QTD totals, and once for YTD totals.

To be sure, waiting four hours for a report to finish is not unprecedented. Complicated reports with multiple joins on very large transactional tables may result in a long processing time. In this example, however, using a tool such as Crystal Reports, the same report can be written with a single instance of that table, significantly reducing the time needed for the report to finish.

One last note: Systems in the same tier often have similar types of tables. For example, Tier 1 applications such as Oracle, SAP, Baan, PeopleSoft, and Lawson tend to store data in very similar transactional and summary tables. However, the names of these tables and fields are typically different, as are the relationships among each system's related tables.

Q&A with John Henley

I can think of no better person to provide additional insights into reporting than my friend John Henley. John has over 20 years of consulting experience spanning multiple industries, including healthcare, non-profits, government contracting and professional services. John runs Decision Analytics, a consulting firm located in Arlington, VA, providing software development support services to a number of diverse organizations. Decision Analytics focuses on Lawson technical projects and specializes in reporting, customization/modification, data conversion, and integration.

PS: How often are you asked to rewrite a report that existed in a client's legacy system but does not come delivered in an ERP?

JH: That happens quite often, which I think points to a larger issue beyond reporting itself. One of the prevailing themes underlying an ERP implementation is that of the organization modeling their new system to look just like the legacy system being replaced. While there are sometimes valid reasons for doing so—perhaps to retain a key core competency—it's often done to avoid confronting change and alienating end-users who are comfortable with their current operating processes and reports. An ERP implementation is a unique opportunity in the organizational lifecycle for re-invention. Frankly, I think that many organizations fail to embrace that idea.

PS: Generally speaking, what are some of the most common reporting requests that clients give you?

JH: What I see most often in smaller organizations using Lawson is that the finance people are either content with Excel exporting tools or the well-established financial ad hoc reporting tool, or they're much larger and they use some other reporting system/application like Hyperion or Microsoft FRx to generate their financials. The ones in between are the ones who usually contact me for developing financial reports. Procurement and materials end-users tend to be more technical and database savvy and are able to generate their own reports using SQL or Crystal Reports. For HR and benefits, the HRIS administrator is usually good at satisfying the easier requirements but not with more complicated reports like staffing plans and turnover.

PS: How often do clients change their minds once they see reports they have asked you to create?

JH: Report development is an iterative and collaborative process. It's a lot like a remodeling or building project. Sometimes a homeowner sees how a concept translates into a reality and then asks the builder to move the stairs or change the windows. It's the same with building a report. You try to accommodate the changes as best you can, and—unlike with most building projects—you sometimes do start over when the client decides what they were asking for wasn't really what they wanted. And just like those remodeling jobs, reports often do end up costing more than the estimate!

PS: What drives most of your clients to you? Do they lack time or experience?

JH: I would say it's generally both. Take a new customer who's just purchased Lawson applications or Lawson Business Intelligence (LBI). Lawson has about 2000 tables. That's pretty intimidating to even a veteran developer. By leveraging my experience and understanding of the Lawson data structures and concepts like primary keys, complex joins, using Lawson's subset indexes, database-specific "null dates," and syntax, etc., a new client can get a pretty good jump start on delivering efficient high-quality reports to their users. But even still, most of my business is from repeat customers. I have some customers who go back eight or ten years, and even for them it's still a mix. Some of them just don't have the resources to create the report or aren't interested in making an investment in training their developers in the idiosyncrasies of how Lawson stores data. If you're only developing a handful of reports every now and then, it's probably not a good investment to have a high-caliber reporting person on your staff; it's more cost-effective to outsource it to someone they trust.

PS: What are some of the reporting tips that you would give an organization implementing a new system?

JH: Organize the report development project into a mentoring process. Bring in some outside help to guide you through the development of some of the more difficult reports. Catalog and prioritize your requirements. You can't create all of the reports at once. Another piece of advice is to take some of the techniques used in software development and apply them to report development. Have peer reviews or use the pair-programming methodology. We can all learn from each other—I know I do—when we don't work in isolation. And it's usually a lot more fun! Design patterns, which have been used very successfully in software development, can also be applied to report development.

PS: In your experience, are clients satisfied with the standard reports that they receive from ERPs? What about their satisfaction with system-delivered ad hoc tools?

JH: Well, I can only really speak from the Lawson perspective, but for the most part it depends on the audience. A number of the standard reports end up being "good enough," and there are some tools that ship with Lawson that can be used to augment the standard reports. For instance, HR users who take the time to learn Lawson's HR report writer seem to be happy enough with it. As for ad hoc tools, I think a lot of clients who purchase the Lawson Business Intelligence (LBI) suite end up never really using it. It's just too wide-open. It's really a big set of tools, and it's really hard for them to get started. And they end up never using very much of it, if any.

PS: How often are you asked to rewrite a report that an end-user has attempted? Are you typically able to make the report more efficient?

JH: I tend to work with developers probably more often than with end-users, as sort of a mentoring "super-developer." I can demonstrate various techniques to the developers based on my experience and understanding of the Lawson data structures; they can leverage my experience to create more efficient reports. I have a good friend who worked at a client who once gave me the advice that if a report didn't produce results within 90 seconds, it needed to go back through an efficiency analysis. I constantly use that as a guideline.

Interface Issues

Now, let's move on to the related but separate topic of interfaces. Any time that an organization retires its legacy system, it must rewrite its inbound and outbound interfaces. This is no small chore. Interfaces to other vendors, banks, and/or financial institutions are imperative for a successful system activation. Examples of common inbound and outbound interfaces include:

- Direct deposit and "positive pay" interfaces
- Third party benefit provider interfaces such as 401(k) contributions or health plan enrollments
- Supplemental employee data interfaces to external vendors, such as employment verification services
- Interfaces to any additional internal systems

Interface Tools for Clients

Clients have a head start writing interfaces to and from the new system. Vendors almost always provide very detailed specifications on both the type and format of the data required. These specifications are extremely granular and will specify the field length, starting point of a field, and so on. For example, the interface developer will not have to guess where to store employee social security numbers. That field should start on position 10 of the interface and contain nine digits: 123456789.

Second, these vendors have many clients, some of which may very well run the same system that the client is implementing. End-users at an organization implementing SAP HR, for example, can find colleagues at other organizations hardly new to SAP that have essentially written that same interface. User groups allow clients to network with others who face the same challenges.

Issues and Limitations

Clients are not completely out of the woods, however. Because vendors have many clients, they cannot devote extensive resources to any one organization's testing. Typically, coordination well ahead of time can mitigate this factor. However, it is unreasonable for end-users to expect a vendor's complete attention just because they are in the middle of testing. Remember, the vendor may have 100 or more other clients in production and/or in testing. End-users should tell vendors well in advance that they will be remitting test files.

A client can only expect a vendor to unearth data and formatting errors. Vendor import programs typically have functionality that automatically rejects records due to improper format. For example, an employee social security number of "1234578" does not have the requisite nine digits. Also, a "1234567a" record would be rejected because "a" is not an integer.

Many clients do not realize that the vendor's validation stops at a certain point. In all but the most exceptional of circumstances, the vendor will not validate the accuracy of the incoming data. If Elaine's benefit election is "single coverage" in a test system, then the vendor will accept this value if formatted and transmitted correctly. Now, if Elaine's value should be "Single+1," then the vendor will not know this.

Both vendors and clients tend not to look at the results of interfaces during testing as closely as they would in a live, production environment. As a result, sometimes end-users discover issues only at the tail end of an implementation.

Other interface issues may surface during testing, including questions about current legacy system interfaces that may not have been documented very well. What's more, an interface's original designer may no longer work for the organization. As a result, an implementation team may not know exactly which data it is currently sending to a vendor.

Summary

In most organizations, the writing of custom reports and complex interfaces has been typically performed by a very technical individual. New systems obviate the need for reports to be the exclusive purview of the IT department. Regardless of who writes the report or interface, the absence or inadequacy of a formal design specification will result in, at best, inaccurate data being sent to a vendor or report recipient. Quite possibly, the vendor will reject the interface or the report recipient will make incorrect business decisions based on the inaccuracy of the information contained. End-users should *not* take testing and approving interfaces and reports lightly.

Organizations should understand that end-users cannot start working on interfaces and reports until key design decisions have been made and a prototype system has been built. Moreover, while essentially any interface or report can be written, the "back and forth" among end-user, developer, and vendor (in the case of interfaces) typically increases the time required to complete these tasks. The organization or consultancy that ignores these points and devotes insufficient time to these tasks is entering a world of pain.

I wish I had an answer to that because I'm tired of answering that question.

-Yogi Berra

CHAPTER 15: DOCUMENTATION ISSUES

Introduction

One of the items that typically falls through the cracks during the implementation of a new system is documentation. Proper system documentation is imperative in the event that one or more of the following occurs:

- A key team member leaves the company or takes ill
- The organization expands and has to hire employees with key setup, data entry, or processing responsibilities
- Particularly for an organization governed by Sarbanes-Oxley, auditors decide that the new system needs appropriate checks and balances

Organizations that minimize the need for comprehensive documentation expose themselves to major risks and additional costs.

Types of Required Documentation

During an implementation, organizations should formally document reports, interfaces, system design, testing results, and so on. This is not merely a matter of "CYA"—consultant-speak for "cover your ass." The following table lists the common types of documentation required and when each *should* begin:

Table 15.1: Common Documentation Types

Type of Documentation	Ideal Beginning Phase	Notes
Business Processes	Project Planning	Client sign-off is typically necessary to move forward.
Reporting Requirements and Design Specs	Project Planning	Tends to be deficient
System Configuration	System Design	With revisions throughout project as needed; Client sign-off is typically necessary to move forward.

Type of Documentation	Ideal Beginning Phase	Notes
Testing Results	System Testing	Typically needed for internal or external auditors
Issues	Ongoing	Should be documented as soon as discovered.
End-User Guides	System Design	Should be revised and kept up to date as organization changes/enhances application
Training Guides	System Design	Should be revised and kept up to date as organization changes/ enhances application

This begs the question: If there are so many types of documentation and these types are so critical to an organization while preparing to go live, then why is it commonplace for documentation to be so lacking? There are two main reasons.

Delays from Previous Phases and the Need to Catch Up

When new system implementations fall behind schedule, PMs and executives look for ways to make up time. One of their favorite places to "trim the fat" is documentation. For example, a PM pressured to get a project back on track may determine that the six weeks initially slated for creating proper training manuals, procedure manuals, and contingency plans can now be done in two. Obviously, this is almost always a poor decision.

Just Do It: Wishful Thinking and the Limitations of Multi-Tasking

Clients and consultants typically face enormous pressure to hit key dates on system implementations, given the "best practice" of going live at the beginning of a quarter or a year, financial pressures, etc. Therefore, team members may devote more time to fixing issues and testing a system than to documenting the "error resolution process" or a "new hire training manual" for that system.

Even the best-intentioned client or consultant may intend to go back, after going live, and properly document—via detailed steps and screen shots—how a business process should be conducted in the new system. However, issues in a production world need to be addressed immediately and documentation is typically relegated to the back burner.

Many PMs erroneously believe that documentation can be done in a client's or a consultant's "spare time." While this is certainly possible, most people produce their best documentation in dedicated blocks of time, not with fifteen minutes here and an hour there. The latter scenario typically results in missing steps and an overall inferior product.

Wilson Case Study: Good Design but Lack of Resources

In this case study, we will look at a large retail chain—Wilson Retail—implementing a new system with recommended design. Unlike the Portnoy and Lifeson case studies, Wilson's design was very straightforward with no major system customizations. The implementation failed due to a number of factors, not the least of which was its lack of internal resources. This dearth directly caused the following:

- Wilson's implementation to go significantly over budget (and miss repeated deadlines)
- Many daily problems for end-users immediately after going live
- Wilson to miss a key opportunity to redefine a new business process

Wilson illustrates the difficulty of key players having two jobs during an implementation as well as the need for projects of this type to be appropriately staffed from the beginning.

Background

Wilson operates in 48 states and runs weekly payroll for its approximately 10,000 employees. Most of its employees work in the stores or "in the field." Due to the nature of its business, many employees may work only during the holiday season, and it is common for employees to be rehired several times over the course of their lifetimes. Many of Wilson's employees are teenagers wanting to be paid every week. While it may seem foolish to have teenagers dictating business practice, retail turnover is high enough that weekly payroll is often an important consideration for seasonal workers—that is, those who work only during the holiday season.

The logistics of paying upwards of 10,000 employees weekly in 48 states should not be understated. Retail margins are not high and, as a result, Wilson runs a pretty tight ship with respect to personnel. In addition, the degree of employee turnover, particularly in the field, poses significant challenges:

- Accurately paying employees
- Providing timely and accurate government reporting
- Ensuring that employee benefit deductions and taxes are correct

Impetus for Change

Wilson's prior HR and payroll system contained limited reporting capability and lacked real-time data. The legacy system constantly placed IT in the middle of all reporting requests. End-users did not "own" the system. Wilson management decided that a new system with superior reporting capability would democratize the data. No longer would IT need to provide headcount reports, payroll information, and the like. Impressed with several of the vendor presentations, Wilson made the decision to purchase and implement Tier 1 ERP. Such a system could meet Wilson's growing business needs, empower end-users, and reduce administration costs. Wilson also initially selected the vendor to serve as the consultancy.

Aside from increased functionality, cost was also an important factor in Wilson's decision to retire its legacy system. The ERP would allow Wilson to save extensively on software licensing and mainframe hosting changes down the road.

It is important to note that Wilson did not use this opportunity to switch to a biweekly or semi-monthly payroll. We will see how this decision compromised the implementation from the beginning and set the stage for recurring problems after system activation.

Implementation Challenges

Wilson faced significant challenges throughout the implementation, some of which affected organizations in the previous case studies. Unlike many of Wilson's counterparts crossing the technological Rubicon, however, a core business process was the root of most of its problems. Specifically, Wilson's weekly payroll created a formidable set of issues that plagued the implementation from day one.

On the reporting front, things were a mess. Resources assigned to produce custom reports had no knowledge of the ERP's functionality, fields, tables, or the entire database structure. Previous attempts to create reports were either flat-out incorrect or, at best, wholly inefficient. Wilson brought in a consultant to manage the reports towards the end of the implementation. Jeff knew the system cold but had enormous difficulty obtaining anything remotely resembling a formal reporting specification from Wilson end-users. Jeff's expertise allowed him to build many reports without this key information but he was certainly not a mind reader. Reports merely described as "transaction listing" left him scratching his head.

The vast majority of Wilson's functional end-users were simply too busy to provide detailed reporting specifications, much less learn how to create reports themselves. Their day jobs kept them so busy that they had no time. They would simply tell Jeff what they wanted and he would try to create those reports, publishing them on a dashboard for electronic distribution. The hours that Wilson's end-users devoted to learning how to create reports were few and far between, hardly a successful recipe for transferring and retaining knowledge.

Inadequate Staffing and Acceptance of the New System

First, the decision to implement the ERP did not mean that Wilson's "normal" world would stop turning. On the contrary, employees still had to perform their day jobs in the legacy system while (in theory) learning, configuring, and testing the new system. For a company that processes biweekly or bimonthly payroll, staff members typically have periods of relative "down time" in which they can devote attention to a new system. This was not the case at Wilson. Without much time to relax, Wilson staff members were left with small pockets of time to do critical things such as define custom reporting requirements, learn and test the new system, meet with external consultants, and participate in training. These are not items that are best accomplished in half-hour increments. End-users must devote significant blocks of time to these accomplish mission-critical tasks.

Perhaps because of their workloads effectively doubling, Wilson end-users were not very receptive to the new system from the beginning. (To be fair, those end-users ran weekly payroll—not exactly conducive to "down time.") Still, they neither embraced nor owned the new system, nor did they spend the requisite time validating data to be converted into the new system. They were simply too busy doing their day jobs to understand and learn the new ERP effectively. As a result of the end-users' lack of time and interest in the new system, Wilson relied excessively on external consultants to provide expertise.

Wilson eventually changed partners, citing a need for more experienced consultants. However, the new consultants faced similar challenges in getting "face time" with end-users. It is very difficult for even the best consultant to come in from outside an organization and effectively set up a system without very much time spent with existing end-users. The situation is exacerbated when end-users lack sufficient documentation on current business practices.

The sheer amount of work involved in weekly payroll in a high transaction environment such as retail made formal training of team members nearly impossible. Initially, some employees participated in classroom training away from their desks. Unfortunately, this took place too early in the project, well before the system could be tested. During the second round of training (held at their desks), end-users were typically distracted: answering phones and emails or dealing with employees knocking on their doors.

By giving its employees too much work, Wilson was left doubly exposed to the risk of employee turnover. On the core team, if any one of four key employees left, the project may well have come to a halt right then and there. While just about every organization today is lean and faces this risk to some extent, the issue was particularly pronounced at Wilson. For instance, no one knew how to do the payroll manager's job and, as stated, existing documentation was sparse. Throw in weekly payroll and not only could the project have ceased, but Wilson would have had a difficult time cutting employee checks from the legacy system. Wilson simply would not have been able find a suitable replacement and provide sufficient training in such a short period of time.

Data Challenges

From a data perspective, Wilson's legacy system stored data in a fundamentally different way than did its new ERP. Given the number of transactions and the data quality issues, creating the conversion files proved extremely vexing. One particularly daunting challenge involved converting payroll history, an essential component for an organization activating a new system in the middle of a year due to government W-2 requirements. Payroll history was essential to going live. In the words of the IT director responsible for the conversion programs:

> The biggest challenge was creating the payroll history load with data for nine months of weekly payrolls. A close second was the validation effort. While a lot of work went into creating accurate conversions, the data was only as good as the source systems. Without a proper (independent) way to validate values, we were open to inaccurate values that only revealed themselves during go-live. While performed extensively, parallel testing never really reflected reality. Managers dismissed many issues with statements such as, "We'll fix this after go-live."

Beyond the unexpected challenges extracting and validating payroll history, Wilson did not anticipate about 80 percent its issues. Wilson management staffed the project based on the assumption that it would find minimal errors. Nothing could have been further from the truth. Among the tsunami of errors discovered throughout the project, some of the most significant included tax setup errors by prior consultants. Attempts to load data revealed significant setup issues. A compromised series of parallel system tests resulted in end-users not testing fixes and "workarounds" before Wilson's final conversion (i.e., the one prior to going live).

An Unresponsive Senior Management
Again, Wilson did not staff the implementation team sufficiently. Key internal resources identified the inadequate resource level to senior management, both during the first weeks of the project and routinely during steering committee meetings. Had senior management increased the number of internal resources devoted to the project— specifically by hiring two functional experts with prior ERP experience— the team would have found and resolved key issues quicker. What's more, Wilson would have spent much less money on external consultants.

Two years into the project, management was close to pulling the plug altogether. By this point, the project was several hundred thousand dollars over budget. A key team member suggested to senior management that the project was not going to be cost-effective and that the team members were not learning the new system. Management rejected this suggestion and, by sheer force, decided to "plow through the issues."

An Overreliance on Consultants Due to Inadequate Internal Staffing
Wilson heavily relied upon external consultants throughout the project at a cost of hundreds of thousands of dollars outside the initial budget. Specific consultant responsibilities included everything from the purely functional (determining setup of items such as tax codes) to the purely technical (building conversion/interface programs and analyzing their results). Consultants set up the payroll, benefits, and HR rules and created almost all of the required custom reports. External consultants performed nearly half of the implementation tasks, minimizing knowledge transfer to Wilson's end-users.

The Go-Live Decision
Lack of comprehensive validation and end-user knowledge throughout the implementation came to a head during system

activation. Fortunately, on a particularly vital payroll issue, Jeff provided a key solution to a showstopper. Wilson printed its first checks in the wee hours of the morning and, a few days later, discovered a key interface issue for employee direct deposit that required manual intervention.

Wilson's final decision to activate the system was predicated on risk and cost. While known issues existed, Wilson management knew that failure to go live would have delayed the project an additional four months and cost another $500,000. The implementation team believed that the data were sufficiently accurate and the issues minor enough to make the decision to move forward.

Outcomes

In the end, the project took over three years and exceeded its budget by more than $2M. The organization learned the hard way that an ERP implementation is much more difficult than just acquiring some software and learning how to use it on the fly. In retrospect, end-users realized that they need to find additional internal project resources early and train functional teams on how the applications work throughout the process, not as the first production payroll is being run.

After going live, Wilson end-users encountered additional issues immediately, stemming from a core implementation problem: End-users did not become experts in the applications that they needed to support. For one, payroll needed to watch individual employee taxes, making adjustments manually before cutting additional checks. Reports that end-users had formally approved needed to be changed, indicating that they never really looked at them in any detail during testing. End-users did not have enough time to fix all issues in the first week and were still trying to triage issues six weeks after going live. Much to senior management's dismay, several end-users still relied exclusively on the same costly external consultants to find and resolve issues.

After the project began, Wilson management estimated that the organization needed three years to realize a positive ROI on the new system. After the project, management revised that number to just over eight years. On the positive side, six weeks after system activation, data flowed to the end-users much more easily than before. Some began to perform analytics on data previously unavailable to them.

Phase I contained only the basic functionality of HR, benefits, and payroll. Phase II calls for employee self-service and online open enrollment. However, based on the issues encountered during Phase I and the related budgetary debacle, it is unlikely that Wilson will be undertaking a major ERP initiative in the near future.

Wilson can be rated on the failure scale as a Big Failure. Its IT director offers the following advice for organizations going through a new system implementation for the first time:

> Reject anyone on the core team who doesn't want the formal training. This is really a primer for the rest of the project. Insist that they invest the week to get the basics and also to learn the third-party add-on products. I also suggest that companies hire employees with at least three years of related knowledge and experience to be added to each functional area. They are the ones who will lead your existing staff on how the application works. Nothing beats experience. This comes from someone with thirteen years of experience with the ERP and 21 years in the industry. I'm still learning every day.

Julian Case Study: Building its Own System

The next case study is quite different from the rest on a number of levels: It focuses on a custom-built system for a very small company. This case study will show how strikingly different companies and systems often face identical issues. It illustrates that large organizations are not the only ones that tend to fail when implementing off-the-shelf systems; even small companies that build custom packages exhibit many of the same characteristics as their larger brethren. Finally, it evinces the dangers of both using a completely malleable systems framework and poorly documenting that framework.

Background

Julian Marketing Partners is a small sales and marketing firm with approximately 150 full-time employees. The company grew at a very rapid pace, increasing both employee head count and sales as fast as it could. As is the case with many high-paced, intense startups, employee turnover was a major issue. Julian was constantly hiring and retraining new sales representatives, many of whom were in their mid-20s. Few new hires looked at Julian as a company as a long-term employment option.

Julian operated in a niche market and did not see any current systems off-the-shelf that met its business needs. Using Microsoft's .NET framework, Julian hired external consultants to build a system for tracking sales from scratch. To be certain, .NET is a very flexible framework and many organizations have been able to deploy .NET-based applications with varying degrees of success.

Data and Business Process Issues

Julian's home grown system could certainly track sales as the individual reps entered them. However, the fundamental business question was never asked: What constitutes a sale?

- Does the sale take place when the customer asks for information?
- Does it take place when the customer verbally agrees to make the purchase?
- How about when the paperwork is formally sent out?
- Or does it occur when the signed paperwork arrives by mail?

Asking four different reps would have resulted in four different answers. Julian should have bought a quality off-the-shelf solution or configured its own system appropriately. Either solution would have prevented a sale from being logged seven times, as was the case for some sales by a few of the most ambitious representatives.

Without the business question being answered, Julian's system would allow just about any customer contact to count as a sale. As such, a signed application from a customer might have four "sales" attached to it. The implications for forecasting future sales, much less paying commissions to the "right" representative, were substantial. Employees who stayed longer than a few months discovered that their commissions increased significantly if they entered as many "sales" as possible. Given the low base salaries, employees who logged only true sales received lower commissions than those who did not.

Reporting Issues

Julian did not provide its IT end-users with a robust reporting tool, such as Crystal Reports or Business Objects. Rather, they relied almost exclusively on SQL statements. Functional end-users with legitimate needs to view and analyze data could not do so on their own; they were not programmers and could not code in SQL. They had to ask techies to write custom reports, and invariably, something was lost in the translation. What's more, an employee absence often meant that the report often could not be run.

When a few IT end-users brought these issues to the attention of Julian's senior management, they chose not to address them. In their view, addressing the issues and reconfiguring the system were subordinate to increasing sales. Management opted to put out other fires over shoring up its systems.

Lack of Documentation and Knowledge Transfer

Because its system was developed on the fly, Julian did not maintain a data dictionary, formal documentation, or entity relationship diagrams (ERDs).[36] All of which would have allowed newly hired IT end-users to understand the system. No consultant or end-user at Julian really knew why or how the system did everything that it did. When one of the external consultants accepted a job closer to his home, Julian management panicked. They offered to double his salary and provide local housing. While this was understandable in the short-term, Julian had no long-term plan of bringing system expertise in-house.

Several IT end-users expressed a desire to learn more about Julian's custom .NET system. However, Julian management would not send them to formal training. While a public .NET class obviously would not have covered the specifics of Julian's system, it certainly would have provided end-users with extensive knowledge of that platform's building blocks. No end-user can realistically learn a platform as robust as .NET on lunch breaks.

Outcomes

Julian spent tens of thousands of unnecessary dollars on recruiting and training costs, attempting to replace skilled employees, many of whom left over inadequate commissions. Julian kept its external consultants indefinitely, as it had neither the internal expertise nor the documentation to maintain—much less fix or enhance—its systems independently. Because of its overreliance upon consultants and an inability to track basic sales, Julian can be rated on the failure scale as a Mild Failure.

Summary

Documentation is often inadequate on legacy systems, thus setting the stage for suboptimal documentation during the project. Due to the importance of testing and resolving previously discovered issues, budget and time considerations, and the "firmness" of a go-live date, documentation may continue to suffer. The need to document existing

---

[36] An entity-relationship model (ERM) or diagram (ERD) in software engineering is an abstract and conceptual representation of data. Entity-relationship modeling is a relational schema database modeling method, used to produce a type of conceptual schema or semantic data model of a system, often a relational database and its requirements, in a top-down fashion. (Source: Wikipedia)

and future business practice and processes should not be minimized. Any postponement of documentation should be addressed immediately after going live. Employee turnover, an organizational audit, or newly discovered issues may well bring this underemphasized need to the forefront.

Part Four: The Brave New World of Production Life

Going live with a new system typically proves more challenging than organizations and their end-users anticipate. To be sure, there are typically quite a few stressful moments during "cutover" and "go-live," to use the industry vernacular. During system activation, the sum total of all of the planning, testing, work, and meetings comes to fruition. Ready or not, organizations often go live not knowing or being prepared for their forthcoming challenges, both system- and operations-related.

This section focuses on the issues that organizations will face after activating new systems. Testing has ceased—at least for the time being—as the dream of a new system has hopefully not become a nightmare.

Insanity: doing the same thing over and over again and expecting different results.

-Albert Einstein

CHAPTER 16: ONGOING SYSTEM MAINTENANCE
Introduction
Einstein was a smart man. While this book is intentionally light on absolutes, this is certainly one of them: Organizations and their end-users should learn a great deal throughout an implementation with respect to the system, testing, reporting, and so on. What's more, this knowledge should *not* be confined merely to the functionality of the new application and, fortunately, can be applied immediately after going live. This is imperative, as end-users must maintain the system as well as troubleshoot issues as they arise.

By the time an organization goes live, most end-users have long disabused themselves of the myth of perfect software, if it ever existed. Senior management and end-users are hopefully more realistic than they were during system selection, especially if the implementation was their first. This chapter is devoted to exploring organizations' ongoing *system* challenges while the next focuses on their *operational* challenges.

Reporting and Interface Issues Revisited
Prior to going live, most organizations spend many hours defining, writing, testing, and tweaking custom reports. In the whole scheme of things, however, reporting tends to no receive the required attention prior to system activation. In this sense, it is like documentation. Why is that?

First of all, there are only so many hours in a day for end-users. Remember, most of them are doing two jobs concurrently: their "day" jobs with the legacy system and their "post-legacy system" day jobs. In the latter, they are setting up GL accounts, looking at item masters, and testing payroll. It's understandable that many end-users do not have enough time to properly review the created reports for them.

Second, end-users tend to look at reports more closely that reflect real—i.e., production—data. I have had to redesign many reports that a client had previously approved after the organization has gone live.

The same holds true for interfaces. While carriers provide their clients with file formats, errors will appear if the client interfaces pass data that do not meet the vendors' specifications. Zed's hire date, for example, cannot be sent as "aa/00/2008." Many carriers will spit out error reports based on nonsensical data, even if the data type and format are valid. For example, the employee hire date of 1/1/1753—SQL Server's default null value—is probably not accurate; the employee is not 255 years old. However, many values may sneak through the validation process. To continue with the example, an employee hire date of 1/1/1990 is in a perfectly valid format and date range. However, perhaps Zed's true hire date is 1/1/1999. His seniority date (stemming from his first tenure with the company) is 1/1/1990. Carriers are not responsible for the integrity of their clients' data. An incorrectly sent value can have potentially dangerous consequences, as the Tate case study discussed in Chapter 22 will demonstrate.

Database Views

As discussed in Chapter 14, many functional end-users often have difficulty writing custom reports. For one, since the system is new, they may not know where to find key information. Also, legacy systems store data differently. They often have fewer tables than the transaction-based applications in the ERP world. Data are stored in different places and a novice report writer may not easily be able to extract the desired information in the proper format. While not overly complicated, building custom reports typically requires a fair amount of knowledge of each of the following:

- The reporting tool
- The application itself
- The application's fields and tables and the relationships among them

Beyond the difficulty of building the reports, end-users may complain that they take progressively longer to run each time. This truism stems from the fact that, absent a data purge, there is simply more data in these tables than there were when the organization went live. Let's take a look at an example of a report that needs fields from three separate tables:

Figure 16.1: Example of Three Joined Tables

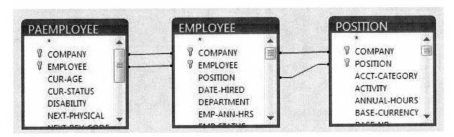

The POSITION table contains information on the employee's position. Both the PAEMPLOYEE and EMPLOYEE tables contain different information related to the employee. A report stitching together these tables might take too long to finish. To eliminate the need to run this report against the three tables in Figure 16.1, IT may decide to create a database view.[37] Relative to three separate tables, a single view offers two benefits:

- End-users require less time to create a report from one report object—not three tables.
- Under certain circumstances, report performance will be superior.

An example of a view based on Figure 16.1 is displayed next:

---

[37] In database theory, a *view* is a stored query accessible as a virtual table composed of the result set of a query. Unlike ordinary tables (base tables) in a relational database, a view is not part of the physical schema: It is a dynamic, virtual table computed or collated from data in the database. Changing the data in a table alters the data shown in the view. The result of a view is stored in a permanent table, whereas the result of a query is displayed in a temporary table. (Source: Wikipedia)

Table 16.1: Consolidated Database View for Three Transactional Tables

COMPANY	DEPT	DATE-HIRED	EMPLOYEE	FULL-NAME	CUR-AGE	POSITION	DESCRIPTION
1	740	2-Apr-62	100123	Paulson, Henry	60	123	REGISTERED NURSE
1	682	15-Aug-70	100396	Spacey, Kevin	56	182	VP, MARKETING
1	704	17-Jun-68	100412	Hayek, Salma	42	403	INTERNIST
1	720	10-Jul-67	100479	Wilson, Steven	54	423	HR SPECIALIST
1	880	16-Dec-68	100792	Mercury, Freddie	42	180	MGR OFFICE SVCS
1	702	17-Jun-67	100958	Cruz, Penelope	41	144	NURSE TECHNICIAN
1	751	2-Jan-68	101147	Cruise, Thomas	46	144	NURSE TECHNICIAN

In other words, the view consolidates all of the desired information from the three separate tables into one single database entity.

Note that most systems do not provide database views out of the box. Kronos Workforce Central is one exception to this rule. The view in Table 16.1 above is a single database entity, expediting report creation and execution. While vendor support will not assist clients in creating or maintaining these views, databases such as SQL Server and Oracle provide relatively easy methods for knowledgeable IT professionals to create and refresh views. These views can be immeasurably helpful, particularly with historical tables holding millions of records that need to be summarized on a report.

Most complicated or large reports *do not* require database views. I have written hundreds of efficient reports against large transactional tables native to the application and database. However, reporting skill cannot overcome a massive quantity of data. For example, if a report requires summary information on three distinct multimillion-record tables with complex joins, then a view may be the way to go, especially if that report needs to be run in the middle of the day while other users are accessing the system.

Data Areas

During the implementation, organizations and their end-users should have learned about the importance of testing and training. To that end, once up and running with a new ERP or major system, organizations should devote the required resources to maintaining different data areas.

The production data area—typically called PROD—should store all current data. Everything from regular payroll to P&Ls stem from PROD. However, foolish is the organization that maintains only one data area. Yes, they exist. Where will new employees need to be trained? What about testing new system functionality or applying patches? The organization that attempts to do all of these in PROD dramatically increases its chances of encountering issues of all sorts.

Because of these different needs, organizations need to have a minimum of three different data areas in addition to PROD:

- A training data area (TRAIN) in which to train new employees
- A development data area (DEV) in which to store current and future setup but no employee, financial, or procurement transactions
- A testing data area (TEST) in which to test upgrades, patches, new functionality, and reports

This may seem like overkill, but organizations are wise to devote the time and resources necessary for maintaining these different data areas. Each has an important and distinct purpose.

Upgrades

Typically, a major release of a software version has a shelf life of about six to eight years, give or take. Examples include PeopleSoft version 8, Lawson version 8, and Oracle version 11i. These major releases do not include "cyclicals" such as PeopleSoft 8.1, Lawson 8.1, and Oracle 11.5. Cyclicals are *not* major releases. Rather, they represent some improvements or changes from the vendor's last major release, short of the next major one.

Vendors change and, one would hope, improve their software over time. An organization that purchases annual support from a vendor can expect a number of years of support for its current version. Eventually, however, vendors refuse to support older versions of their products. For example, an organization running Oracle Applications version 9 is on a burning plank if Version 11i is the current "preferred" version and has been for a while. Oracle will eventually decommission version 9 at some point and Oracle version 9 clients will have to do one of the following:

- Upgrade to a supported version
- Find alternative support mechanisms

- Continue using version 9 unsupported

Consider Gilmour, Inc., a company that runs Oracle financials, procurement, and HR. Gilmour is an Oracle "shop," as they say. Unlike the legacy systems that Gilmour had built and previously controlled, now it is somewhat at the mercy of Oracle with regard to upgrades and support. Gilmour implemented Oracle version 9 in 2000. Suppose that, in 2008, Oracle announced a decommission date of May 15, 2009, for version 9. Newer versions of Oracle (11i and above) will become the standard. To prepare for the upgrade, Gilmour loads version 11i applications into its TEST data area for extensive testing well before the May deadline. PROD remains the system of record—with application or "apps" version 9—until that time.

As previously discussed, most organizations will eventually opt for the upgrade for two reasons: the risks of being unsupported and the perceived benefits of the upgrade do not justify remaining on an unsupported version. While virtually no upgrade is as costly and resource intensive as the initial implementation, the upgrade is a major endeavor requiring a great deal of planning and execution. What's more, issues identical to those of a new implementation may well present themselves.

Enhancements
Remember that many organizations opting for a phased approach implement essential modules early, activating nonessential modules later. For example, a company might go live with payroll but not with time and attendance tracking until six months later. This approach will be discussed extensively in Chapter 22.

Suffice it to say that, much like a true upgrade, enhancements are typically major endeavors. They are not of the same scope as a new implementation, but depending on the new modules under consideration, may be comparable to an upgrade in terms of human and financial resources required. As such, lack of planning, data validation, and testing all represent potential obstacles.

Patches
Vendors and clients typically find issues in current versions of the software. In either case, in the event of a true bug, vendors will issue patches or service packs—basically a group of patches—that supported clients can download from the vendor's support site. Because it is not completely unprecedented for a patch to fix the problem but break

something else, these fixes should first be applied in a TEST data area, as discussed earlier in this chapter.

Customizations

Organization may be tempted to customize their systems after going live. As discussed in Chapter 9, customizations are not to be taken lightly. To be sure, not all customizations are created equal; there are degrees. A database administrator (DBA) may create a custom view of invoice data to facilitate historical reports. That's a far cry from changing that system's batch program to match invoices. Individuals who do not know what they are doing in those instances may well cause a problem that cannot easily be fixed or reversed.

Any system customization ought to be viewed skeptically. If the benefits of the customization do not outweigh the costs by a significant margin and the organization does not have the resources to support it, then the organization would be wise to "stay vanilla." Remember that vendors have form design tools allowing clients to pretty up screens without changing the underlying software code or data structure. Finally, the organization considering a customization should extensively test it in a different data area—i.e., not in PROD. Testing the customization should be coupled with testing programs *not* ostensibly affected. Sometimes changing one program or form leads to breaking another. Depending on the level of support purchased, the client may be on its own to fix an unintended consequence.

The bottom line is this: Organizations considering customizations should look very carefully at their available options, ideally with the help of a very experienced technical consultant.

Backup and Disaster Recovery

The system administrator's motto states, "If it wasn't backed-up, then it wasn't important." This chapter has discussed the importance of maintaining different data areas for different purpose—TRAIN, DEV, PROD, and TEST. However, IT departments need to do more than merely maintain these data areas. As a part of routine system maintenance, organizations should take backups or snapshots of their data and move them to secured areas on a different server.

One of my favorite maxims is, "It's better to have it and not need it then to need it and not have it." To that end, a number of things may cause an organization to restore data from one of its backups:

- Complete or partial loss of key data caused by security breach, software bug, "orphaned" batch job, and so on
- Corruption of key data caused by security breach, software bug, "orphaned" batch job, and so on
- End-user massive error

A client's need to restore data often comes unexpectedly. For example, Stevenson Hospital a few years ago experienced a major issue, the resolution of which would have been much less painful if it had had such a backup. Rich, the HRIS manager, felt that some of the payroll tables were too large for his reporting needs. He ran a purge program in PROD and eliminated millions of rows of data that others in the organization—particularly finance—needed. What's more, Rich did this during a major upgrade. The consultancy running the upgrade essentially had to stop the project and recreate the data from the purged table(s). This process took a considerable amount of time because Stevenson did not have a recent backup of its data. Needless to say, Rich was not too popular with the IT and finance folks.

Summary

Once an organization has activated its system, it has entered the real world. This chapter has described the system-related challenges associated with maintaining new systems—i.e., after testing has ceased. At some point, even a smooth system implementation and activation will face issues related to reports, interfaces, upgrades, and patches. Organizations and their end-users should be sufficiently prepared for these challenges. The next chapter explains why this is sometimes not the case.

Life is a risk.

-Diane Von Furstenberg

CHAPTER 17: OPERATIONAL CHANGES

Introduction

Up to this point, the book has focused on organizations migrating from legacy systems to more contemporary ones, such as ERPs. However, the world is not a static place; people, processes, and systems are dynamic in nature. Organizations face challenges of all kinds *after* activating their new systems. To be sure, these challenges are typically not as significant as those associated with going live. Still, senior management and end-users should never assume that system activation means that everyone is home free. Systems are hardly self-sufficient and issues always appear. This chapter focuses on the steps that organizations can take to minimize operational risks.

Consider an organization that has successfully activated its new system. Over the last two years, its end-users have gone about their jobs without major incident, entering data and performing regular processing. At some point, however, the organization will see a kink in its armor. It is inevitable that organizations fortunate enough to smoothly make the transition from old system to new will experience one or more of the following issues, ultimately threatening this utopian existence:

- Key Employee Movement
- Change in Major Business Process
- Acquisition

Key Employee Movement

Mason Footwear successfully implemented a new system five years ago. Since that time, Mason has avoided software bugs, major upgrades, and system disasters. This is no coincidence. Prior to beginning the project, Mason's senior management, hiring managers, and recruiters worked very hard to ensure that its implementation team was staffed with skilled and dedicated individuals. Since activation, Mason has retained all of its key employees—i.e., those essential to successfully supporting the new system. However, this is about to change.

Mason's management knows that, from a systems perspective, not all employee movement is created equal. In other words, different types pose different risks. While not a definitive list, the following factors determine the severity of the risk posed by an employee's departure:

- The employee's role
- Organizational "bench strength"
- The type of move (internal vs. external to the organization)
- The amount of notice given by the employee

Figure 17.1 shows the risks associated with each type of employee move:

Figure 17.1: Employee Movement Risk Matrix

	Notice		
Destination	**None**	**Short**	**Long**
Internal	Medium	Medium to Low	Low
External	High	High to Medium	Medium

Note that, for the sake of simplicity, Figure 17.1 holds constant the importance of employee role and organizational bench strength. **Suffice it to say that critical roles without suitable replacements make organizations most vulnerable to employee turnover.**

Let's look at two examples. If Nicole, one of Mason's four AP clerks, becomes ill and takes a medical leave of absence, one of her colleagues can at least temporarily pick up the slack. In this case, the overall risk to Mason is low. On the other hand, consider Alexandra, Mason's IT manager. She is solely responsible for creating new user accounts, maintaining security, applying patches, and overseeing upgrades. No one else knows how to do these things. If she were to abruptly leave the organization or even give two weeks' notice, Mason would need to scramble to find a suitable replacement. While Mason cannot guarantee that Alexandra does not win the lottery or prevent her from being hit by a bus, it should certainly have in place a succession plan for the IT manager position.

Internal Movement
Figure 17.1 manifests the obvious: Generally speaking, internal employee movement poses less risk to organizations than employee

departures. Whether via promotion or lateral move, employees often take on new roles within the same organization. In either event, several factors mitigate organizational risk in these cases:

- Within reason, organizations can control when employees begin their new positions, maximizing both knowledge transfer and the time needed to find replacements from the external labor market if necessary.
- Organizations typically set aside time for incumbents to mentor their eventual replacements.
- If replacements still have questions after the mentoring period ends, then they can call their predecessors as needed.
- The circumstances surrounding an incumbent's transfer or promotion tend to be reasonably pleasant, thus minimizing any tension between incumbent and predecessor.

External Movement

The era of unabashed employee loyalty ceased long ago and does not require rehashing in this book. Compared to twenty years ago, organizations today face a much greater risk of losing key employees to competitors, especially in concentrated geographic areas. What's more, by virtue of implementing a widely used system, an organization typically makes its end-users much more marketable than they were *before* the project began. It's hardly an exaggeration to say that certain organizations are so lean that the sudden loss of a single key employee could cause their systems to fail.

Figure 17.1 leads to the following natural conclusions surrounding employee exits:

- Organizations cannot always control when incumbent employees leave, potentially minimizing both knowledge transfer and the time needed to find replacements from the external labor market if necessary.
- Organizations may not be able to set aside sufficient time for departing incumbents to mentor their eventual replacements.
- New employees with unanswered questions after the mentoring period probably cannot call their predecessors.
- Incumbents departing under less than ideal circumstances may not be willing to impart their knowledge to their predecessors.

Of course, not all turnover is voluntary. Organizations sometimes terminate employees for gross misconduct, allowing for *no* time for knowledge transfer or "on the job" training of a replacement. The following example is true, although the company name has been changed: About six years ago, a medium-sized company (Gumble) fired its payroll manager (Barney) because he was giving himself raises. Barney figured that, even if caught, Gumble management would not do anything about it because he was the only one who knew how to run payroll. While this is hardly an excuse for this type of conduct, Barney was absolutely correct in one regard: *He was the only one who knew how to run payroll.* Gumble had not documented any part of its payroll process. To cut employee checks, Gumble had to fly me in on very short notice. Obviously, this is not an ideal situation.

External Labor Market

As it pertains to the successful maintenance of systems, the relative increase in voluntary employee turnover over the last twenty years has created both problems and opportunities. As discussed, key end-users may be more apt to walk away, especially now that they have participated in the implementation of a commonly used system.

The possibility of losing key employees is particularly acute on adversarial projects, such as that of the Page and Plant Company first discussed in Chapter 1. Certain P&P end-users may have endured the turbulence of the Bonham Software project specifically to make themselves more marketable to other companies either running Bonham or in the process of implementing it. For instance, if P&P's HRIS manager (Colin) decides that he is underpaid, rest assured that Bonham will appear prominently on his resume along with the role that he played on the project. Should a recruiter call with the promise of more money, he can hardly be blamed for listening to the sales pitch.

For P&P, however, that same problem represents an opportunity. The fact that many companies use Bonham means that, if Colin leaves, P&P should have an easier time finding a suitable replacement. The pool of available applicants is, in all likelihood, much larger than that for P&P's legacy system. Again, Bonham is a widely-used application.

This is not to say that P&P should view its employees as replaceable cogs. They are not. Let's say that P&P is able to poach the HRIS manager (Zach) from The Mercury Group, a competitor that also runs Bonham. Mercury and P&P will each have different system configurations, interfaces, and reporting requirements. Zach's learning curve may not be terribly steep but, rest assured, it does exist. P&P

should not make the mistake of assuming that Zach can hit the ground running, especially if P&P lacks comprehensive system documentation.

Change in Major Business Process

Much less frequent than key employee turnover, an organization sometimes decides to change a major internal process, prompting a "mini-implementation" within a live system. For example, Deacon Entertainment activates its new system and, three months later, decides to start paying its employees on a biweekly basis—rather than weekly. While this may not seem like an enormous project (and it really should not be), Deacon should *not* minimize the amount of work involved. Deacon will have to change specific settings in its system for employee paychecks to be correct. Employee taxes that were taken every week will now need to be taken every two. End-users need to run update programs in the new system. IT will have to modify interfaces to send accurate amounts to carriers. Reports that audited data for anomalies will need to be tweaked, if not completely rewritten.

Larger process changes require more work than smaller chances. Consider an organization that fundamentally changes its accounting basis from cash to accrual. To think that this can be accomplished from a systems perspective with a mere click of the mouse is the acme of foolishness. **A significant change in business process may require major system ramifications vis-à-vis setup, processing, and reporting. To be certain, organizations should extensively test such changes *before* rolling them out. Organizations that do not devote the required time and resources to changes of this magnitude dramatically increase the risk of either immediate or forthcoming system issues.**

Acquisition

Organizations sometimes acquire or merge with others, typically resulting in challenges of many different fronts, including systems. For example, Woods Construction acquires Mickelson Plumbing. As a result of the merger, Woods' management decides to integrate Mickelson's setup and data into its current system. Rare is the acquisition in which both companies are using the same payroll, GL, and procurement systems. This is no exception. In this case, Woods uses SAP while Mickleson never retired its legacy system. Even if both companies had used the same system (and version), Woods would still have to convert all of Mickelson's data into its ERP in order to process all transactions in the combined entity from the same system.

Organizations involved in acquisitions have a number of different data and system options. Each option is presented in the order of expected difficulty. Note that the expected outputs of each option vary in direct relation to its expected inputs. To get more out, organizations have to put more in.

Complete Integration

As was the case above, Woods can fully migrate Mickelson's data to SAP. While this is the costliest and most time-consuming, complete integration eliminates the need for Woods to maintain Mickelson's legacy system—or pay for its support. It also facilitates standard business processing and reporting.

Partial Integration

Woods can migrate Mickelson's data to SAP but store that data in a separate SAP configuration. While this solution represents a decent amount of work for Woods, it will not have to pay support costs on more Mickelson's legacy system. What's more, Woods will not have to maintain two separate systems; it will have a central repository of all data after the merger. Note that partial integration means that data from the two organizations will *not* be standardized, resulting in complicated reporting and increased processing time.

Zero Integration

Woods may choose to leave Mickelson's legacy system alone. This choice represents the least amount of work for Woods. However, it also means that Woods will have to maintain two different systems, pay additional support costs, and lack a central data repository.

A Brief Word about Vendor M&A Activity

While certainly not a common occurrence, sometimes vendors acquire one another. Two prominent recent examples include PeopleSoft's acquisition of JD Edwards in July of 2003 and Oracle's subsequent—and highly contentious—acquisition of PeopleSoft in January of 2005. M&A activity often and justifiably gives pause to clients running the software of the acquired companies. For example, many PeopleSoft clients expressed concern over eventually having to move to Oracle applications upon completion of that merger. (In fact, one of my clients involved in system selection at the time actually avoided both PeopleSoft and Oracle because of the uncertainly regarding the merger.) Up to this point, that fear has not been realized; Oracle as of this writing fully supports PeopleSoft applications.[38] Of course, this could change at any point.

On a general level, a client happily running a vendor's applications *may* find itself in a precarious position at some point in the future as a result of M&A activity. All else being equal, smaller, publicly-held vendors are much likely to be acquired than larger, privately-held organizations. The Oracle acquisition of PeopleSoft, however, proves that even very large companies can be gobbled up.

Summary

The only constant with any widely used system is change; no system exists in a vacuum. This chapter focused on the effects of operational decisions on organizations' systems. Changes in personnel, business practices, and organizational structure can take place at any point. Wise is the organization that anticipates such changes with succession planning, end-user backups, formal succession planning, and comprehensive system documentation. Danger and risk are always lurking with new systems, just as they did with the old ones. Organizations need to be prepared.

---

[38] Oracle continues to support the existing Oracle and PeopleSoft product lines for current users. By retaining current applications and supporting the move to Fusion when appropriate, Oracle may be attempting prevent customer defections to rival Enterprise Resource Planning vendors. (Source: Wikipedia)

Part Five: Maximizing the Chance of Success

The final part of this book focuses on specific steps that organizations can take to limit their risk of system failures. At a minimum, organizations should attempt to avoid the pitfalls mentioned in previous sections and case studies. For example, organizations would be wise not to start off on the wrong foot by selecting a "fly by night" consultancy, designing their systems with excessive interfaces, insufficiently staffing their implementation teams, and expecting end-users to effectively do two jobs concurrently for a year. These are obvious steps in the wrong direction; examples of what *not* to do.

Avoiding the obvious is not enough. Organizations can do many positive things to increase the odds that their new systems not only realize the benefits promised by the vendor during system selection, but do so in a timely, budget-conscious fashion.

The perfect is the enemy of the good.

-Voltaire

CHAPTER 18: MID-IMPLEMENTATION CORRECTIVE MECHANISMS

Introduction

As a general rule, implementations do not just spontaneously combust. Failures tend to stem from the aggregation of many issues. While some issues may have been known since the early stages of the project (e.g., the sales cycle or system design), implementation teams discover the majority of problems during the middle of the implementation, typically during testing. This chapter focuses on the different mechanisms available to the organization that has reached the point of no return. Specific measures include:

- Adding Resources
- Replacing Individual Consultants
- Replacing the PM
- "Losing" the PM Altogether
- Changing Consultancies
- Mid-Implementation Audit
- Moving Non-Critical Items to Phase II

Adding Resources

Many PMs and implementation teams do not anticipate the time and resources required during testing. Faced with delays from previous phases of the project, their stopgap solution is to throw more people into the fray. For example, a company has tasked its HR, payroll, and finance managers with data validation. However, those three people are not terribly skilled in related tools such as Microsoft Excel or Access. To remedy the situation, the organization involves IT more than originally planned. IT must create an automated tool that performs the validation electronically. On the less-technical end, employees not critical to the project might be asked to spot check some transactions from the new system and see if they match the same transactions from the legacy system.

Note that the simpler the task required the quicker end-users can perform them. It does not take a rocket scientist to look at two paper or electronic paychecks or purchase orders and note any differences. Very little formal training should be required for tasks as simple as these. If shown how to do something or given a formal script, the end-user should be good to go. However, for more involved tasks, it is unrealistic to show previously uninvolved and inexperienced end-users how to perform them and expect quick turnarounds. In these cases, the adding of resources may actually be a net negative.

Let's consider the example of Atlanta Medical. Henry is the payroll manager on an implementation that is in the middle of a critical testing point. In trying to make up time, he involves Aaron, the payroll clerk who had previously been peripheral to the implementation. Aaron attended training six months ago but really has not touched the system since that time. It may take so much time for Henry to show Aaron how to process payroll that the time spent explaining the tasks actually exceeds the time it would take for Henry to simply do it himself. Even assuming that Aaron is a quick study, he no doubt will have questions about what to do if and when issues arise, thus taking Henry away from his original task.

Adding more resources can have mixed results. If the right people are involved at the right time to perform tasks within their abilities, then the benefits will outweigh the costs. The bottom line is that adding more people will not always fix an issue and make up for lost time. There is no guarantee that these steps will put a project back on course. What's more, an experienced PM should know this. When unsure about whether this tactic will work, the PM should ask his or her seasoned consultants about the expected outcomes *before* committing resources.

Replacing Individual Consultants

From the client's perspective, there are several reasons that any individual consultant might need to be replaced. The first and most important is an inability of that consultant to contribute at a level mandated by the client. As discussed in Chapter 8, the type of consultancy selected often drives the type of consultants placed on the project. The larger firm might send in a team of consultants, some of whom are more junior than the "project lead." To be sure, not all consultants possess the same background, skills, and expertise in any system or with the individual applications within that system.

Client senior management may remove a consultant from a project for two major reasons:

- The consultant lacks the ability to contribute at the required level
- The consultant has a personality conflict with other team members

This has happened to almost every seasoned consultant, including yours truly. Sometimes clients and consultants just get off on the wrong foot. For example, more technical consultants might come off as abrupt with "warm and fuzzy" end-users, causing conflict.

Clients certainly have the right to remove a problematic consultant at any point during the project, as they are the ones paying the bills. However, the effectiveness of this strategy is not guaranteed for a number of reasons. The following general rules apply for replacing external consultants.

First, timing matters. Organizations in the latter stages of an implementation will have greater difficulty in finding a suitable replacement. What's more, organizations close to system activation should almost never replace a consultant—absent some sort of gross misconduct. It is very difficult for an organization to expect a consultancy to quickly locate and deploy a suitable consultant who can hit the ground running at this critical stage.

Second, trying to address personality conflicts among existing team members is typically more effective than bringing in a new consultant. In other words, as the project progresses, the institutional, system, and business process knowledge of an external consultant may become irreplaceable. Also, it is important to understand the source of the conflict. Is the client upset that a delivered feature in the software being implemented does not work as advertised or as it does in the legacy system? If this is the case, then the consultant is simply the bearer of bad news. Supplanting that consultant will not resolve the underlying problem. A new consultant may provide the answer using different words or in a different voice but the overall message to the client is the same: The software does not work as the client wants it to work without some type of customization.

Third, the greater the depth and breadth of that consultant's skills, the less willing the client should be to replace that consultant. Replacing the seasoned consultant who diplomatically challenges poor client decisions with a more malleable but less knowledgeable, less skilled consultant may appease a client in the short-term. In the long-term, however, that switch may lead to setup, testing, or validation issues. Perhaps the original consultant knew the ultimate outcome of poor setup or processing decisions and was simply trying to avoid them, not merely being difficult.

If a consultant comes across as abrasive from day one, then the best course of action for both the consultancy and the client is to attempt to address the issue immediately. Sometimes it's simply best to cut the cord right from the start. If a personality conflict exacerbates over time, then the resolution is much less clear. Client perceptions matter and no one should have to tolerate demeaning comments or actions from a consultant on site at $200 per hour. However, client end-users should tolerate an expert consultant who means well and simply wants the project to be successful, even if he or she is a little "quirky." (Working on projects like these tends to make people a little eccentric.) After all, that consultant brings a great deal to the table and will not be around forever.

Replacing the PM

PMs are not replaced nearly as frequently as individual consultants for several reasons. For one, PMs are coordinators more than they are "worker bees" and product experts. The latter can come across as condescending to apprehensive end-users who may fear the unknown of a new system. By their very nature, most PMs should try to bring people together, ensure that goals are met, and soothe conflicts as they arise. As such, they are less likely to provoke daily conflicts with end-users.

On a second and equally important note, PMs are harder to replace because consultancies employ fewer of them. This is particularly true for boutique firms. Generally speaking, consulting firms have more consultants than PMs. As a result, PMs tend not to be "on the bench" as much as individual consultants.

This is not to say that an organization should tolerate consistently deficient performance from a PM, a subject addressed in Chapter 13. However, clients should understand the often considerable logistical difficulty of replacing a PM from the same consulting company. To that end, organizations may want to consider two additional options for the PM consistently not meeting expectations: "losing" the PM (and keeping the consultancy) or changing consultancies altogether.

"Losing" the PM

Perhaps an organization values the contributions of the consultancy as a whole—and the individual consultants–but cannot live with the current PM. Rather than find a new consulting partner (a drastic step to be discussed next), the client requests a replacement from the firm's senior management. That firm has no short-term replacement available. The client opts to remove the PM from the project and will either permanently or temporarily manage the project and the individual consultants using internal team members.

This approach is fraught with risks. For example, Lars is a full-time employee at DM Metal, a large organization implementing an ERP. DM's management was not happy with Robert, the PM from its partner, RTL Consultants. As a result, DM appoints Lars as the *de facto* PM of the project but keeps Kirk and James, the RTL consultants. From a practical standpoint, Lars has insufficient expertise in the new system. Second, Lars is going to lean more often and more heavily on Kirk and James for updates than did Robert. The net impact is that the consultants will have less time to do their "day jobs," and the project may suffer as a result.

Changing Consultancies

On occasion, an organization is so dissatisfied with its partner that it opts to bring in a new one. The client finds its partner's promises of skilled consultants and an organized approach lacking. Rather than attempt one of the strategies previously discussed, the client pulls the plug. Before deciding on a new partner, senior management should understand the nature of the fractured relationship. True consulting or PM incompetence from the beginning is certainly grounds to sever the relationship. However, rarely is the situation that obvious. Organizations should look in the mirror to determine the true source of the conflict and consider the following questions:

- Can the issues be easily fixed with different personnel from the same consultancy?
- Can the issues be easily fixed with different personnel from the client?
- Can the issues be fixed with a different strategy?
- Do the issues stem from the type of contract signed?
- Are the implementation issues a function of the consultancy or of the new system? Is the consultancy simply the

messenger of client-based issues—e.g., bad data, insufficiently skilled end-users, and so on?

- Is the consultancy "working to rule?" Or is it perceived as "obstinate" because it is simply attempting to implement the system in a traditional manner—i.e., one that is known to work?
- Is another consulting company going to be appreciably better?
- What is the overall impact of changing consultancies on the project timeline and budget?

The answers to these questions will help guide an organization towards the right decision. In order to replace consultancies, clients should remember the following:

- The net benefits should exceed the costs of keeping the existing consultancy by a considerable margin. For example, the organization spending $2M on an implementation should not oust its consultants two months before going live solely to save $50,000 in consulting fees; the risks do not justify the rewards.
- The closer to going live, the tougher it is for a client to replace individual consultants, much less the entire consultancy, and still make the desired go-live date.

Many implementation issues stem from overly ambitious vendor promises, bad data, and reluctance on the part of client end-users to "get on board." Simply changing consultancies will in no way guarantee that a project will turn around. New consultancies may very well tell clients virtually the same thing as their predecessor, simply in a different voice.

Mid-Implementation Audit

Larger consultancies can deploy some type of "delivery excellence" team tasked with periodically assessing project issues and impacts mid-stream. Typically, these teams have no specific system knowledge. This is not sold as a limitation; an "outsider" perspective is supposed to be an advantage. By focusing on different types of systems, these teams can look at projects from 30,000 feet and make observations ostensibly lost on both client end-users and consultants heavily involved in the project's day-to-day activities.

The mid-implementation audit aims to identify technical, functional, and "people" issues that may cause the implementation to fail. The audit that brings important issues to the attention of senior management is certainly valuable. If the PM had previously broached these issues, then the audit will confirm what senior management already knows. If the PM had not, then manifesting them as early as possible can potentially right the ship.

On the downside, the audit requires the time and resources from end-users who are already juggling their day jobs with the additional responsibilities required by the implementation. Also, the auditors bring with them broad perspectives and may well not be able to appreciate some of the specific complexities that, while possibly appearing trivial, are actually driving the issues. Everything looks simple at 30,000 feet and auditors often do not know the implications of their specific recommendations. They may not know what they do not know.

In the end, auditors may make completely impractical and facile recommendations that do more harm than good. I worked on one project in which an auditor proposed an additional parallel test late in the project. There was no time to conduct this test under the existing project plan but this did not concern him. After all, he would not be personally involved in this additional round of testing and client senior management could hardly argue with more testing on a problematic implementation.

Sunk Costs and Avoiding the Point of No Return
Most organizations hold meetings at the *end* of their implementations to determine if they should activate the systems on which so many have been working for so long. Given the amount of time and money already spent on the project, organizations almost invariably decide to proceed with their system activations, *irrespective of the number and severity of the issues facing them*. In the end, this "go/no go" meeting is almost always a mere formality.

On a well-run implementation, the client's senior management and consultancy's PM are much more proactive than this. Rather than wait until the decision is essentially made for them, the intelligent organization holds a formal meeting after the project has launched but *before* it has reached the "point of no return." The point of this meeting is for senior management—along with critical input from its consulting partner—to determine whether or not the implementation should continue. If the implementation is unlikely to result in a successful system activation, then senior managers need to realize that their organizations cannot recoup their project's sunk costs.[39]

Under these dire circumstances, organizations should fight the urge to throw good money after bad. Of course, executives have options short of completely pulling the plug on a problematic implementation, one of which is discussed next.

Facing Reality: Moving Non-Critical Items to Phase II

Many delayed implementations have not hit previously planned system activation dates. The levers mentioned earlier in this chapter— e.g., adding consultants, replacing the PM, and so on—may *not* have resolved the issues. However, while employee and consultant hours tend to increase as projects near their magic dates, efforts cannot simply be redoubled by wishful PMs or senior management. If an implementation is considerably behind schedule and over budget and the go-live date is etched in stone, then the client and PM should make hard decisions about which features will "make the cut." Removing system features modules from Phase I is a much less drastic step than nixing the consultancies or pushing the go-live date. In fact, it may be better for all concerned.

Table 18.1 displays modules on a fictitious implementation viewed under the "essential" microscope:

---

[39] In economics and business decision-making, sunk costs are costs that cannot be recovered once they have been incurred. Sunk costs are sometimes contrasted with variable costs, which are the costs that will change due to the proposed course of action, and prospective costs which are costs that will be incurred if an action is taken. In microeconomic theory, only variable costs are relevant to a decision. Economics proposes that a rational actor does not let sunk costs influence one's decisions, because doing so would not be assessing a decision exclusively on its own merits. The decision-maker may make rational decisions according to their own incentives; these incentives may dictate different decisions than would be dictated by efficiency or profitability, and this is considered an incentive problem and distinct from a sunk cost problem. (Source: Wikipedia)

Table 18.1: List of System Modules for an Implementation

Module	Essential
Payroll	Yes
Benefits	Yes
GL	Yes
Position Management	No
Activity Management	No
Inventory Control	Yes
Web-Based Reporting	No

Many organizations mistakenly believe that every module of the new system is essential for Phase I. In Table 18.1, the Payroll module happens to be mission-critical, as are GL, Inventory Control, and Benefits. However, organizations can implement items such as position management—in which employees are tied to positions for budgeting purposes–at later date without causing significant operational problems. The same applies to items such as Web-Based Reporting. If reports have to be generated locally—and not delivered via email—from day one, the organization will survive.

Alternatively, organizations using a phased approach may consider postponing entire parts of the organization to a later phase. Returning to the example of Byrne Healthcare in Chapter 9, unexpected delays stemming from poor data and end-user resistance have left Byrne management two choices. First, it can carry on and risk major issues with all five hospitals in Phase I. Second, it could focus its resources on the three "easiest" implementations as shown below:

Table 18.2: Phased Approach for Byrne Medical, Revised

	Modules			
Hospital	HR	Payroll	GL	Procurement
Victoria	Phase I	Phase I	Phase II	Phase III
Winfield	Phase I	Phase I	Phase II	Phase III
Mattingly	Phase I	Phase I	Phase II	Phase III
Gamble	Phase IA	Phase IA	Phase II	Phase III
Jackson	Phase IA	Phase IA	Phase II	Phase III

Because of issues discovered at Gamble and Jackson Hospitals, Byrne senior management postpones their implementations until the end of Phase I. Internal resources and consultants will spend two months working exclusively with end-users from these sites, thereby maximizing the chances that those hospitals will go live successfully. While these may be viewed as individual failures, the Victoria, Winfield, and Mattingly sites will go live on the desired date. In other words, from the perspective of the entire project, two Mild Failures are preferable than one Unmitigated Disaster. Had Byrne pushed through, it would have run the risk of *all* hospitals missing their go-live dates—arguably an Unmitigated Disaster or, at the very least, a Big Failure.

In an ideal world, Byrne would activate each module at the same time at each hospital. However, as discussed, the entire project is in jeopardy of missing its go-live date. The intelligent PM should have made senior management aware of this possibility as soon as this became realistic, not at the last minute.

Petrucci Case Study: Trying to Boil the Ocean

The following case study illustrates a number of significant pitfalls on system implementations, including the following:

- An organization that tried to do too much too soon
- The danger of a client PM gone wild
- The inability of the consultant PM to control a client

Background

Petrucci General is a large, single-site hospital with 4,000 employees. Petrucci management bought an ERP and wanted to do all of the following *at the same time:*

- Implement a completely new HR/payroll system with employee and manager self-service, including relatively new modules that had yet to gain a footing in the larger user community.
- Implement a completely new finance/GL system with self-service.
- Implement a completely new procurement system with requisition self-service.
- Create and activate multiple interfaces to and from the hospital to different TPAs, banks, and other organizations.
- Enhance the core application by using almost all of the vendor's add-on tools to enhance the system's default functionality.
- Implement a completely new, largely untested security structure.

This project was simply enormous in scope and cost. In other words, rather than opting for a phased approach (which is typically the norm), Petrucci management decided to go for broke—"all in," in the poker vernacular. Note that organizations are not compelled to immediately use each piece of a new system upon activation. Unlike the Portnoy case study, which dealt with an organization attempting to integrate a number of disparate systems, Petrucci management at least had the intelligence to retire its legacy systems and implement a single new one. To lead this endeavor, Petrucci selected The Lemmon Group, an experienced partner of the vendor.

Petrucci management completely bought into the vendor's promises about the power of the new system. It would transform their business, reduce administration costs, empower employees via self-service, provide meaningful business analytics and email alerts, and unlock the power of their information. Petrucci management made the new system the centerpiece of a large organizational change and communication effort.

As is the case with implementations of this size, internal politics played a significant role. A key employee (Nick) was determined not to go live any earlier than the January 1st of the next year. Now, if the project was scheduled for completion in November, then someone hemming and hawing for a few months would not have been that problematic. However, the system was initially scheduled and, more important, budgeted for a go-live date in June or, at the latest, July. In order to extend the project by almost half a year, Nick would have to manufacture six months of delays and issues, creating reasonable doubt every step of the way.

Implementation Issues

On projects of the type of scale mentioned above, priorities can become completely convoluted. Mission-critical items, such being able to correctly pay vendors and employees, are certainly paramount to items such as the ability to electronically track expenditures tied to several governmental grants. In the whole scheme of things, Petrucci end-users would survive if they had to wait six months to roll out this functionality. In other words, in comparison to being able to pay employees accurately, submit government reporting, and so on, grants are pretty small potatoes. Unfortunately, Petrucci's PM (Dorothy) vehemently disagreed and the PM for the consultancy (Andy) would routinely refuse to confront Dorothy.

Compounding matters further, Dorothy insisted on perfection in all phases of testing. Her stance violates a central tenet of testing and, specifically, the conversion programs discussed earlier: It is simply not possible to import hundreds of thousands of often suspect records from an old system to a new system without incident. Alternatively stated, from Dorothy's perspective, a single error in an employee hire date on a data conversion program caused her grave concern. Never having been responsible for the implementation of a system of this scale before (much less this ERP), Dorothy would panic, call for emergency meetings, and stop both consultants and employees from continuing with their work on more pressing matters.

Andy failed to manage Dorothy and assure her that errors were part of the process. He would simply listen to her complaints and make promises about new dates, additional work from existing consultants, and more consultants. Andy made the critical mistake of making these promises before consulting with his own team: the experts who then had to make good on these new, overly aggressive deadlines and expectations.

By focusing on the minutiae and holding superfluous meetings, Dorothy contributed heavily to the implementation running further and further behind. In an attempt to make up for lost time, Dorothy demanded that different phases of testing occur in different data areas simultaneously. In other words, payroll testing in Environment A would take place while related—but separate—testing took place in Environment B. Forget the processing difficulties of trying to juggle two major tests at once; it was logistically difficult for all concerned to remember who did what to whom and when. Were errors the result of a design issue, timing, a missed step, bad data, a true software glitch, or something else? While consultants investigated issues in Environment A, they ignored issues in Environment B, exacerbating the situation.

The "double threading" was an Unmitigated Disaster, giving fodder to Nick and his quest to postpone the system until January 1st. When errors appeared in testing, he would say, "I told you so" or ask the rhetorical question, "How do I know that something else is not wrong?" Somehow, Petrucci end-users put the onus on Lemmon consultants to prove that every check, every deduction, check, and transaction was correct to the penny; Dorothy and Nick did not need to find issues or provide evidence of an error. This juxtaposition of the burden of proof added to the frustration of the consultants. Had Andy been willing or able to manage the client properly, the situation would never have become a crisis.

A Vicious Cycle of Retesting

Delays compounded and Andy constantly revised the project plan, with fewer and fewer days devoted to critical tasks. What's more, the plans were overly aggressive; there was no margin for error. As soon as one major task would be theoretically completed, another equally important task was supposed to start–often that very day. Therefore, a delay to one phase would reverberate throughout the project plan. Andy's project plans were predicated on the notion that the team would complete tasks without incident. Despite never having completed a single major task on time throughout the project, Andy would tinker with the plan to "back in" to Petrucci's desired go-live date, despite the objections of the consultants who knew that the dates were untenable.

On the software side, because Petrucci management decided to implement so much relatively new software, many of the issues discovered by the consultants had never been reported to the vendor by any client. As such, there were no existing patches. At any point towards the end of the implementation, the team had roughly ten critical tickets pending with the vendor. Petrucci management considered the vast majority of these issues "showstoppers" and pressured the vendor's support staff to find issues immediately. In these cases, the individual consultants could do nothing to move the issue forward; the issue rested solely in the hands of vendor support specialists.

Vendor "fixes" or patches often did not resolve the issues. On more than one occasion, a patch fixed one problem but caused another.

Systematic Chaos

A prime example of Nick's obstinacy occurred at a key point during testing. Pete, a Lemmon consultant, electronically stitched together legacy data with test data, kicking out differences on employee checks. For example, let's say that a nurse was paid $2,000 (gross) in the legacy system with a net amount of $1,200 for a two-week period. In testing, that same nurse was paid $1,950 with a net amount of $1,150. Pete produced spreadsheets showing only differences greater than a user-defined amount. In other words, an employee paid the same amount in both systems (both gross and net) would not have appeared on the report because the records were correct and did not warrant further validation or investigation. Pete's tool could potentially bring the project back on track.

Rather than use Pete's slick tool, Nick insisted that all checks from both systems for the same period be printed out and compared *manually*. If Petrucci employed fifty employees, then this process would not have taken very long. Petrucci was much larger; *end-users and consultants printed thousands of pages as the team stayed well into the night trying to identify discrepancies that Pete had already provided in a very user-friendly spreadsheet.*

Now, manual validation of a handful of records is very common during implementations. To be sure, paper makes people feel good and client end-users benefit in simply seeing how data will appear on new standard reports, forms, checks, invoices, and the like. However, there is no remotely compelling or logical reason to refuse to take advantage of accurate electronic validation tools, especially when a project is grossly behind schedule. Efficiency aside for the moment, Nick's scattershot approach may well have identified some issues but missed many more. Making matters worse, Nick insisted that the same process be repeated for the next round of testing. The term "systematic chaos" comes to mind.

While Dorothy's and Nick's motives were very different, their net effects were the same: The project became highly contentious between many client end-users and consultants. Both consultants and employees worked endlessly, routinely cancelling trips home for the weekends and skipping previously scheduled vacations.

Misplaced Concerns

Dorothy did not realize—or care—that, with the sole exception of Nick, everyone on the implementation team wanted Petrucci to go live as quickly as possible with as few issues as possible. No one wanted hundreds of hospital vendors and employees paid incorrectly and/or late. Reports needed to work and Petrucci's end users should have been able to conduct business as usual upon system activation. However, no one can rationally expect a project of this scope to go live without at least a few minor issues. Cutting checks with a 99 percent accuracy rate during the first payroll run, for example, is a home run. What's more, the ERP contained many well-tested error correction tools—e.g., adjustments for payroll, reversing journal entries, and the like. Refusing to confront reality, Dorothy and Nick pressed on in their question for perfection.

It is interesting to note that even though Petrucci decided to use technology in a much superior fashion to Portnoy, both projects suffered from two similar issues:

- Deficient project management by the consultancy
- Refusal of client PMs to listen to consultants

Outcomes
Petrucci ultimately went live with relatively few issues in late September of that year. The project missed major deadlines and came in hundreds of thousands dollars over budget. Petrucci received significant financial concessions from Lemmon. In the end, this project derailed due, in large part, to the unwillingness of both the PMs to accept the basic premise that one cannot boil the ocean. In the end, Petrucci can be rated on the failure scale as a Big Failure.

Summary
The organization with a project gone awry has a number of tools in its arsenal. Many times, the organization's focus is outward-bound; for example, the vendor made false promises, the consultants are not sufficiently skilled, etc. While these may be true to some extent, the intelligent client also looks inward. Rather than placing all of the blame on the easiest targets, the sage organization assesses its own resources, data, and internal politics. Clients that simply replace Consultancy A with Consultancy B—and fail to address core issues–will in all likelihood find themselves soon looking at Consultancy C.

> If you don't know where you are going, any road will get you there.
>
> -Lewis Carroll

CHAPTER 19: AUDITS

Introduction

Implementations result in one of two basic outcomes: the new system is activated or it is not. With respect to the first outcome, most organizations go live with an imperfect system. The real question is whether the implementation team identified the risks that could cause the newly implemented system to truly fail. The success of the new system hinges directly on the implementation team's ability to quickly identify and resolve system-related issues. For organizations that fail to go live, the finger-pointing begins, with vendors and consultants being the most easiest and visible targets.

This chapter focuses on pre- and post-implementation audits. Unfortunately, organizations do not utilize these tools nearly to the extent that they should.

The Need for an Organizational Readiness Assessment

Many organizations begin the system implementation without sufficient forethought. Senior management somewhat arbitrarily picks a date, calculates a budget, submits RFPs, selects its vendor and consulting partner, and jumps in feet first. Perhaps members from senior management at similar organizations compare notes prior to undertaking a project of this magnitude.

Consider Rudess Healthcare, an organization about to implement a new system. Rudess' management believes that its new system will cost $1M to purchase and another $1.5M to implement, with support costs running about $200K per annum. Albert The IT director decides to do some due diligence. His friend Boris recently implemented a similar system at Roscoe Healthcare. Albert asks Boris the same questions and receives the following answers:

- How long did the implementation take? Two years.
- What functionality did Roscoe implement? Full HR/payroll, financials, and procurement
- How many consultants did Roscoe employ full-time? One functional expert in each (three total) and one technical consultant

- How much did the project cost? $2.5M

Boris also provides Albert with a breakdown of the costs of the implementation at Roscoe, simplified as follows:

Table 19.1: First Year Costs of Implementation at Roscoe Healthcare

FT consultants	4
Hourly consultant rate	$175
Weeks per consultant	60
Total money spent on consultants	$1,440,000
Software license plus first year support	$600,000
Hardware upgrade cost	$820,000
Total Cost	**$2,500,000**

To be sure, ballpark figures such as Boris' serve as useful guides for determining items such as funds required, resources, and project timing. However, these answers should serve as guides and approximations, not as gospel. Each organization has its own set of challenges that individually and collectively can have enormous impacts on just about every facet of the project.

Beyond comparing notes, the single best thing that Rudess can do prior to even purchasing a new system is to determine whether the organization is ready to go down this road in the first place. Rudess should perform this analysis well *before* it signs millions of dollars in contracts and commits months or years of their employees' time.

Rudess' can appoint an internal team to conduct a study on the feasibility of this project. Second, it can ask an external consultancy to determine if Rudess is ready for such a massive undertaking. It has in mind Burns Consultants, a firm that wants to win the implementation business. Third, it can ask a separate, autonomous consultancy (The Wright Group) with no stake in the outcome to conduct this vital assessment

Option number two is a catastrophic mistake, as Burns would be tempted to suggest two things at the end of the feasibility study:

- Rudess is ready for the implementation.
- Rudess should choose Burns, as it has intimate knowledge of the organization.

Option two is fraught with peril. How can Rudess ensure that Burns conducted an objective analysis? Rudess management fears that an internal team may also be biased from the start. Management ultimately and wisely chooses option three, as The Wright Group offers the greatest objectivity. Roscoe management contracts The Wright Group specifically to conduct the readiness assessment. Wright has tremendous expertise in the field and is not affiliated with any vendor or delivery-based consultancy. Wright is on site for a period of two months at a cost of $40,000. During that time, Wright delves deeply into the crux of Rudess' organization.

From a purely financial standpoint, Rudess is behooved to discover as soon as possible if it would face any significant dangers by implementing a new system. Wright's analysis will include following emphases:

- Data Readiness
- Business Practice Variation within the Organization
- People and Organizational Readiness
- System Readiness
- Documentation
- Political Obstacles

Data Readiness
Wright sees vast inconsistencies in Rudess data across its many hospitals with regard to pay practices, GL setup, reporting, and the like. As a result of the differing setups and business rules, the data are wildly divergent. The clean-up effort alone should take about four months. Rudess does not currently possess the internal expertise required to clean up its data. As a result, it will require additional funds for extra consultants.

Business Practice Variation within the Organization
Beyond simply cleaning up the data, however, Rudess must decide on the extent to which it wants to standardize business practices and policies across the organization. Different parts of the Rudess organization currently employ very different pay and accounting practices. Rudess management cannot simply issue a decree consolidating them throughout the organization. If employee paychecks

change, then Rudess must conduct an employee and management communications blitz. Nor can Rudess management standardize its GL throughout the organization without input from the staff in each area's finance department.

People and Organizational Readiness

Wright personnel meet with each hospital's end-users to understand their jobs as well as to assess their individual capacities to potentially handle the new system. Wright also notes the level of work at each site, an important factor when considering resource allocation. Wright notes that employees at certain hospitals are so swamped with work that they would only have, on average, roughly four hours per week to devote to a new system implementation.

Beyond the actual work involved, Wright notes that these employees have not had to learn any new system functionality in over fifteen years. Very few of these people have even heard of the new system, much less had any experience with it. The training need is particularly acute in the payroll departments of several hospitals. In fact, a few of the payroll managers are very close to retiring and may not have much desire to learn a new system—or much time to use that system after going live. Wright recommends that payroll managers continue to work on the legacy payroll systems. However, Rudess should hire new payroll managers for these hospitals who have previous experience with the new system.

Rudess implemented new medical billing and OR (operating room) systems a few years back, resulting in some bumps throughout the organization. Fortunately, Rudess has addressed these issues and the scars have healed. Further, Rudess' senior management has in place a very solid IT structure. Wright determines that these other systems would pose minimal risk to Rudess' implementation of a new system. In other words, the internal staff members at Rudess who implemented— and currently support—the billing and OR systems have those issues under control.

System Readiness

Wright's technical consultant discovers some hardware issues at Rudess. Specifically, the company's existing servers and databases do not have the capacity to handle the new system. Whatever the limitations of the legacy system, it is fast; current end-users have come to expect a certain performance level. Without significant purchases of new hardware, Wright does not see how the new system can provide the same speed, a requirement in Rudess' high-transaction environment.

On the reporting front, Rudess would have to create many custom reports from the new system. No system to Wright's knowledge comes with the array of custom reports ostensibly required by Rudess personnel. End-users would need to retire a significant number of reports and opt for the new system's standard alternatives. Wright's final report notes this as a red flag.

Documentation

Wright finds that certain pockets of Rudess have better documentation than others. Any external consultant who arrives on site will certainly need to review any documentation in order to understand Rudess' functional and technical requirements. Rudess should "get its ducks in a row" with regard to documentation *before* deploying expensive consultants. Wright has often seen consultants arrive at a client site only to discover that this vital information is not available or simply does not exist.

Political Obstacles

In meeting with end-users and senior management, Wright notices that certain executives and key end-users do not believe in the need for a new system. The "if it ain't broke don't fix it mentality" is more prevalent in certain pockets.

In its final analysis, Wright determines that Rudess faces significant risks related to the implementation of a new system. The net result is a roughly 40 percent chance that the project would suffer from considerable budgetary and timeline issues if started today. Wright proposes a number of specific recommendations and the costs associated with each one.

Armed with Wright's organization-specific analysis—not merely ballpark numbers from Roscoe, Rudess' management considers the anticipated costs of the implementation:

Table 19.2: Comparison of First Year Costs of Implementation

	Roscoe - Actual	Rudess - Expected	Percentage Difference
FT consultants	4	4	0%
Hourly consultant rate	$175	$175	0%
Weeks per consultant	60	80	33%
Total money spent on consultants	$1,440,000	$2,240,000	56%
Software license plus first year of support	$600,000	$600,000	0%
Hardware upgrade cost	$820,000	$820,000	0%
Total Cost	$2,500,000	$3,660,000	46%

While the above example is fictitious, it is instructive on a number of fronts. For one, Rudess' senior management knows its risks before it has even committed itself to the project. What's more, via Wright's recommendations, it knows the steps that it can take to address those risks. Finally and most important, Rudess management can trust that Wright's findings are unbiased, as Wright is not in the systems delivery business.

Rudess spent a very small fraction of the overall anticipated project costs ($40,000) for extremely valuable information on whether it should even undertake this project. Rudess management can now:

- Walk away from a possible train wreck at minimal cost
- Opt to delay the project for a number of months or years until it overcomes some of the aforementioned hurdles
- Proceed with the project knowing the risks well ahead of time

Regardless of its ultimate decision, Rudess is in a far superior position to meet its time and budgetary goals once it makes this critical decision. For the sake of argument, Rudess opts for number two, delaying the implementation. As a result, it can expect to realize a number of significant benefits. For one, during system testing, internal staff and external consultants will not have to fix issues that should have been identified in advance. Addressing these issues in advance will mean that team members will not have to work fourteen hour days, minimizing the risk of key employee turnover. What's more, Rudess' management will probably not have to make its go-live decision under duress.

Should Rudess proceed, it will certainly have its challenges, expected and unexpected. Unlike the vast majority of organizations, however, Rudess can rationally assess the pros and cons of the project in relation to a detailed set of known risks *from the beginning*.

Intelligent organizations ask these questions beforehand. Unfortunately, for many reasons, most organizations find themselves behind the eight ball, wishing that they knew about project-threatening issues months ago.

The Postmortem: A Unique Opportunity to Learn

To paraphrase a Chinese proverb, in crisis there is opportunity. Consider an organization that has pulled the plug on its implementation, wasting millions of dollars in the process. The Portnoy case study in Chapter 11 was one such example. Immediately after pulling the plug, Portnoy management should have carefully analyzed what went wrong and why. Less extreme than Portnoy's cancelled project is an organization like Wilson that activated its systems with considerable and known issues because it had no other realistic choice.

Regardless of a project's outcome, organizations have unique opportunities for self-assessment after their system implementations. Organizations can learn a great deal about their employees, data, business processes, and politics from even a failed implementation, much less a relatively successful one. A postmortem will shed light on the specific issues that delayed or derailed a project

Who Should Perform the Postmortem?

Much like the pre-implementation audit, an unbiased and seasoned independent consultancy or individual should perform the postmortem. The objectivity of the third party is crucial here. For example, let's return to Lifeson, the subject of the third case study. Lifeson spent $5M and ended the project after repeated delays, overruns, and limited results. Remember that opposition from senior management played a key role in that project's demise. If those same senior managers drive the postmortem, then they will surely minimize their own culpability, blaming the vendor or the consultancy (frequent targets of misplaced blame). Wilson needs to understand the core issues before it even thinks about undertaking a project of that scope and budget again. If senior management does recognize and ultimately address those issues, then the next system implementation will more than likely yield similarly unsatisfactory results.

A project need not be an Unmitigated Disaster to benefit from a post-mortem. Remember that the successful implementation is far from perfect. Management may have tabled issues, allowing the project to continue. Perhaps management is still unaware of existing issues. Returning to the Oates Healthcare example from the Chapter 1, if management had performed an audit immediately after going live, it might have identified:

- The problem with the payroll setup causing overtime issues
- The need to hire more technical end-users and to provide additional training for current end-users
- The need for a more robust reporting tool

In the end, a postmortem can provide valuable insight into the organization's implementation, irrespective of the outcome of that project. Aside from identifying past problems, this type of analysis can list possible (if not likely) future issues that may arise and the methods to address them.

Managing and Auditing Data

The data clean-up and migration efforts from a legacy system to a new one is typically quite significant. Because of previously discussed differences among the ways in which different systems store data, the very process of mapping old to new will manifest inconsistencies and inaccuracies in any data set. As a general rule, larger and older data contain more problems than smaller, newer data.

To be sure, organizations will realize major outputs from these painful inputs: A new system represents a unique and opportune time for organizations to purge and/or correct historical inaccuracies that have long plagued end-users and made reports less meaningful. Organizations should audit their data routinely to ensure the following:

- Incipient problems are nipped in the bud
- End-users are sufficiently trained
- Reports contain meaningful and accurate information

As Chapter 22 will show, hybrid employees are perfect for this type of work. They tend to understand the "front end" (the functionality of the system) as well as the "back end" (how the data are stored in fields and tables).

Summary

Pre-implementation, post-implementation, and ongoing data audits are invaluable tools for organizations. Used judiciously by knowledgeable and impartial resources, audits can detect, avoid, and/or minimize issues that can derail a successful implementation or cause a live system to fail. Rather than view them as superfluous expenses, organizations would be wise to conduct them at key points throughout the system's lifecycle.

Hope for the best but prepare for the worst.

-Proverb

Chapter 20: Build in a Margin for Error
Introduction

As has been discussed at length, many projects suffer delays and do not have the requisite time to overcome them with existing resources. The result is either the project goes over budget, misses its deadline, or both. At this point, the myth of the "delay-free" system implementation should be shattered. Perfection on projects of this scope and cost—regardless of tier—is virtually non-existent.

One of the simplest things that organizations can do is remarkably obvious yet almost always overlooked: build in a margin for error. While no panacea, project plans with reasonable amounts of slack minimize the chances of outright failures. Project without such buffers undertake enormous risks.

Example

Two companies—Lebowski and Sobchak—are implementing the same ERP at the same time using consultants of the same caliber. Let's assume that the two companies face identical challenges vis-à-vis data, testing, design changes, and personnel. The final stretches of the two organizations' project plans are represented in Table 20.1:

Table 20.1: Original Project Plans for Lebowski and Sobchak

Task	Lebowski		Sobchak	
	Start Date	End Date	Start Date	End Date
Conduct System Testing	12/1/2008	12/15/2008	11/10/2008	11/24/2008
Final End-User Training	12/16/2008	12/17/2008	12/3/2008	12/6/2008
Readiness Assessment	12/18/2008	12/21/2008	12/11/2008	12/14/2008
Final Preparation for Production	12/22/2008	12/28/2008	12/18/2008	12/22/2008
System Activation/Go-Live	12/28/2008	12/30/2008	12/28/2008	12/30/2008
Post Implementation Audit	1/11/2009	11/13/2008	1/11/2009	1/13/2009

Note how the tasks in Lebowski's project plan are sequential and have no room for error. As soon as one task ends, the next is immediately scheduled to begin. In other words, should a major task suffer a delay, all subsequent tasks will suffer. Now, should the same issue confront Sobchak, dates can be tweaked and the dates of other phases may *not* need to be moved. Most important, the requisite time required for each phase can be left intact.

In mid-November, both organizations discover a bug with the vendor's software issue previously unreported. The vendor has promised to make this a relatively high priority but, since both organizations are not yet live, will not assign it "critical" status. The ETA of a patch is one week.

Despite the similarities of their projects, the net impact of this delay on each company is dramatically different. Sobchak was prescient enough to anticipate such problems and, as a result, built in a margin for error early in the project planning stages to be used if and when such a delay or issue presented itself. Lebowski did not, and as a result, is in danger of missing its date. Certainly, senior management at Lebowski will escalate the issue with the vendor, and perhaps a resolution can be expedited. Lebowski is left with the following ugly alternatives:

- Move its date and face increased consulting and support costs
- Compress tasks to "back into" a date. In this case, it can attempt to perform the testing in one week instead of the necessary two. To do so, Lebowski must push consultants and internal staff harder and effectively complete work originally set for two weeks in only one

Table 20.2: Revised Project Plans for Lebowski and Sobchak

Task	Lebowski		Sobchak	
	Start Date	End Date	Start Date	End Date
Conduct System Testing	12/8/2008	12/15/2008	11/17/2008	11/30/2008
Final End-User Training	12/16/2008	12/17/2008	12/3/2008	12/6/2008
Readiness Assessment	12/18/2008	12/21/2008	12/11/2008	12/14/2008
Final Preparation for Production	12/22/2008	12/28/2008	12/18/2008	12/22/2008
System Activation/Go-Live	12/28/2008	12/30/2008	12/28/2008	12/30/2008
Post Implementation Audit	1/11/2009	11/13/2008	1/11/2009	1/13/2009

Lebowski management opts for the second alternative. In the process, Lebowski has increased its risks of failure considerably. Two weeks of system testing cannot be accomplished in one, even if employees and consultants work sixteen hours per day. Under that kind of pressure, it is also very likely that employees and consultants will miss certain issues due to fatigue. While Sobchak management cannot be happy about the software bug and its resultant effect on the project, its pain is not nearly as severe as that of Lebowski.

In the above example, the major benefit of including a margin for error in a project plan is that a sudden, unexpected crisis does not necessarily imperil the go-live date. However, there are also many side benefits of using slack. For one, employees and consultants can use the time to catch up on tasks that may have been delayed—documentation and report writing come to mind. Second, organizations can use this period for supplemental training and knowledge transfer. Finally and often overlooked, the time could be used as a "down week" in which everyone can relax. Employee hours worked during implementations, especially as organizations prepare to go live, can be quite onerous. Well-rested employees and consultants are better prepared for the final, critical hurdle: going live.

Challenges, Realities, and Aligning Interests

Admittedly, the margin for error often does not exist in many project plans because its very notion faces an uphill battle. First, the consultancy asking the client to accept a margin for error in the project plan runs the risk of appearing weak and ostensibly less organized, as if it expects the project to fail. Translation: It may not win business in the first place.

For example, Manilow Entertainment has purchased Oracle applications and is soliciting bids for the implementation work. It receives two responses to its RFP. Maiden is a large firm with many practices. It promises to perform the work in ten months sans delays and prices the project at $400,000 on a time and materials (T&M) basis. Judas is a boutique shop, specializing in Oracle. It commits to a full year with potentially unnecessary margins for error at the price of $450,000, also on a T&M basis. All else being equal, Manilow may naively and immediately rule out Judas for cost reasons. However, the $400,000 submitted by Maiden may balloon to $500,000 or more with issues and delays.

Maiden needs to position its bid as follows. Maiden very much wants Manilow to implement Oracle successfully. In its experience, comparable organizations need about a year to do this. Rather than "under-price" its bid, Maiden commits to a year, with built-in margins for error. Maiden assures Manilow management that it has every intention of implementing Oracle in a timeframe and manner minimizing costs and maximizing client ROI. Specifically, if the project plan's margins for error are not necessary, then Manilow and Maiden will jointly accelerate individual tasks in a fashion conducive to their successful completion. Aside from potentially saving Manilow money, this approach sets a very positive tone from the beginning and aligns consultant and client interests. Think about it. Oracle may actually go live ahead of schedule and under the proposed budget. Perish the thought!

Of course, progressive consultancies often make this argument in vain. Clients need to listen to the argument and not race to the bottom on consulting rates and total cost. Remember from Chapter 8 that sometimes consultancies intentionally price bids on a T&E basis on the low side based on a strict list of business requirements. Clients that deviate from this list must submit change requests for out of scope items. That is, both the initial budget and timeline ultimately increase, often considerably.

The need for a margin for error will become particularly acute for a system activation scheduled at the end of the year. Forget for the moment that employees tend to take time off during this time. More than that, the realities of their day jobs often set in. Accounting folks have month-end, quarter-end, and year-end balancing. Payroll has to process W-2s each year. These are examples of non-negotiable items that end-users have to complete in a timely manner. Project plans should be sensitive to end-users' availability during such periods.

Summary
While hardly rocket science, organizations that bake in margins of error at natural breaking points are better able to withstand invariable last-minute delays. Foolish is the PM, consultancy, or senior manager who assumes that perfect execution is attainable.

> Good management is the art of making problems so interesting and their solutions so constructive that everyone wants to get to work and deal with them.

> -Paul Hawken

CHAPTER 21: EMPLOYEE AND CONSULTANT-BASED STRATEGIES

Introduction

This chapter focuses on the most important part of a system implementation: people. Very often, the talents of individual consultants and end-users can make the difference between success and failure on an implementation and beyond. This is *not* to say that the most talented and dedicated employees and consultants can always or even often overcome poor system design, bad data, horrible project planning, or last-minute crises. They cannot. However, finding and then retaining quality people is one of the single best things that an organization can do to maximize their chances of successful system implementations.

Specific employee- and consultant-based strategies include:

- Finding and retaining consultant and employee hybrids
- Using employee retention bonuses during an implementation
- Immediately removing or redeploying difficult employees
- Bringing in a hired gun
- Preempting key employee turnover

Finding and Retaining Hybrids

As discussed, most "worker bees" on an implementation fall into one of two categories: technical or functional. There are two reasons for this distinction.

Consultants

Consulting companies hire and train new consultants at often considerable costs. It typically takes freshly hired consultants anywhere from three to six months to gain certification and become proficient enough with a product to guide clients effectively through an implementation, although some take quite a bit longer. After this period, consultancies rightfully expect a return on their investment—i.e., consultants need to start billing clients as soon as possible. After obtaining their certifications, consultants should not expect to attend very many training sessions on a vendor's "add on" products. Down the road, ambitious individual consultants may have opportunities for to expand their skill sets. However, in the short- and near-term, it is not reasonable for consultancies to produce "techno-functional" super-users.

While consultancies place a great deal of emphasis on billing, the individual consultant typically possesses a tremendous desire to maximize bonuses. Such bonuses are almost always tied to employee utilization. In tandem, these incentives tend to create consultants with a great deal of depth in an individual application but not nearly as much breadth. A GL consultant at a large firm, for example, may know invoice matching inside and out but know very little about fixed asset management. Alternatively, many payroll consultants know a great deal about how the application processes employee paychecks but nothing about the fields and tables updated by each payroll program in the process.

Let's look at an example at one organization with a traditional, purely functional payroll consultant (Donna) interacting with the client's designated report developer (Sam):

- The payroll manager needs a payroll report from the system.
- Donna creates the reporting specification, leaving out key technical pieces of information.
- Sam attempts to create the report but cannot without additional information. He emails Donna.
- Donna receives the email but is fully engaged in system testing. She is unable to answer Sam's questions for three days.
- Donna asks client end-users to elaborate on the reporting requirements.
- Donna finally provides the information to Sam, who then creates a template of the report and sends an example to Donna.
- Donna reviews the report with end-users and makes some changes.
- Frustrated, Sam receives the changes requested and has to recreate the report from scratch because it contains tables and joins that make the original version of the report useless.
- After a month of back-and-forth, the report is ready for sign-off.

This is hardly an ideal process, especially if the report is essential and the project is running behind schedule. Now, let's look at the same process spearheaded by Pete, a highly-skilled functional consultant with extensive experience in Crystal Reports:

- The payroll manager needs a payroll report from the system.
- Pete asks them specifically what they want to see, already thinking about the required tables and fields.
- Pete knows that the number and size of the required tables will cause this report to take six hours to complete soon after the client goes live; he does not even attempt to build the report using the traditional tables because he knows that the effort is futile.
- Pete quickly puts together a formal reporting specification and creates a custom view in the database that aggregates this information. He provides the code for this view to the IT department for sign-off.
- Pete creates the report and provides a sample with data.
- The report is spot-on and takes minutes to run. The payroll manager signs off on it one week later.

Now, multiply this process by fifty—a fairly common number of custom reports required by a client during an implementation. Isn't the hybrid consultant worth 20 percent more?

An organization's desire to keep *initially expected* consulting costs at a minimum often results in their staffing projects with consultants who wear only one hat. Remember the example of "Joe the Independent" in Chapter 8. His rate exceeded that of Rena by a considerable margin, but he brought a great deal more to the table. **Depending on the role required, hybrid consultants are almost always well worth their premiums.** Organizations **that hire hybrids often find that they spend less in total consulting expenses throughout the project.**

Employees

On the client side, remember that legacy systems typically resulted in segregated responsibilities for many end-users. Let's return to reporting, first discussed in Chapter 14. In many organizations, legacy systems and/or traditional roles did not permit functional end-users to write reports and extract system data. As a result, reporting, has historically been viewed as an "IT function" and most client end-users do not have very much experience in that vein.

While an implementation may represent an ideal time for curious end-users to learn new reporting applications, there are only so many hours in a day. Consider a benefits manager involved in an implementation. Her day job requires her to attend to current employee enrollment issues. In her spare time, she needs to set up and learn the new benefits application of the ERP. She probably does not have a great deal of time to devote to learning how to create custom reports.

Many organizations staff their projects with end-users who wear only one hat. This typically results in an discovering issues relatively late in the process, often well into testing. Consider the following examples:

- A payroll manager with a decent amount of GL experience could tell during system design that a decision will have a negative or unexpected GL impact.
- An HRIS Manager adept at Crystal Reports knows that a poor setup decision will limit the organization's future ability to extract key employee information.
- A database administrator (DBA) realizes that the organization's desired security setup with prevent the distribution of key reports.

Again, a single, isolated, and relatively minor issue uncovered relatively late in an implementation tends not to derail a project singlehandedly. However, to the extent that projects scheduled to go live on a particular date may already be pushing that date, these issues collectively increase the risk of a system failure. Clients are best served by employing experienced, *hybrid* end-users.

Applicant Questions

Prior to beginning a system implementation, organizations may determine that existing staff members do not have sufficient experience with the new system. Consider Terrence Pet Supplies, a large company about to implement SAP, along with Alvin Consulting, its partner. While Terrence management believes that its employees can be trained on SAP, it simultaneously realizes that a team staffed exclusively with newly trained team members would benefit a great deal from the presence of at least one experienced super-user. Such an employee would also potentially decrease the number of required external consultants.

Terrence is in luck. Unlike its legacy system, the available pool of prospective employees familiar with SAP is quite large. While there may be geographical and budgetary restrictions, Terrence can find and hire individuals who already possess deep expertise in SAP. In other words, its existing team would not need to start with a blank slate. Terrence makes the decision to proceed with filling the position.

When Terrence recruiters go to job search boards, such as monster.com, and perform a keyword search on "SAP," thousands of prospective candidates appear. Before continuing, a note of caution is in order for Terrence. **Different implementation projects and teams require individuals to play different roles. As a result, candidates may or may not have performed the tasks indicated on their resumes.**

Terrence finds Ricky and Ronnie, ostensibly ideal candidates, who claims to have "extensive experience configuring and testing SAP." Here's the problem: They may actually have been light SAP users. To the extent that Terrence and its end-users have not yet implemented SAP, its hiring managers may very well not be able to assess the candidates' SAP proficiency accurately. What should it do?

While a formal examination SAP may not be practical, Terrence should ask its implementation partner, Alvin, to interview Ricky and Ronnie and ask many detailed questions related to SAP. Terrence needs to ensure that it is hiring a true SAP expert, even though its management and end-users are not in positions to make that call. Alvin's consultants should probe each candidate about their SAP experiences, either alone or in conjunction with Terrence's hiring managers. In the end, Alvin personnel should make a recommendation to Terrence management about each candidate's SAP proficiency and suitability for the position.

I have seen job candidates exaggerate their roles on previous implementations more than once. An end-user on one project who was only peripherally involved claimed on her resume to be a key member of the team after leaving the organization. Also, in the Portnoy case study, management hired an alleged super-user who grossly embellished her experience with the system.

Behavioral Interviews

How can an organization guarantee that it is hiring a true system expert? In short, it cannot. There is no scientific way of determining expertise in an application. One method that *should* weed out "posers" is the behavioral interview.[40] In this type of interview, the interviewer asks the applicant a question such as, "Tell me about a specific challenge that *you* faced on an implementation."

The interviewer should tell the applicant to frame responses in terms of three things:

- The background or situation establishing the issue
- The tasks or actions that *the individual* took to resolve that issue, not the team
- The outcome or results of those actions

A useful acronym for behavioral interviews is *STAR*: Situation, Task/Action, and Result. Returning to the Terrence example, consider the following two responses from Ronnie and Ricky:

---

[40] Behavioral-based interviewing aims to discover how an interviewee acted in specific employment-related situations. The logic is that how you behaved in the past will predict how you will behave in the future—i.e., that past performance predicts future performance. (Source: about.com)

Table 21.1 Comparison of Applicant Responses in Behavioral Interview

	Ronnie	Ricky
Situation	As we were about to go live with SAP, I discovered a data issue with a key financial conversion program.	We had problems with as we were about to go live
Task/ Action	I alerted senior management of the issue and researched the options. I wrote extensive queries isolating the suspect data and distributed it to end users, emphasizing the need for immediate action. I coordinated the validation of that data. Also, I found a patch on the support site and alerted the IT manager, who installed the patch in a TEST data area. I tested the patch and determined that it resolved the issue. I recommended that it should be applied to the PROD data area.	IT handled the issue. I kept people informed.
Result	The patch resolved the issue. We activated the system as scheduled.	The patch resolved the issue. We activated the system as scheduled.

Note how Ronnie can articulate the specific actions that he took to identify and resolve the problem. Ricky can only speak in general terms about the problem and the resolution and, as such, appears to be an inferior candidate. At this point, Terrence should ensure that Ronnie's references check out.

In behavioral interviews, the outcome of a situation is not nearly as important as the steps taken by each individual in response to that situation. The applicant who did everything possible to resolve an issue may not have been able to save the day through no fault of her own. Conversely, the individual who acted as though "things would work themselves out" may have been right. More than the outcome, the interviewer should look for what each applicant did and did not do in response to the problem.

Using Employee Retention Bonuses during an Implementation

Internal staff members are critical not only to a system implementation and activation but to that system's ongoing performance after system activation. During an implementation, additional resources may well be hired, even beyond external consultants. The fact remains, however, that the workloads of key team members increase significantly throughout the implementation, often by considerable amounts. For the most part, these key members will not be freshly minted college graduates. Often in their mid-30s at least, these employees are very likely to have families. An increased workload means a great deal of personal sacrifice on their parts.

To address such issues, intelligent organizations do more than merely recognize these personal sacrifices. While a pat on the back is always nice, a financial incentive for key team members to remain with the organization during and after the implantation is often wise for at least two reasons. First, it tangibly rewards key contributors for the extra work and hours that they will devote to the project. Second, such a carrot decreases the likelihood of employee turnover, particularly at critical and stressful points of the project.

Obviously, both parties must keep these bonuses confidential. The last thing that a team member not receiving a bonus needs to hear is that her colleague is going to be compensated beyond her additional salary. As for amounts, there is no one magic formula. To quote my old compensation professor, George Milkovich,[41] the amounts should equate to "meaningful hits." For example, an employee pulling 60-plus hours per week for six months may well view $1,000 as a slap in the face. After all, that employee probably did not sign up for two jobs when joining the company: a day job as well as additional responsibilities related to the implementation. However, $20,000 is probably excessive, especially if the team member is not entirely essential to the project.

This is Risk Mitigation 101. Organizations that understand the need to retain and reward key contributors, particularly on high-visibility projects such as system implementations, are simply protecting their assets. Used appropriately, the retention bonus can be an extremely effective mechanism in counteracting the sometimes natural desire of a frustrated, burned-out employee to simply walk away at a critical point in the project.

---

[41] http://instruct1.cit.cornell.edu/courses/ilrhr769/biosketch.html

Preempting Key Employee Turnover

Hybrids are rarely wanting for job offers, if they decide to look or not. The functional GL consultant who also knows how to run a payroll or match invoices has quite a bag of tricks at her disposal. Remember that HR and payroll end-users tend to be much less technical than financial and procurement folks. Rare is the functional HR/payroll individual who can also build complicated Crystal Reports and/or Microsoft Access applications to address complex issues like the one encountered by Oates Healthcare in Chapter 1. Hybrids often eliminate the need to bring in expensive external consultants to solve system and data problems. Aside from a retention bonus during an intense implementation, the smart organization should consider the items mentioned in this section to preempt valuable hybrids from jumping ship.

Formal Training

Hybrids like to learn and develop their skill as much as possible. Going back to Chapter 13, they are the very definition of "willing and able." To be certain, much of this learning takes place on the job. Hybrids like to get their hands dirty and dive into issues; the unknown does not scare them. However, most applications and products are so robust that no one can effectively learn them one hour at a time on relatively slow days. Dedicated classroom time is often required to learn an advanced product with the intent of applying that knowledge within the organization. Hybrids repeatedly denied chances to participate in formal training for whatever reason may become frustrated and may be more apt to listen when a recruiter calls.

Compensation

Hybrids do not fall easily into many traditional job descriptions. While they often have a primary source of expertise, hybrids tend to do a little bit of everything. Key, but often overlooked, is the fact that many hybrids interface extremely well with everyone in an organization, from the purely functional to purely technical and everything in between. Aside from their vast knowledge, they often know how to speak both languages; many know when to dial up or down more technical language as the audience and situation warrants. This in turn expedites the resolution of all sorts of issues, minimizing the "back and forth" between these two disparate groups. Less is lost in translation when a fluent interpreter is present.

All of these skills add up to a considerable amount value for the organization. Management should recognize hybrids' contributions by paying them above-market salaries. After all, hybrids are exceptionally hard to find and replace.

Strategic Input

Money and training may go a long way but hybrids often want something else: involvement in organizational decisions. As people who typically solve the problems created or exacerbated by others, they often have keen insight into the ways in which technologies can be effectively deployed in the present and future. The converse holds true as well: They are more likely than not to have strong opinions about what should *not* be done and what will cause problems usually unanticipated by others. While turning the entire IT or finance department over to a hybrid may not be feasible, organizations should seek out the input of hybrids for key systems-related decisions *before they are made.*

Immediately Removing or Redeploying Difficult Employees

As shown in Chapter 13, some end-users on a project may *not* be willing and able to perform necessary tasks in the time allotted. Those with good intentions but without the requisite skills—willing but not able—may need help. As a result, the implementation team might have to augment or remove end-users. Now, consider ABNWs (Able but Not Willing) and NWNAs (Neither Willing nor Able). Ideally, management would never have assign them to the project in the first place. However, sometimes these characters hide their true colors until after the implementation begins. Sometimes the organization is simply so lean that it simply has no other choice. It has to bite the bullet and assign potentially problematic employees to implementation teams.

Client end-users may pose problems for a variety of reasons. Some people may find the new system too complicated. In the words of Niklaus Wirth,[42] "A primary cause of complexity is that software vendors uncritically adopt almost any feature that users want." That is, legacy systems may have been "easier" to use because they simply did not do

---

[42] Niklaus Emil Wirth (born February 15, 1934) is a Swiss computer scientist, best known for designing several programming languages, including Pascal, and for pioneering several classic topics in software engineering. In 1984, he won the Turing Award for developing a sequence of innovative computer languages. (Source: Wikipedia)

as much. Today, organizations buy, build, and rent systems that offer much more functionality than did their predecessors. Patience and training may not quell end-users' fears or help them assimilate to a new system. Faced with an uncertain future, they may kick and scream throughout the project.

If the carrots and sticks mentioned in Chapter 13 do not do the trick, then it is best simply to remove or redeploy problem employees as soon as possible. The longer that organizations wait to remove internal obstacles—particularly those in key roles, the greater the risk to that the project. Going back to the Petrucci General case study, had management reined in Nick from the beginning, the project may have not failed to the extent that it did.

Emergency Triage: Send in "The Wolf"

One of my very favorite movies is *Pulp Fiction*. Trust me. I am going somewhere with this. I particularly enjoy the scenes involving Harvey Keitel's character, Winston Wolfe, a.k.a. "The Wolf." Hit men Jules (Samuel L. Jackson) and Vincent (John Travolta) have accidentally shot a man in their car, the inside of which is now covered in blood. They arrive unexpectedly at the house of Jules' friend, Jimmy. Aside from needing to dispose of the body and clean themselves up, they must sanitize the car within an hour, as Jimmy's wife is due home from work soon. Panicked and unsure about how to handle the situation, Jules calls his boss, Marsellus, who is able to calm Jules down by telling him that he is sending in The Wolf.

The Wolf arrives at Jimmy's house less than ten minutes after receiving the call from Marsellus. The Wolf quickly gathers information, assesses the situation, and starts telling Jules and Vincent what to do. Told abruptly to clean the car, Vincent snaps that "a 'please' would be nice," prompting the following exchange:

THE WOLF: Set it straight, Buster. I'm not here to say "please." I'm here to tell you want to do. And if self-preservation is an instinct you possess, you better (expletive) do it and do it quick. I'm here to help. If my help's not appreciated, lots of luck gentlemen.

JULES: It ain't that way, Mr. Wolf. Your help is definitely appreciated.

VINCENT: I don't mean any disrespect. You know I respect you. I just don't like people barking orders at me.

THE WOLF: If I'm curt with you, it's because time is a factor. I think fast, I talk fast, and I need you guys to act fast if you want to get out of this. So pretty please, with sugar on top, clean the (expletive) car.

In the end, everything turns out alright—sort of. Jimmy and Jules dispose of both body and car, Jimmy's wife never finds out about the murder, The Wolf gets breakfast, and Jimmy receives several thousand dollars for a new bedroom set for his trouble.

So, what does *Pulp Fiction* have to do with systems implementations? In short, organizations in dire situations may need to "send in The Wolf." In other words, distressed clients may need to turn to highly skilled and compensated hired guns at key points in an implementation in an attempt to solve major problems. Examples of situations requiring "The Wolf" include when:

- Essential setup decisions still need to be made.
- Reports or interfaces are well-behind schedule.
- Testing is lagging and not manifesting issues in a timely manner.

If left unaddressed, these issues will result in missed activation dates and budget overruns. In order for the hired gun to be successful, all end-users—even external consultants—need to fall in line, much like Jules and Vincent. The Wolf needs to have complete authority and cannot be bothered with knowledge transfer or ensuring that end-users are comfortable with the process. End-users need to quickly and comprehensively answer The Wolf's specific questions concerning anything—setup, testing, report requirements, etc.

While probably not quite as coarse as the Harvey Keitel character, the hired gun has one primary objective: to get the project back on track. The organization needs the hired gun to work his magic. To that end, excessive meetings, diplomacy, and end-user hand-holding must go by the wayside. The Wolf is there to provide results and everyone needs to follow his orders precisely.

The hired gun *cannot* guarantee a successful outcome. Some situations are so dire that they are beyond rescue, even for The Wolf. For example, no one person can configure and test an entire system in two days. Superman himself cannot completely validate an organization's GL or payroll setup at the last minute. Even a reporting guru like Ken Hamady cannot knock out 100 custom reports in a weekend. Still, for the implementation on life support, sending in a hired gun may be the only available option short of postponing the go-live date or scrapping the project altogether.

Summary

Client end-users on a system implementation should lead, follow, or get out of the way. Organizations lucky enough to have hybrids should take steps to ensure that they remain satisfied employees. Followers may not have the skills that hybrids do but at least they are "on board." Management should either not staff projects with problem employees or put them on short leashes from the beginning. While this approach may seem draconian at first and people certainly see the light, organizations opting to utilize potential problem employees increase risk to the overall project. As a last resort, bringing in a hired gun may salvage a project or a go-live date.

We go out in the world and take our chances.
Fate is just the weight of circumstances.
That's the way that lady luck dances.

-Neil Peart

CHAPTER 22: INTELLIGENT EXPANSION
Introduction

One of my favorite board games is *Risk*.[43] In an attempt at world domination, players deploy their armies throughout the globe, roll the dice, and conquer countries. To be sure, there is a huge luck component in the game. However, the player who knows how to manage "risk" (specifically in the game, when to be aggressive and when to pull back) is at an advantage. That player will not take unnecessary risks and, in the end, stands the best chance of winning. While no outcome is certain, using an intelligent strategy often overcomes some bad rolls of the dice.

Most of the time, organizations will go live with at least a few known issues with the ultimate intent of fixing them. Any thoughts of a "pain-free" implementation disappeared long ago. Perhaps issues were intentionally tabled for budgetary reasons. Depending on the severity of these issues, an implementation team may either push them aside until Phase II or choose to live with them. However, as a general rule, organizations should address certain the following issues well before even entertaining the thought of system expansion:

- Those that affect data integrity and reporting
- Those that affect system performance and stability
- Those that affect system security

---

[43] Risk® is a turn-based game for two to six players and is played on a board depicting a stylized Napoleonic-era political map of the Earth, divided into forty-two territories, which are grouped into six continents. Players control armies with which they attempt to capture territories from other players. The goal of the game is "world domination," to control all the territories—or "conquer the world"—through the elimination of the other players. Using area movement, Risk ignores limitations such as the vast size of the world and the logistics of long campaigns. (Source: Wikipedia)

This chapter focuses on expansion-related risks and the steps that organizations can take to ensure that any additions are successful ones.

Types of Future Enhancements

To be sure, not all system enhancements and additions are equal—much like all post-implementation issues. For the organization to successfully realize the outputs of each enhancement, it must take into account the required and proportional inputs. This section presents each type of enhancement in ascending order of *expected* difficulty and resources required.

Enabling Additional Functionality within a Module of an Existing System

Perhaps an organization's resources during Phase I of an implementation were stretched. A few items originally slated for immediate activation did not make the cut. After a cooling down period following system activation, organizations typically revisit those features, seeking to enhance their systems by adding functionality to existing modules. Examples include the following:

- Creating additional web-based reports for an existing dashboard
- Turning on a new PTO plan within the currently used absence management application to track employee balances
- Increasing the number of government grants tracked

These types of enhancements tend to be the easiest to accomplish. While design, documentation, planning, and testing are all important, each enhancement is *incremental*. As a result, end-users are typically already familiar with the system and each module at this point. Thus, the new functionality simply represents an extension of that which is currently working.

Enabling Entirely New Modules

More often than enhancing functionality within a module, organizations often activate new modules within the existing system. Examples include:

- Enabling asset management to leverage the value of fixed asset inventory and minimize the cost of tracking physical assets

- Enabling the entire absence management module to track employee vacation and sick accruals

These types of enhancements require organizations to devote much more time and resources than merely enabling additional functionality within a module of an existing system. Proper design, documentation, planning, and formal testing are also essential. While end-users are already familiar with applications in the system, they are *not* familiar with these new modules.

Integrating an Entirely Different System

The most expensive, time-consuming of these enhancements is the third-party system integration. Clients tend to go the Best of Breed (BOB) route for a number of reasons. First, right or wrong, client management has confidence in the basic functionality, stability, and performance of the new system. Second, the BOB system offers superior functionality relative to the vendor's alternative, if one even exists. Finally, the client believes that the BOB system addresses a compelling business need that justifies the additional license and support fees, integration costs, and departure from a unified systems strategy.

Examples of such projects include the implementation and integration of the following systems:

- Taleo's Talent Management for applicant tracking and recruiting
- Hyperion's Business Intelligence (BI) tool for enhanced reporting
- Kronos Workforce Central for employee timekeeping purposes

Often times, organizations may have good reasons for going this route. I personally recommended this very approach a few years ago to a large hospital system that had great difficulty with a vendor's electronic recruiting application. That organization met the criteria above; it had tried the ERP vendor's alternative for years and still couldn't get it to work, resulting in a lack of qualified nursing applicants, excessive overtime paid, and a host of other issues. However, before adding any significant functionality or integrating a new system, it is imperative that organizations ensure that their existing hardware, system infrastructure, and end-users can handle the increased demands about to be placed on them.

The following case study illustrates an organization with a total lack of a coherent systems strategy. It not only routinely ignored opportunities to fix post-go-live issues; it actually exacerbated those issues by introducing more systems. It is a prime example of what *not* to do if an organization wants to improve its use of technology. **This case also illustrates, however, that despite lip service to the contrary, some organizations simply do not want to "get better." Systems in these organizations are bound to fail.**

Tate Case Study: Adding on to a Poor Foundation

Publically traded Tate Apparel operates a chain of about 1,000 retail stores throughout the United States and Canada. About 10,000 employees work at Tate, although that number increases during the holiday season. Tate began its implementation of a new ERP in 2000, ultimately going live in 2002. The enormity of the implementation called for a partial or phased approach. Tate did not convert all regions throughout the organization to the new system. As a result, after the implementation, biweekly payroll needed to be processed from three different systems, a time-consuming and inefficient process. In most organizations, such arrangements tend to be ephemeral in nature. However, Tate management never did retire the other two payroll systems.

During the implementation, Tate management made a number of critical mistakes. First of all, it did not upgrade its servers to handle the number of anticipated annual transactions that the ERP would generate. This problem was terribly acute immediately after going live because Tate activated the system with minimal amount of historical data. However, as the number of transactions continued to grow, system performance continued to exacerbate. A mere year after going live, end-users noted a distinct drop in system performance with everything from entering basic information to running simple reports.

Second, Tate spent thousands of dollars implementing the ERP's native self-service product. That application would have allowed Tate employees and managers to view key information, enroll in benefits, and enter important personal information updates—such as name and address changes. However, Tate never rolled it out. This is tantamount to getting all of the buck for no bang. Instead, it opted to build and attempt to integrate a separate system for store-based transactions with the new ERP.

Post-Go-Live Issues

Tate faced a number of expected and significant issues in the months after going live. First, as mentioned, employee and financial transactions grew quickly. The existing server's lack of processing power—and management's unwillingness to buy more powerful boxes—made daily system processing and reporting glacially slow for end-users. Management's stopgap solution was simply to purge important historical data from the PROD data area and move them to a different one (on the same box).

This solution had two effects. System performance improved because there were simply less data in PROD. However, on the flip side, an end-user looking at employee compensation, benefit, or vacation history now had to look in two different data areas if the employee had been with Tate for more than one year. Also, from a reporting standpoint, reports would often need to be run twice, since no data area had comprehensive information, reinforcing Tate's inefficient business processes.

Tate's second major issue stemmed from the fact that data from its home-grown store system did not typically match the data in its ERP. Often, end-users had to key information into both systems or did not know which system contained the correct information. HR and payroll clerks typically had to call individual stores and speak to managers to determine employee hire dates, rates of pay, and job titles.

Tate was at a fork in the road with regard to new technologies. The dispersion, redundancy, and inconsistency of its organizational data left it with two options: fix the problem or ignore it. Lamentably, Tate management chose the latter. A perfect example was its annual open enrollment, a process for which Tate used the carrier's separate enrollment system. Tate refused to use the ERP vendor's similar application because it would force the organization to clean up the bad data in its ERP. The carrier's software could be used in relative isolation—i.e., sans data cleanup, although the data generated by the system would ultimately need to be imported into the ERP for employee deduction and interface purposes. In other words, the short-term solution of using relatively independent applications only exacerbated the long-term, underlying data and system problems.

Third, adding to the chaos, Tate suffered from extensive turnover at corporate headquarters. Many of its end-users were relatively new to the system at any given point. Tate refused to train its staff properly and opted for an "on the job" approach. As a result of this lack of internal expertise, Tate end-users made many errors in the system, adding more superfluous records to the system and rendering many transaction-based reports essentially meaningless.

Finally and most important, Tate lacked both proper internal controls and a coherent system strategy. Collectively, these caused inaccurate and inconsistent government reporting on a number of vital levels. Aside from financial discrepancies and irregularities, Tate also lacked the ability to track and properly audit transactions from its employee stock purchase program. Tate not only followed poor and inconsistent business processes, but the company could not even sufficiently document them. Conscientious employees made senior executives aware of these issues but management routinely turned a blind eye; it did not even attempt to reconcile known differences, improve its processes, and create proper documentation. Ultimately, management would pay for its willful ignorance.

Misplaced Priorities and an Aversion to Change

Faced with four major post-go-live issues, Tate attempted to address only one. It recognized that it needed more internal bandwidth and hired two very knowledgeable and talented super-users—Sharon and Scott. Both had a great deal of previous experience with the ERP and reported to Renee, the director of Payroll and HRIS.

Hiring "rock stars" will not automatically avert or correct a system failure at an organization. In this case, Tate did not use its new resources to optimize existing systems and stop the bleeding. Scott and Sharon *could* have helped address known issues, enhance automated reporting and distribution, provide end-user training, and ultimately improve system performance and data consistency. On a larger scale, Renee could have deployed them on a system integration project, the intent of which would be to run payroll every two weeks from one system, as opposed to three. Renee chose not to pursue either option.

Rather than address the existing issues, Tate executives—at the behest of Laura, its Senior VP of HR—decided to purchase and implement a BOB performance management system (PMS) at the cost of over $1M. Although well aware of the status quo, Renee chose not to oppose this decision. Renee knew that Laura was not an "operations" person and would not appreciate Tate's current and future data challenges, much less care to fix them. Laura was hell-bent on a new PMS and, as a result, Tate marched on with the third part system. Renee put Sharon in charge of the project.

On the reporting front, Tate had deployed web-based Crystal Reports to a very limited extent but relied almost exclusively on old-fashioned mechanisms such as Microsoft Excel. Scott immediately saw opportunities to improve Tate's systems, data, and business processes. He approached Renee and made his case for rewriting Tate's reports to allow for automated scheduling and electronic delivery via Crystal. She told Scott in no uncertain terms "that's not how we do things here." Scott would have to continue Tate's wholly inefficient process of manually cobbling together reports each month, a process requiring days of error-prone work.

In other words, despite having superior reporting functionality and delivery mechanisms *already at its disposal*, Tate insisted on continuing the same antiquated methods of report generation and distribution. Aside from frustrating Scott, this decision had the additional effect of minimizing the time that he could spend cleaning up inconsistent and/or inaccurate data. As a result, Renee effectively minimized Scott's contribution, negating his:

- Extensive knowledge of the ERP on both the functional and technical ends
- Previous consulting experience with many organizations (with resultant knowledge of best practices and system limitations)
- Strong desire to streamline manual processes
- Ability to clean up bad data

As it turned out, Renee never wanted Scott to improve Tate's systems and data, although she preached the need to do those very things during the interview process. Despite her public goals to improve Tate's systems, Renee knew that Scott's work ethic and skill set would eventually unearth major data, configuration, integration, and processing issues. In fact, Scott was already uncovering such issues and attempting to address them within the ERP. To be blunt, Renee wanted no part of fixing them. Although Tate's systems were in disarray, from Renee's perspective, neither the organization in general—nor her boss in particular—was exactly in a hurry to fix them.

Rather than viewing him as an asset, Renee now saw Scott as a threat that could bring down the whole house of cards. If Scott made—or attempted to make—improvements to the system, then he would expose the company's vast system and data inconsistencies, not to mention its complete lack of internal controls. Even with the lurking fear of a Sarbanes Oxley audit, Renee continued to hide known issues. She certainly did not want Scott—or anyone else for that matter—discovering any new problems and trying to fix them at their core. Scott was soon asked to leave the organization.

Outcomes

Rather than improve its recently implemented ERP, Tate chose to spend over $1M on a third-party system. Tate management should have used those resources to solidify its ERP and internal controls. Not a year after the PMS project began, Tate was the subject of a formal Sarbanes Oxley (SOX) audit. In the end, Tate's misguided priorities, lack of internal controls, and poor systems directly—or indirectly—resulted in the following:

- The dispersal of even more organizational data to even more disparate places (including the newly implemented PMS), further compromising reporting and data integrity
- Core system issues remaining unaddressed
- The SOX audit that found material weaknesses[44] with respect to Tate's internal controls
- The restatement of three years of earnings
- The plummeting of its stock
- The departure of its CEO

While the PMS was certainly superior to the ERP vendor's equivalent, Tate was in absolutely no position to add any system to its existing architecture. Tate's initial system activation resulted in a Forthcoming Failure. However, because management wantonly ignored major system issues, and actually created more after going live, Tate can only be classified as an Unmitigated Disaster.

Summary

Systems are dynamic in nature. They change—hopefully, for the better—as do organizational end-users. As the Tate case study shows, organizations should enhance or expand their systems only on stable system platforms with knowledgeable end-users, proper testing, and coherent long-term systems strategies. If an organization has

---

[44] A material weakness is a significant deficiency or combination of significant deficiencies that result in more than a remote likelihood that a material misstatement will not be prevented or detected. (Source: McGladrey & Pullen LLP website)

widespread system problems, its worst course of action is to add more systems and/or functionality. Expansion for the sake of expansion is at best ill-advised and, more often than not, outright dangerous.

Organizations can certainly activate systems without every feature under the sun, growing into additional modules at later points. In other words, clients need not do everything at once. As a general rule, they should activate systems with critical functionality and with as many "desirable" features as is plausible. Clients can and should revisit functionality dropped from Phase I in future phases, often after the dust settles from their initial implementations.

Get the facts, or the facts will get you. And when you get them, get them right, or they will get you wrong.

-Dr. Thomas Fuller

CHAPTER 23: CONCLUSIONS AND GENERAL RULES OF THUMB

Introduction

This book has been intentionally light on absolutes for two reasons. First, all implementations are unique. No two organizations face identical challenges with respect their implementations' internal politics, consultancies, budgets, timeframes, issues, and end-users. Second, even heeding all of the advice in this book cannot guarantee a successful system activation. No text, consultant, or vendor can promise that an organization will not have major issues. To be sure, organizations benefit a great deal from skilled consultants, conscientious PMs, dedicated client end-users, and responsive vendors. However, no one person or entity can honestly guarantee a successful outcome to a system implementation.

The best-managed project may fail while a horribly managed project may come in under budget, ahead of schedule, and do everything that the vendor promised at the onset. In reality, however, organizations are very unlikely to find themselves in one of these extreme scenarios. On a fundamental level, successfully activating and utilizing a new a system is about minimizing risk from day one until the end of the project and beyond. The organization that can do this stands the best chance of averting failure.

With that disclaimer out of the way, this chapter lists some of the book's more salient points and "relative absolutes" with respect to system implementations, broken into categories.

Pre-Implementation

Check the Engine and Tires before Getting in the Car

Before even considering the implementation of new system, an organization should honestly assess if it can stomach the costs, remove its significant internal political roadblocks, clean up its data, and provide the requisite human and financial resources. Even before the onset, an organization should first overcome these obstacles before attempting an endeavor of this time, magnitude, and cost.

Don't Reinvent the Wheel

Organizations should stick to their knitting and purchase tested and proven systems rather than build them from scratch. The amount of time, money, and effort required to build a new system dissuades most organizations. Undeterred organizations should consider that back office systems present no sustainable business advantage. Organizations that want to reinvent the wheel better have enough bandwidth, documentation, and backup if and when the brakes fail.

Keep it Simple

More complicated systems face much greater chances of failure than simpler ones. A system designed and configured intelligently—according to the best practices espoused by knowledgeable consultants—stands a much greater chance of withstanding the rigors of testing and the challenges of an implementation. Overly complex configurations increase the odds of encountering problems before, during, and after system activation. This is true in both the short- and long-terms.

Bigger isn't Necessarily Better

As Clint Eastwood said in *Sudden Impact*, "A man's gotta know his limitations." In terms of systems, organizations should not "overreach." In other words, clients need to view the alleged advantages of a new system within the context of the organization itself. If not tested and used properly, superior functionally from more costly applications does more harm than good. The organization that attempts to implement a critical system—irrespective of that system's tier—needs to budget enough time and money to properly test that system. Spending $1M on a software license and support and $50K on its implementation is a recipe for disaster.

Know Your Organization

Organizations with old systems, old data, relatively high profit margins, and little competition will face difficult system implementations. Organizations need to be aware of their own limitations and tendencies from the very beginning of a project—while selecting a system and a consulting partner, planning a project, and assigning timelines and resources. Management at a mature multi-site healthcare organization should not delude itself into thinking that it can implement a system in the same time and within the same budget as a small telecommunications company.

Take Vendor Promises with More than a Grain of Salt

Vendor demonstrations can be outright dazzling. Prospective clients will never hear the word "no" from salespeople in response to a question such as, "Can your software do this?" To be sure, the answer to this question may not be a complete misrepresentation of the truth. After all, anything is possible. For the prospective client, the burning question for the vendor should be, "Does your software do this out of the box?" Should the salesperson answer in the affirmative, the follow-up question should be, "Can you please show me now?"

Get it in Writing

Senior management should insist upon strict contract language, especially if the organization is using the vendor and consultancy for the first time. While time-consuming and arduous in nature, such language serves as the ultimate insurance policy if a client's partner misrepresented items (not) covered during the sales cycle. More than a CYA maneuver, a client's process of documenting its business requirements will help it identify areas for potential improvement with the new system.

Find a Trusted Partner for Vendor Selection

Organizations that use consultancies to assist with vendor selection should adhere to the "all or nothing" principle: Find partners either with experience in multiple systems or no specific system—i.e., vendor-agnostic organizations. A consulting firm with a vested interest in the outcome tends to produce skewed findings.

Don't Skimp on Internal Staff

Organizations wanting to minimize the number of external consultants on an implementation first must ensure that their internal resources are devoted almost exclusively to the implementation of that new system. Beyond time, those internal resources must have sufficient expertise in that system—via training, previous experience, or both. Clients should augment implementation teams with external talent, especially when current end-users have no experience with the new system. Hybrid employees often cost a premium but, over the course of the implementation and beyond, more than justify their increased compensation.

Not All Consultants are Created Equal

Organizations should not make the mistake of assuming that all consultancies and individual consultants are equal. By the same token, clients should not choose a consulting firm solely on the basis of cost.

More expensive consultants may in fact be worth a premium and save the client money in the long-term.

The bottom line with independents is that organizations get what they pay for. An independent's rate is a direct reflection of the experience brought to the table. The organization that opts for the less expensive independent should not expect the same level of performance that it would receive from a more seasoned—and expensive—one.

Expect and Plan for Project Delays from the Onset

Organizations that bake in delays and gaps at natural breaking points are in a better position withstand invariable last-minute delays. Foolish is the PM, consultancy, or senior manager that assumes that perfect execution is imminent.

Mid-Implementation

Listen to Consultants and Allow them to Freely Disagree

Organizations that insist on complicated or cumbersome system configurations create problems down the road that can threaten entire projects. Consultants should guide the setup of the system such that it meets with best practices, lest the client be left with a system that it cannot easily support. Consultants able to challenge questionable client decisions can prevent or minimize long-term issues.

Data Conversion is Never Easy

Vendors and consultants trumpet the ease of loading data into a newly purchased system via conversion or load programs. In other words, in all but the most severe circumstances, client end-users will *not* have to hire temps to key 10,000 employees or 2,000 vendors into the new system. However, loading data is almost never as easy as clients believe. The conversion process involves much more than extracting the old and loading the new. This crucial oversight can significantly impact the timeline and budget of an implementation. Organizations must kick the tires on their conversions as soon as possible, even if all individual decisions with respect to data values have not been made.

Allow End-Users Sufficient Time to Play

Application Exploration should focus extensively on items targeted for the first phase of the implementation but not at the risk of completely ignoring future phases. Configuring the application with the knowledge that it will need to be substantially changed after go-live is ill-advised. Also, functional end-users should participate in training immediately before the AE phase, as it will reinforce what end-users have learned in class. Technical users need to attend training before AE, as their jobs mandate that they create data areas, set up security, and perform other tasks required to start the project in earnest.

Replacing a Consultancy is not an Elixir

Many implementation issues stem from overly ambitious vendor promises, bad data, and reluctance on the part of client end-users to get on board. Simply changing consultancies will in no way guarantee that a project will turn around. New consultancies may tell clients virtually the same thing as their predecessors, simply in a different voice. In the words of Ernest Hemingway, "Never mistake motion for action."

Consider Postponing Sites and Functionality

System activation is not an "all or nothing" principle. While organizations ideally want to activate new systems at all sites and with all applications as initially planned, project delays may make that impossible. If an implementation has gone wildly awry, organizations have options beyond blindly "powering through" and pulling the plug altogether. Rather than forcing the issue and potentially causing an Unmitigated Disaster, organizations should strongly consider partially going live—i.e., postponing functionality or certain sites until a later phase.

Post Activation

Expand Cautiously

Before even considering additional functionality, organizations must ensure that their existing systems and end-users can handle the increased demands about to be placed on them. Building on a poor foundation is never wise; shore it up before adding on.

Audits Work

Audits can be invaluable tools for organizations at many different phases, especially after system activation. When performed judiciously by knowledgeable and impartial resources, they can detect, avoid, and minimize issues that can derail an implementation or cause a would-be successful one to fail. Organizations should not view audits as superfluous costs; they typically more than justify their costs.

Shore Up Documentation

Upon going live, organizations should ensure that end-user documentation is accurate and comprehensive. End-users often intend to "get around" to documenting any last-minute tweaks in regular processing, interfaces, setup, and data entry. However, daily realities often cause this to fall by the wayside. When a key end-user exits the organization, that opportunity may be forever lost.

Employee Backup and Succession Planning

After system activation, organizations need to identify or reassess critical roles. Those without suitable replacements pose the greatest risks and should be addressed immediately. Organizations should ensure that they have adequate backup in the event that a key end-user decides to suddenly leave. While a valuable source of talent, the external labor market is not a panacea to an immediate staffing crisis. While two organizations may run the same version of the same software, replacement employees always have learning curves, especially when documentation is lacking.

Summary

Sixty percent of IT projects fail for all sorts of reasons. The examples and case studies in this book revealed the different causes—and combination of causes—of many system failures. Differences aside, the implementation and activation of a system is a major endeavor for any organization. Perils exist around every corner. While the advice dispensed in this book cannot by any means guarantee success on any given project, one thing is certain: Organizations that follow principles detailed in this book stand a much better chance of being part of the fortunate forty percent.

Bibliography

Berkun, Scott. Making Things Happen: Mastering Project Management (Theory in Practice). O'Reilly, 2008.

Brooks, Frederick P. The Mythical Man-Month: Essays on Software Engineering. Addison-Wesley Professional, 1995.

Champy, J.A and Hammer, Michael. Reengineering the Corporation: A Manifesto for Business Revolution. Harper Business Books, 1993.

Peters, Thomas J. and Waterman, Robert H. In Search of Excellence: Lessons from America's Best-Run Companies. Collins Business Essentials, 2004.

Index

Printed in the United States
210954BV00002BA/1/P